Breaking the Conflict Trap

Civil War and Development Policy

**A World Bank
Policy Research Report**

Breaking the Conflict Trap

Civil War and Development Policy

Paul Collier
V. L. Elliott
Håvard Hegre
Anke Hoeffler
Marta Reynal-Querol
Nicholas Sambanis

A copublication of the World Bank
and Oxford University Press

Contents

Foreword   ix

The Report Team   xiii

Acronyms and Abbreviations   xv

Overview   1
    Let Them Fight It Out among Themselves?   1
    What Can We Do about Ancestral Hatreds?   3
    The Conflict Trap   4
    The Rising Global Incidence of Conflict   5
    Nothing Can Be Done   6

PART I. CRY HAVOC:
WHY CIVIL WAR MATTERS   11

1. Civil War as Development in Reverse   13
    Costs during Conflict   13
    Legacy Effects of Civil War   19
    Conclusion   31

2. Let Them Fight It Out among Themselves?   33
    Neighborhood Effects of Civil War   33
    Global Effects of Civil War   41
    Conclusion   48

PART II. WHAT FUELS CIVIL WAR?   51

3. What Makes a Country Prone to Civil War?   53
    Understanding Rebellion   55
    The Conflict Trap   79
    Conclusion   88

4. **Why Is Civil War So Common?**   93
   Changes in the Global Pattern of Civil War   93
   Changes in the Incidence of Civil War   98
   Unpacking the Global Incidence of Civil War   100
   Conclusion: Poverty and the Conflict Trap   117

PART III. POLICIES FOR PEACE   119

5. **What Works Where?**   121
   Conflict Prevention in the Successful Developers   122
   Marginalized Countries at Peace   125
   Ending Conflicts   140
   Reducing Postconflict Risks   150
   Conclusion   171

6. **An Agenda for International Action**   173
   Precedents for International Action   174
   International Policies for Peace   175
   Conclusion: A New Goal for 2015?   186

Appendix 1. Methods and Data   189
   Data Set and Model   189
   Data Sources   193

Appendix 2. A Selected Bibliography of Studies of Civil War and Rebellion   197
   Economic Factors   197
   Role of Ethnicity and Nationalism   198
   Anatomy of Rebellion   199
   Role of the State   199
   Negotiation and Implementation of Peace   200
   Bibliography   200

References   211

Boxes
1.1   Violent conflict and the transformation of social capital   16
1.2   Refugees and IDPs in Liberia and Sudan   20
1.3   Angola   28
1.4   Psychological trauma   29
1.5   Landmines: A bitter legacy for Cambodians   31

2.1   Regional arms races   34
2.2   Eritrea   40

3.1   Modeling the risk of civil war   58
3.2   Oil and demands for secession in Nigeria   61
3.3   Inefficient counterinsurgency measures in Indonesia   73
3.4   Financing the Chechen rebellion   78

3.5   Modeling the duration of civil war   80

4.1   Recurrent conflicts example 1: Afghanistan   104
4.2   Recurrent conflicts example 2: Angola   105

5.1   A comparison of Botswana and Sierra Leone   127
5.2   Transparency of oil revenues in Chad   131
5.3   The rough diamond trade and the Kimberley process   143
5.4   The Khmer Rouge and the logs of war   145

Figures
1.1   GDP per capita before and after civil war   14
1.2   Total number of refugees, 1962–2002   18
1.3   Increase in mortality rates due to civil war   24

2.1   The flow and stock of refugees, 1951–2002   36
2.2   The stock of refugees and civil wars, 1951–2001   37
2.3   Refugees and cases of malaria, 1962–97   38
2.4   Opium production, 1986–2001   43
2.5   Cocaine production, 1986–2001   43
2.6   Opium production in Afghanistan and heroin seizures in Europe,
       1980–2001   45
2.7   Estimates of annual opiate and cocaine use in the late 1990s   45

3.1   Ethnic fractionalization and the risk of civil war   59
3.2   Risk of civil war for the typical low-income country with and
       without ethnic dominance during a five-year period   59
3.3   Risk of civil wars from natural resources endowment   61
3.4   The risk of civil war in democracies and nondemocracies
       at different levels of income   65
3.5   Improved economic performance and the risk of civil war   67
3.6   Military expenditures and the risk of civil war   72
3.7   Natural resources and the risk of civil war for low-income
       countries   76
3.8   How chances of peace evolve worldwide   81
3.9   Duration of civil wars over time   82
3.10   The risk of civil war for a typical civil war country, just before
       and just after war   83
3.11   Diasporas and postconflict risk   85
3.12   Military spending and the risk of renewed conflict in postconflict
       countries   86

4.1   The global incidence of civil warfare, 1950–2001   94
4.2   Simulating the effects of the waves of decolonization,
       1950–2020   95
4.3   Proportion of civil wars that end each year   96
4.4   The global self-sustaining incidence of civil war, by decades   97
4.5   Factors changing the global risk of conflict   99
4.6   The changing rates of conflict termination   100
4.7   Divergent risks: marginalized countries relative to
       successful developers   102

4.8 Development of risk of civil war for the marginalized and successful developers, 2000–2020   103

4.9 The conflict trap: risk of civil war relative to a country with no recent war   106

4.10 The conflict trap by type of country   107

4.11 Risk components for marginalized countries in the conflict trap, relative to the same countries preconflict   107

4.12 The conflict trap in 2000: annual flows into and out of conflict   109

4.13a The conflict trap in 2020: annual flows into and out of conflict   111

4.13b The conflict trap in 2050: annual flows into and out of conflict   111

4.14 The incidence of civil war in South and East Asia and in Oceania, 1950–2001   112

4.15 The incidence of civil war in Latin America and the Caribbean, 1950–2001   113

4.16 The incidence of civil war in Eastern Europe and Central Asia, 1950–2001   113

4.17 The incidence of civil war in the Middle East and North Africa, 1950–2001   114

4.18 The incidence of civil war in Sub-Saharan Africa, 1950–2001   114

4.19 The incidence of civil war in Africa and other developing countries, 1950–2001   115

5.1 The contribution to peace of faster growth in the successful developers   124

5.2 The contribution to peace of faster growth in the marginalized countries   135

5.3 The contribution to peace of shortening conflicts   141

5.4 The contribution to peace of successful postconflict policies   151

6.1 The contribution of the policy package to peace   187

Tables

1.1 Major refugee and IDP populations, 2001   19

1.2 Mortality rates among children under five in refugee and IDP camps, selected conflicts   25

1.3 Effects of civil war on public health   26

1.4 HIV prevalence in the military, selected countries and years   27

2.1 Production of opium and coca, selected countries and years, 1990–2001   42

2.2 Prevalence estimates of opiate and cocaine use, selected industrial countries and years   46

3.1 Size of rebel organizations, selected countries and years   55

Foreword

WHY SHOULD THE WORLD BANK FOCUS ON CIVIL WAR? Basically, there are two reasons. First, civil war usually has devastating consequences: it is development in reverse. As civil wars have accumulated and persisted, they have generated or intensified a significant part of the global poverty problem that is the World Bank's core mission to confront. Part of the purpose of this report is to alert the international community to the adverse consequences of civil war for development. These consequences are suffered mostly by civilians, often by children and by those in neighboring countries. Those who make the decisions to start or to sustain wars are often relatively immune to their adverse effects. The international community therefore has a legitimate role as an advocate for those who are victims. The second reason why the World Bank should focus on civil war is that development can be an effective instrument for conflict prevention. The risk of civil war is much higher in low-income countries than in middle-income countries. Civil war thus reflects not just a problem *for* development, but a failure *of* development. The core of this report sets out the evidence on the efficacy of development for conflict prevention and proposes a practical agenda for action. The World Bank and its partner development agencies can undertake parts of this agenda, but other parts depend on international collective action by the governments of industrial countries. One important forum for such action is the Group of Eight.

Our research yields three main findings. First, civil wars have highly adverse ripple effects that those who determine whether they start or end obviously do not take into account. The first ripple is within the country: most of the victims are children and other noncombatants. The second ripple is the region: neighboring countries suffer reduced incomes and increased disease. The third ripple is global: civil war generates territory outside the control of any recognized government, and such territories have become the epicenters of crime and disease. Many of these adverse consequences persist long after the civil war has ended, so that much of the costs of a war occur after it is over.

The second finding is that the risks of civil war differ massively according to a country's characteristics, including its economic characteristics. As a result, civil war is becoming increasingly concentrated in relatively few developing countries. Two groups of countries are at the highest risk. One we refer to as the *marginalized* developing countries, that is, those low-income countries that have to date failed to sustain the policies, governance, and institutions that might give them a chance of achieving reasonable growth and diversifying out of dependence on primary commodities. On average, during the 1990s these countries actually had declining per capita incomes. Such countries are facing a Russian roulette of conflict risk. Even countries that have had long periods of peace do not seem to be safe, as shown by recent conflicts in Côte d'Ivoire and Nepal. It is imperative that such countries are brought into the mainstream of development. The other high-risk group is countries caught in the *conflict trap*. Once a country has had a conflict it is in far greater danger of further conflict: commonly, the chief legacy of a civil war is another war. For this group of countries the core development challenge is to design international interventions that are effective in stabilizing the society during the first postconflict decade.

The third finding is that feasible international actions could substantially reduce the global incidence of civil war. Although our proposals are wide-ranging, including aid and policy reform, we place particular emphasis on improving the international governance of natural resources. Diamonds were critical to the tremendous economic success of Botswana, but also to the social catastrophe that engulfed Sierra Leone. The Kimberley process of tracking diamonds is intended to curtail rebel organizations' access to diamond revenues. The "publish what you pay" initiative, launched by the nongovernmental organization Global Witness, is intended to increase the transparency of natural resource revenues to governments. Transparency is, in turn, an input into enhanced domestic scrutiny of how such revenues are used. If rebel finances can be curbed and citizens come to believe that resources are being well used, civil war will be less likely. A third element in a package of improved international governance of natural resources is to cushion the price shocks that exporters commonly face. Price crashes have been associated with severe recessions that directly increase the risk of civil war and have sometimes destabilized economic management for long periods. At present the international community has no effective instrument to compensate for these shocks.

International collective action has seldom looked so difficult, but the cost of failure will be measured in violence and poverty.

Nicholas Stern
Senior Vice-President
  and Chief Economist
The World Bank
April 2003

The Report Team

THIS REPORT WAS PREPARED UNDER THE SUPERVISION OF Nicholas Stern, chief economist and senior vice-president. It was written by a team led by Paul Collier (director, Development Research Group) and consisting of V. L. Elliott, Håvard Hegre, Anke Hoeffler, Marta Reynal-Querol, and Nicholas Sambanis.

The report builds on research by the Economics of Civil War, Crime, and Violence project in the World Bank Development Research Group. The project was initiated and directed by Paul Collier and has been ongoing since 1999. Ibrahim Elbadawi, Håvard Hegre, Marta Reynal-Querol, and Nicholas Sambanis were the project's core staff. In addition, the project has commissioned a large number of studies from researchers outside the World Bank. The project received funding from the Norwegian, Swiss, and Greek governments; the World Bank Post-Conflict Fund; and the World Bank Research Committee.

The project has been collaborating with United Nations Studies at Yale, the International Peace Research Institute in Oslo, the Agence française de développement, the Economic Commission for Africa, and the African Economic Research Consortium. Conferences have been held in Addis Ababa, Irvine, Kampala, New Haven, Oslo, Paris, Princeton, and Washington, D.C.

Many of the project papers are referred to in the text of the report, and most of them are posted on the project's web site: http://econ. worldbank.org/programs/conflict. Selections of the papers have also been published as special issues of the *Journal of Conflict Resolution, Defence and Peace Economics,* the *Journal of Peace Research,* and the *Journal of African Economies.* A set of country studies is being prepared for publication under the supervision of Nicholas Sambanis.

We thank for their excellent work Polly Means, who did the graphics; Audrey Kitson-Walters, who processed the report; Alice Faintich, who edited it; and Susan Graham, who was in charge of production.

The judgments in this policy research report do not necessarily reflect the views of the World Bank's Board of Directors or the governments they represent.

Acronyms and Abbreviations

CPIA	country policy and institutional assessment
DALY	disability-adjusted life year
DDR	disarmament, demobilization, and reintegration
ELN	Ejército popular de liberación (Colombia)
ETA	Euskadi ta azkatasuna (Spain)
EU	European Union
FARC	Fuerzas armadas revolucionarias colombianas (Colombia)
GAM	Gerakan Aceh Merdeka (Indonesia)
GDP	gross domestic product
IDP	internally displaced person
IMF	International Monetary Fund
IRA	Irish Republican Army
LICUS	low-income countries under stress
MIGA	Multilateral Investment Guarantee Agency
MNC	multinational corporation
NATO	North Atlantic Treaty Organization
NGO	nongovernmental organization
OECD	Organisation for Economic Co-operation and Development
RENAMO	Resistência nacional Moçambicana (Mozambique)
RUF	Revolutionary United Front (Sierra Leone)
STD	sexually transmitted disease
UN	United Nations
UNHCR	United Nations High Commission for Refugees
UNITA	União Nacional para a Independência Total de Angola (Angola)
UXO	unexploded ordinance
WHO	World Health Organization

Overview

MOST WARS ARE NOW CIVIL WARS. EVEN though international wars attract enormous global attention, they have become infrequent and brief. Civil wars usually attract less attention, but they have become increasingly common and typically go on for years. This report argues that civil war is now an important issue for development. War retards development, but conversely, development retards war. This double causation gives rise to virtuous and vicious circles. Where development succeeds, countries become progressively safer from violent conflict, making subsequent development easier. Where development fails, countries are at high risk of becoming caught in a conflict trap in which war wrecks the economy and increases the risk of further war.

The global incidence of civil war is high because the international community has done little to avert it. Inertia is rooted in two beliefs: that we can safely "let them fight it out among themselves" and that "nothing can be done" because civil war is driven by ancestral ethnic and religious hatreds. The purpose of this report is to challenge these beliefs.

Let Them Fight It Out among Themselves?

PART I INVESTIGATES THE ECONOMIC AND SOCIAL COSTS OF civil war. The costs the active participants in combat bear account for only a trivial part of the overall suffering. The damage from a war ripples out in three rings. The inner ring is the displace-

1

ment, mortality, and poverty inflicted on noncombatants within the country, and this is the subject of chapter 1. The United Nations High Commission for Refugees is currently assisting more than 5 million internally displaced persons as a result of civil war. Many of these displaced people are forced to move to areas where the partial immunity they have acquired to malaria is no longer effective, and so their mortality rate rises. By the end of the typical civil war incomes are around 15 percent lower than they would otherwise have been, implying that about 30 percent more people are living in absolute poverty. However, the end of a civil war does not end the costs arising from it. Many of the economic costs, such as high military expenditure and capital flight, persist for years after the conflict. So too do heightened mortality and morbidity rates. Approximately half of the loss of disability-adjusted years of life expectancy due to a conflict arise after it is over. These economic and health costs of conflict are not usually compensated by any postconflict improvements in economic policy, democratic institutions, or political freedom. On the contrary, all three usually deteriorate. The typical civil war starts a prolonged process of development in reverse.

Chapter 2 focuses on civil wars' spillover effects beyond the country. The second ring of suffering affects neighboring countries. Refugees stream across borders carrying and spreading the infections to which they have been exposed; for example, for every 1,000 international refugees the host country sees around 1,400 additional cases of malaria. Neighboring economies also suffer in other ways: growth rates are significantly reduced and neighbors increase their military expenditure in a chain reaction of local arms races. Often the costs of a civil war to the combined neighboring countries are of the same order of magnitude as the costs to the country itself. Through all these routes civil war is a regional public bad.

The outer ring of suffering is global. Civil war creates territory outside the control of any recognized government. One major use for this territory is to produce and transport drugs: 95 percent of the global production of hard drugs occurs in countries with civil wars and the major supply routes run through conflict territories. A more speculative possible global cost of civil war is the current AIDS pandemic. Some evidence suggests that this was triggered by the rapid spread of a highly localized infection caused by mass rape during a civil war. A further global shock to which civil war has contributed is Al Qaeda. When international terrorism is conducted on a large scale, the organization needs a safe haven that can probably only be provided in territory outside the control of any recognized government. Al Qaeda chose to locate in Taliban-held territory in Afghanistan, even though most of its recruits were not Afghans. It also used the war in Sierra Leone to generate profits from the trade in conflict diamonds and to store its wealth. The global mortality caused by hard drugs and international terrorism is a significant toll, but the wider social costs are immense. The World Bank estimates that the September 11 attacks alone may have increased global poverty by 10 million people.

We have no reason to think that those who decide to embark on civil war—the active participants, especially a few leaders—take all this suffering of others into account. Furthermore, many of these adverse effects are highly persistent. The typical civil war lasts long enough, around seven years, but the damage persists well beyond the end of the conflict. Once disease has set in, a country may need many years of peace to revert to its preconflict morbidity and mortality rates. Similarly, once an economy has experienced a wave of capital flight and emigration, this tends to continue even when the conflict is over. In addition, the regional escalation in military expenditure can persist because of insufficient coordination to reduce it. In many cases most of the costs of a civil war occur only once it is over. Again, those who have the power of decision are unlikely to take these consequences into account. Thus, in practice, the attitude let them fight it out among themselves gives license to a few thousand combatants and a few dozen of their leaders to inflict widespread misery on millions of others.

What Can We Do about Ancestral Hatreds?

CAN THE INTERNATIONAL COMMUNITY DO ANYTHING TO reduce the global incidence of civil war? If violence is simply determined by ancestral ethnic and religious hatreds, outsiders can probably do little. Part II turns to the underlying factors that determine the global incidence of civil war.

Chapter 3 discusses what makes some countries prone to civil war. Of course, each civil war is different and has its own distinctive, idiosyncratic triggers, be they a charismatic rebel leader or a provocative government action, but beneath these chance circumstances patterns are apparent. Some social, political, and economic characteristics systematically increase the incidence of civil war, and we show that ethnicity and religion are much less important than is commonly believed. Indeed, societies that are highly diverse mixtures of many ethnic and religious groups are usually safer than more homogenous societies. By contrast, economic characteristics matter more than has usually been recognized. If a country is in economic decline, is dependent on primary commodity exports, and has a low per capita income and that income is unequally distributed, it is at high risk of civil war. This cocktail is so lethal for several reasons. Low and declining incomes, badly distributed, create a pool of impoverished and disaffected young men who can be cheaply recruited by "entrepreneurs of violence." In such conditions the state is also likely to be weak, nondemocratic, and incompetent, offering little impediment to the escalation of rebel violence, and maybe even inadvertently provoking it. Natural resource wealth provides a source of finance for the rebel organization and encourages the local population to support political demands for secession. It is also commonly associated with poor governance. Disputes often fall along ethnic and religious divisions, but they are much more likely to turn violent in countries with low and declining incomes.

The Conflict Trap

ONCE SUCH A COUNTRY STUMBLES INTO CIVIL WAR, ITS RISK of further conflict soars. Conflict weakens the economy and leaves a legacy of atrocities. It also creates leaders and organizations that have invested in skills and equipment that are only useful for violence. Disturbingly, while the overwhelming majority of the population in a country affected by civil war suffers from it, the leaders of military organizations that are actually perpetrating the violence often do well out of it. The prospect of financial gain is seldom the primary motivation for rebellion, but for some it can become a satisfactory way of life. This is a further reason why the participants in a civil war should not be left to fight it out among themselves. Some evidence suggests that decade by decade, civil wars have been getting longer. While this may be due to circumstances in individual countries, it more likely reflects global changes that have made civil wars easier to sustain by allowing rebel groups to raise finance and acquire armaments more easily.

The Rising Global Incidence of Conflict

THE INCIDENCE OF CIVIL WAR HAS INCREASED SUBSTANTIALLY over the past 40 years. As this has been a period of unprecedented global economic development, it might appear evident that development has not been an effective remedy for violent civil conflict, but to make sense of the patterns we need to distinguish between different groups of countries. This is the subject of chapter 4.

Many developing countries have either already reached middle-income status or have policy and institutional environments that should put them on track to do so. Around 4 billion people live in such countries. Currently, as a group, they face a risk of civil war four times as high as the negligible risk societies in countries of the Organisation for Economic Co-operation and Development (OECD) face; however, 30 years ago their risk was five times as high, so they are converging with the group of countries already in secure peace.

Nevertheless, more than a billion people live in low-income countries that have been unable to adopt and sustain policies and institutions conducive to development. On average, these countries have been in economic decline and have remained dependent on natural resources or other primary commodities. This group of countries face far higher risks: typically around 15 times as high as OECD societies. Indeed, these risks have been rising as economies have deteriorated. Forty years ago there were many fewer independent, low-income countries. Most low-income countries were under the imposed peace of colonialism or were fighting liberation wars. As countries gained independence they started, in effect, to play Russian roulette with civil war risk. Many of them stumbled into conflict, and where this happened the conflict trap implied an even higher risk of further conflict. This is the group that increasingly accounts for the global incidence of conflict.

Thus the overall trend in the global incidence of conflict is made up of two radically divergent components. For most of the world's population development has been significantly reducing risks, but a significant minority of people live in low-income countries that have not shared in development. For them the risks have been increasing.

If these two opposing forces persist, the global incidence of conflict will not continue to rise indefinitely, but neither will development secure global peace. The world will find itself stuck with a self-sustaining incidence of civil war, determined predominantly by the large and persistent pool of nondeveloping, low-income countries. These countries will account for a small and diminishing share of global income, but they will be responsible for a high share of the regional and global spillovers from civil war.

Nothing Can Be Done

PART III TURNS TO THE POLICIES THAT MIGHT BE EFFECTIVE IN reducing the global incidence of conflict. Some of these require action at the national level and others at the global level. Until recently, superpower rivalries made an international policy toward civil war unrealistic. Developing country governments lined up on one side or the other, and many rebel movements could count on some degree of cover from the opposing superpower. Therefore the question of what international responses were appropriate has only been worth posing in the past decade. Because asking the question had made little sense, the analysis to guide post–Cold War responses was not in place. Relative to many other questions the analysis is still seriously incomplete, but we are no longer completely in the dark. We now know enough for a reasonable basis for action.

Economic development is central to reducing the global incidence of conflict; however, this does not mean that the standard elements of development strategy—market access, policy reform, and aid—are sufficient, or even appropriate, to address the problem. At the most basic level, development has to reach countries that it has so far missed. Beyond this, development strategies should look different in countries facing a high risk of conflict, where the problems and priorities are distinctive. In addition, some policies that are not normally part of development strategy affect the risk of conflict, such as the presence of external peacekeeping forces, the tendency toward domestic military expenditures, and the design of political institutions. In designing a strategy for risk reduction a useful approach is to view all the interventions that significantly affect risk in an integrated way. For example, different interventions are most effective at different phases, and so may best be sequenced. Because different actors who are not used to working together determine the interventions, to date this has not been common practice.

The global incidence of conflict is made up of four very different components, each of which needs a distinctive approach. This is the subject of chapter 5. The first is the relatively low risk of conflict that is faced by a large group of middle-income countries and by some low-income countries that are on track to becoming middle-income because of good policies and rapid growth. For this class of countries the main risk probably comes from sudden economic crashes, such as that Indonesia experienced in the late 1990s. These crashes are in any case disastrous, and the heightened risk of conflict simply adds a further reason why both national and international action needs to be taken to avoid such shocks and to cushion them when they happen. This is the group of countries that has already participated in global growth. Accelerating their growth would make a modest, but significant, contribution to global peace.

The second component of the global incidence of conflict is the much higher risk stagnant or declining low-income countries face. This group has basically been missed by development to date, and is in effect locked in a game of Russian roulette in which the probability of war is dangerously high. Igniting development in this group would make a far more substantial contribution to global peace, but is difficult because it has not been achieved to date. A particularly helpful aspect of development for these countries would be to help them diversify out of dependence on primary commodity exports.

The third component of the global incidence of conflict is the countries currently in conflict. If the typical conflict could be shortened, then the global incidence of conflict would decrease significantly. Past international interventions to shorten conflict have not been systematically effective; however, some evidence suggests that conflicts can be shortened by squeezing rebel organizations of their sources of external finance. Yet in the absence of other interventions shortening conflicts is not particularly effective: countries in the conflict trap simply pass in and out of war more frequently.

The final component of the global incidence of conflict is those countries that are in the first decade of postconflict peace. For this group the risks of further conflict are exceptionally high: approximately half will fall back into conflict within the decade. This is the area that probably has the most scope for effective international interventions to reduce the incidence of conflict. What is most likely required is a coordination of external military peacekeeping for the first few years with a buildup of large aid programs during the middle of the decade. Both military peacekeeping and aid could be made conditional on the rapid reform of government policies and institutions, so that by the end of the decade the society is reasonably safe from further conflict. We show that an integrated approach involving external military support, aid, and policy reform could, over the course of two decades, take postconflict countries well out of the zone of high risk and reduce their risk of conflict to only a quarter of its initial level.

No single intervention is decisive in reducing the global incidence of conflict; however, different measures complement each other and cumulate. Our simulation of a package of development measures suggests how the global incidence of conflict could be reduced to less than half of its present level. Some of the actions needed for such an improvement come from the governments of developing countries, and some require action at an international level.

Chapter 6 sets out a specific agenda for international action. Because those who decide whether to initiate civil wars and whether to accept a settlement ignore the large and adverse spillovers from civil war, this gives the international community both the moral right and the practical duty to intervene to prevent and shorten conflicts.

International interventions have recently had some important successes, such as the launch of the Kimberley process to regulate trade in diamonds and the international ban on antipersonnel mines. We consider three further sets of interventions: aid, the governance of natural resources, and military peacekeeping.

Aid has substantial potential for conflict prevention, particularly in postconflict settings, and in the past donors have probably not got their aid policies right. Aid has usually flooded in during the immediate postconflict period, when the country is prominent in the international media, and then rapidly tapered out. Based on our analysis, overall aid should have been larger during the first postconflict decade, but it should have gradually tapered in during the decade. There is also considerable scope to retarget aid toward low-income countries: the international community has provided much aid to middle-income countries where conflict risks are usually quite low.

Natural resource endowments have the potential for poverty reduction, but historically have often been associated with conflict, poor governance, and economic decline. Because the adverse effects of natural resources work through a number of routes, several distinct interventions could be helpful.

One global objective might be to make securing finance more difficult for rebel organizations. The Kimberley process has this objective, and it needs to be monitored. If it is successful, it could be replicated for some other commodities. If it is unsuccessful, the present voluntary agreement may need to be strengthened by legislation. There is also scope to supplement the tracking of commodities with the tracking of the financial flows that are their counterparts, and the international banking system is now rightly coming under pressure to provide more effective scrutiny of the transactions it administers. A further source of rebel finance is from ransoms and extortion. Obviously such activities are already illegal, but the scale of payments can probably be reduced by government action in the OECD countries in which targeted companies are based. For example, the recent emergence of a market for ransom insurance is probably undesirable in that it escalates payments. A final source of rebel finance is from illicit primary commodities, notably coca and opium. The current OECD regulatory environment makes territory outside the control of a recognized government extremely valuable, and this clearly facilitates conflict. Many options for redesigning drug policy are available that would moderate this dangerous effect.

A distinct reason why countries dependent on natural resources face problems is their exposure to price shocks. OECD governments, and indeed charities, have been good at responding to such photogenic shocks as earthquakes and hurricanes, but have utterly failed to respond to the much more severe shocks caused by price crashes. There is considerable scope for both the international financial institutions and bilateral donors to provide better cushioning of these shocks and to conduct their commercial policies in such a way as to reduce price shocks in the first place.

A final reason why countries dependent on natural resources face problems is that their revenues are often used inefficiently or corruptly. The Monterrey consensus emphasized that both industrial and developing country governments have responsibilities in this context. There is a case for a template of governance of natural resource revenues to which governments could choose to adhere. Such a template would include transparency and effective scrutiny. It could potentially be used as a signal of reduced exposure to political risk, and so help to attract more reputable resource extraction companies to low-income environments. The international financial institutions have a potential role here in aggregating revenues from the individual accounts of resource extraction companies and publishing the resulting estimates of revenue in a way that integrates the information with budgetary data.

Especially in postconflict situations, government military spending tends to be excessive. High spending tends to increase risks rather than to contain them. Through powerful regional arms races, this high spending becomes a regional public bad. There is scope for regional political organizations to negotiate mutual reductions in spending. The international financial institutions may have a role here as honest brokers monitoring that countries actually implement agreed reductions in spending.

Finally, and more speculatively, we consider the coordination of external military interventions with aid and policy reform. We suggest that in many postconflict environments neither aid, nor policy reform, nor even new democratic political institutions can realistically secure peace during the first few years. External military intervention may be the only practical guarantor of peace. An effective sequence might be that large aid inflows are phased in during the middle of the postconflict decade, generating a growth spurt that may enable a substantial reduction of the military presence. As the conflict-related aid program tapers out at the end of the decade, if the government has used the decade well to accelerate reforms, it should be in a position to sustain the rapid growth that can make the society safer.

In securing a safer world, no single intervention is likely to be decisive. Conflict risk works through multiple channels, and so calls for a package of complementary solutions. Furthermore, most interventions take time to work. However, our simulations suggest that if action is taken now, by 2015—the timetable for the attainment of the Millennium Development Goals—more than halving the global incidence of civil war would be feasible.

At present, reducing the global incidence of civil war is not included as a Millennium Development Goal. Yet both because war is so powerfully development in reverse and because peace is a fundamental good in its own right, it is surely appropriate as a core development objective. It is also much more readily monitorable than any of the other goals and, indeed, is already monitored by the authoritative Swedish International Peace Research Institute. The case for treating the halving of the incidence of civil war as a Millennium Development Goal is the same as that for the current goals: explicit commitments help the international community to sustain collective action. Because the risk of war is so heavily concentrated in the minority of developing countries we have referred to as "marginalized," attaining the overarching goal of halving world poverty without having much impact on the incidence of conflict would unfortunately be entirely possible. The goal of halving the incidence of civil war would help to focus efforts on those countries and people who are at the bottom of the heap.

PART I

CRY HAVOC: WHY CIVIL WAR MATTERS

Cry havoc and let slip the dogs of war.
                    Shakespeare, Henry IV

CIVIL WAR DIFFERS RADICALLY FROM BOTH IN-
ternational war and communal violence. Unlike
international war, it is fought outside any structure of rules and entirely within the territory of
the society. Unlike communal violence, it implies a rebel organization equipped with armaments and staffed with full-time recruits. Such
rebel armies usually have little option but to live
off the land. These features typically escalate the
social costs of civil war above the costs of either
international war or communal violence. For
example, the same conflict between Eritrea and
Ethiopia generated both a civil war and, following Eritrean independence, an international war.
As a civil war the conflict lasted for 30 years and
was ended only by military victory. As an international war the conflict was subject to the full
panoply of international mediation and ended
swiftly in a negotiated settlement. To analyze
civil war we need to know what we mean by it.
We adopt a precise but conventional definition:
civil war occurs when an identifiable rebel organization challenges the government militarily
and the resulting violence results in more than
1,000 combat-related deaths, with at least 5 percent on each side. There are many other forms
of group violence, such as protests, riots, and
pogroms, but we do not consider them here.

The perpetrators of civil war usually adopt
the rhetoric that the war is a necessary catalyst
for social progress. Occasionally this is right, but
more typically war is an economic and social
disaster for the affected country. Therefore, for
those who care about development, civil war is
a major problem. This is the focus of chapter 1:
a theme of the chapter is that civilians, not the
active combatants, suffer the main adverse consequences of civil war, and that many of these
consequences accrue long after the war is over.
Hence the people who determine whether war
occurs are likely to ignore much of its adverse
consequences. Furthermore, civil war has severe
consequences that spill over regionally and globally, and civil war is not just a problem for the
countries directly affected. Thus the attitude
"let them fight it out among themselves" is not
just heartless, it is foolish. This is the subject of
chapter 2.

During a civil war a society diverts some of its resources from productive activities to violence. As a result, the society loses twice over. The diverted resources are lost to productive activity, analogous to the loss from what economists call rent-seeking. Because much of the increase in military spending is on government forces paid for out of the government budget, resources are disproportionately diverted from government provision of useful public goods, such as health care and policing. However, whereas rent-seeking activities are simply unproductive, the increase in violence is harmful. One part of society is producing while another part is destroying.

Most of the costs of civil war accrue from these destructive activities. The power of the gun displaces civil rights. Men with guns, from both rebel and government forces, can steal, rape, and murder with impunity. Behind this veil of havoc, the localized collapse of order extends impunity to criminal and other antisocial behavior. The primary response to the fear of theft, rape, and murder is flight. People try to shift their assets to safety, and they themselves flee. This flight in turn creates massive problems, especially for health, as people are pushed into areas where they lack immunity to disease. They then carry these diseases with them, infecting host populations.

Civil War as Development in Reverse

THIS CHAPTER FOCUSES ONLY ON THE EFFECTS OF civil war within the country that is directly affected. War has economic and social costs. Some of these accrue to the combatants, but many affect people who have no part in the decisions that create and sustain the conflict. Furthermore, many of the adverse consequences of a conflict occur only once it is over and are probably ignored in combatants' decisions. We begin with the costs that arise during conflict and then turn to the legacy effects.

Costs during Conflict

THIS SECTION DISTINGUISHES BETWEEN THE ECONOMIC and social costs of conflict.

Economic Costs

During a civil war a society diverts some of its resources from productive activities to destruction. This causes a double loss: the loss from what the resources were previously contributing and the loss from the damage that they now inflict (figure 1.1).

The first loss can to some extent be quantified, as governments increase their military expenditure during civil war, and this directly reduces economic growth. During peacetime the average developing country, defined as a country with less than US$3,000 per capita gross

13

Figure 1.1 GDP per capita before and after civil war

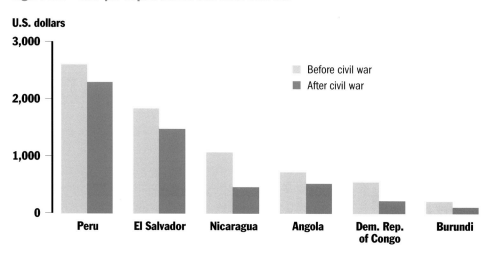

Source: Sambanis (2003).

domestic product (GDP) in 1995, spends about 2.8 percent of GDP on the military. During civil war, on average, this increases to 5 percent. This is likely to cause a decrease in other public expenditures such as those on infrastructure and health. The decrease in the supply of such public goods has consequences for incomes and social indicators, and here we focus on the effects on income. Before taking any of the destructive effects of military activity into account, we can estimate its consequences for crowding out productive expenditures. Knight, Loayza, and Villanueva (1996) quantify the costs to growth of military spending during peacetime. Their simulations suggest that the additional 2.2 percent of GDP spent on the military, sustained over the seven years that is the length of the typical conflict, would lead to a permanent loss of around 2 percent of GDP. Of course, the increase in government military spending is only part of the diversion of resources into violence. The resources rebel groups control are also a diversion from productive activities.

However, the main economic losses from civil war arise not from the waste constituted by diverting resources from production, but from the damage that the diverted resources do when they are used for violence. The most obvious cost arises from the direct destruction of infrastructure. During the war rebel forces target physical infrastructure as part of their strategy. The main targets are the enemy's communication and support lines, such as telecommunications, airports, ports, roads, and bridges. In addition to this strategic destruction of key infrastructure, rebels and government soldiers loot and destroy housing, schools, and health facilities. An example is Mozambique (Brück 2001), where about 40 percent of immobile capital in the agriculture, communications, and administrative sectors was destroyed. The prewar transport system had been a large foreign income earner, as goods were transported from and to the neighboring states of Malawi, South Africa, Swaziland, and Zimbabwe, but 208 out of 222 units of rolling stock were lost or badly damaged between 1982 and 1989. Similarly, during the war in Liberia in the mid-1990s all major infrastructures were damaged and looted. Monrovia, the largest port, suffered major damage during the first few months of the war, most of the electricity generating capacity of the Liberian Electricity Corporation was destroyed, and looting removed much of the distribution and transmission systems. Infrastructure is an important determinant of economic growth (Canning 1998), and so destruction of infrastructure on such a scale is bound to reduce incomes.

Probably a more substantial cost arises from the fear that violence inevitably generates. Frightened people flee from their homes. They also tend to lose the few assets they possess. For example, in a survey of households in Uganda, Matovu and Stewart (2001) found that two-thirds of respondents had lost all their assets. Their houses were bombed or unroofed; their household belongings, such as bicycles and furniture, were looted; and their cattle were stolen by soldiers. In Mozambique less than a fifth of the recorded 1980 cattle stock remained by 1992. Cattle were lost because of direct rebel activity, that is, rebels stole them to feed their troops and killed them to spread terror, and because of indirect effects of warfare, namely, a lack of feed and veterinary attention during the war. Faced with the prospect of such losses, people try to protect their assets by shifting wealth abroad (Collier, Hoeffler, and Pattillo 2002). Prior to conflict the typical civil war country held 9 percent of its private wealth abroad. By the end of the civil war this had risen to an astonishing 20 percent, so that more than a 10th of the private capital stock had been shifted abroad. Even this probably underestimates the extent of overall capital flight, for example, cattle may be moved to neighboring countries and sold.

The disruption of civil war shortens time horizons and the displacement severs family and community links. Both weaken the constraints on opportunistic and criminal behavior. For example, during the Rus-

---

Box 1.1 Violent conflict and the transformation of social capital

Cambodia

Thirty years of warfare all but destroyed most forms of social capital in Cambodia. During the Lon Nol regime, traditional sources of social capital were severely eroded throughout Cambodia. Many villages were forced to reallocate or were split as a result of warfare, bombing, and Lon Nol recruitment. Within villages exchange slowed, and solidarity around the temple dissolved.

The Khmer Rouge ushered in another era of organized violence that included systematic attacks on traditional Cambodian society norms, culture, religion, organizations, networks, and even the family. Community and family members were encouraged to spy on and report on each other, which destroyed trust and planted the seeds of deeply rooted fear. A war against class distinctions was waged, as attempts to level economic status were instituted by making everyone an unpaid agricultural laborer. By destroying all social, political, and economic institutions in this extreme communistic experiment, the brutal Khmer Rouge regime transformed and depleted what little social capital had remained from the Lon Nol period.

Rwanda

During the genocide, social capital atrophied as the country, communities, and families fell prey to hatred and violence. Yet integrative forms of social capital increased within families fighting for survival; among individuals attempting to save or rescue Tutsi; and in the small Muslim community within Rwanda, which never took part in the genocide. Strong, exclusionary social capital also emerged within Hutu extremism, with extremely negative ramifications for those excluded, showing that violence can coexist with, or be the result of, strong bonding social capital among its perpetrators.

Once the killing began, Hutu killed not only Tutsi unknown to them, but also their neighbors and, in some cases, even family members. These indiscriminate yet intimate killings led to the disintegration of communes and families and fragmented social cohesion in general. High levels of social capital existed both vertically and horizontally among Hutu ranks, while bridging social capital that linked Hutu with Tutsi was all but eliminated.

Source: Colletta and Cullen (2000).

---

sian civil war of 1920 the town of Nikolaev was in limbo between White and Red occupation for two days. During those two days local crooks chopped down all the trees lining the main avenue and stole the wood (Figes 1996). During the Rwandan genocide of 1994, those with assets faced a greater risk of being murdered (Andre and Platteau 1998). Colletta and Cullen (2000) analyze the relationship between violent conflict and the transformation of social capital using four case studies: Cambodia, Guatemala, Rwanda, and Somalia (see box 1.1). In response to heightened opportunism and uncertainty, people invest less and retreat into those subsistence activities that are less vulnerable. For example, in Uganda during the long period of social chaos the share of the subsistence sector increased from 20 percent of GDP to 36 percent.

Investigators have used both econometrics and case studies to estimate the overall effect of civil war on the economy. An econometric study finds that during civil war countries tend to grow around 2.2 percentage points more slowly than during peace (Collier 1999). Hence after a typical civil war of seven years duration, incomes would be around 15 percent lower than had the war not happened, implying an approximately 30 percent increase in the incidence of absolute poverty. The cumulative loss of income during the war would be equal to around 60 percent of a year's GDP. Note that this is much larger than the loss directly caused by the resources wasted on extra government military spending, which suggests that most of the costs of war are due to the adverse effects of violence rather than simply to the waste of resources. Stewart, Huang, and Wang (2001) survey data from about 18 countries affected by civil war. For the 14 countries whose average growth rates of gross national product per capita could be calculated, the average annual growth rate was negative, at –3.3 percent. Furthermore, they found that a wide range of macroeconomic indicators worsened during the conflict: in 15 countries per capita income fell, in 13 countries food production dropped, in all 18 economies their external debt increased as a percentage of GDP, and in 12 countries export growth declined.

Social Costs

The most direct human effects of civil war are fatalities and population displacements. In the modern civil war the composition of victims differs radically from the wars of the early 20th century, in that the impact has shifted from military personnel to civilians. At the beginning of the 20th century about 90 percent of the victims were soldiers, but by the 1990s nearly 90 percent of the casualties resulting from armed conflict were civilian (Cairns 1997).

To some extent the rise in civilian casualties is a consequence of new military practices. Rebel recruitment strategies are now commonly coercive, so people flee to avoid recruitment. For example, in response to a recent rebel attack in rural Nepal, "About 35,000 people (out of a population of 75,000) have left the district, mainly young men moving to India to avoid being forcibly recruited by the Maoists" (Holt 2003, p. 23). Furthermore, the military sometimes deliberately targets civilians to create forced migration. Azam and Hoeffler (2002) analyze

Figure 1.2 Total number of refugees, 1962–2002

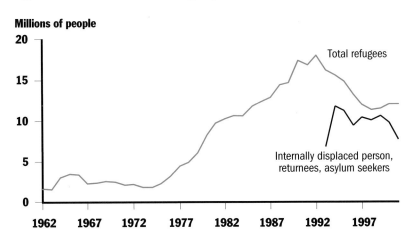

Source: UNHCR (2002).

the different motives for targeting civilians in internal wars. On the one hand, soldiers may terrorize civilians because they need loot to augment their resources. An alternative hypothesis suggests that terrorizing the civilian population plays a direct military role. Using cross-country data from Sub-Saharan Africa they find support for the latter hypothesis. Civilians are targeted mainly because the displacement of large fractions of the civilian population reduces the fighting efficiency of the enemy, as they cannot hide and obtain support as easily.

Forced migration broadly consists of two groups: refugees and internally displaced persons (IDPs). The United Nations High Commission for Refugees (UNHCR) provides data on "people of concern," that is, people who received assistance from the organization. Approximately 86 percent of people of concern are refugees and IDPs. In 2001 the UNHCR assisted about 12 million refugees and about 5.3 million IDPs worldwide (figure 1.2).

Table 1.1 lists the world's major refugee populations by country of origin and the countries with the largest numbers of IDPs. Afghanistan is one of the countries with the largest percentage of displaced populations in the world. During the 1990s almost 40 percent of the Afghan population was living in refugee camps in asylum countries, mostly in Iran and Pakistan. Liberia and Sudan also have exceptionally large percentages of their population either living as refugees in asylum countries or internally displaced (see box 1.2). Such displacements have huge consequences for these individuals and their societies.

Table 1.1 Major refugee and IDP populations, 2001

Country of origin	Years of war	Refugees — Main asylum countries	Refugees — Total in millions	IDPs — Total in millions
Afghanistan	1978–2002	Iran, Pakistan	3.80	1.200
Burundi	1991–ongoing	Tanzania	0.55	—
Iraq	1985–92	Iran	0.53	—
Sudan	1983–ongoing	Central African Republic, Democratic Republic of Congo, Ethiopia, Kenya, Uganda	0.49	—
Angola	1992–2002	Zambia, Democratic Republic of Congo, Namibia	0.47	0.202
Somalia	1988–92	Ethiopia, Kenya, United Kingdom, United States, Yemen	0.44	—
Bosnia-Herzegovina	1992–95	Serbia and Montenegro, United States, Sweden, Denmark, Netherlands	0.43	0.438
Democratic Republic of Congo	1997–99	Burundi, Republic of Congo, Rwanda, Tanzania, Zambia	0.39	—
Vietnam	1960–75	China, United States	0.35	—
Eritrea	1998–2001	Sudan	0.33	—
Colombia	1984–ongoing	n.a.	—	0.720
Sri Lanka	1983–2002	n.a.	—	0.683
Azerbaijan	1991–ongoing	n.a.	—	0.573
Russia	1999–ongoing	n.a.	—	0.443
Georgia	1991–ongoing	n.a.	—	0.264
Serbia and Montenegro (former FR Yugoslavia)	1991–99	n.a.	—	0.263
Liberia	1992–1996	n.a.	—	0.196

n.a. Not applicable.
Source: UNHCR (2002).

Legacy Effects of Civil War

TO THE EXTENT THAT CIVIL WAR HAS A POLITICAL RATIONALE it is as a catalyst for social progress. A rebel leader might honorably accept the terrible costs incurred during war as a high but necessary price to pay for future improvements, but far from being

---

Box 1.2 Refugees and IDPs in Liberia and Sudan

Liberia: A Nation Displaced

While official estimates for IDPs and refugees peak at 70 percent of the population, it is hard to see how a single Liberian family has not been displaced at some stage by Liberia's civil war. Displacement in Liberia has been driven by the conflict, with all its devastating political, economic, and social consequences.

The human costs of displacement are apparent, but hard data have been difficult to collect, and official statistics do not tell the whole story. The last reliable census took place in 1974, with a subsequent exercise in 1984 remaining unfinished. The baseline population figure most often used of 2.6 million at the outset of fighting is an extrapolation based on previous birth and mortality rates. Of this estimated population, at least 750,000 have fled as refugees to neighboring or distant countries, an additional million have been displaced internally, and an estimated 100,000 to 150,000 have died or been killed. The United Nations reports that 1.8 million, virtually the entire remaining population, are dependent on aid. Violence has visited every one of Liberia's 15 counties and territories. The official numbers therefore disguise the fact that all Liberians, from wealthy merchants in Monrovia to peasant farmers up-country, have had their way of life severely disrupted and, more often, destroyed. Most of the refugees are in Côte d'Ivoire.

Sudan

"Civil war, primarily between northern and southern Sudanese from 1955 through 1972 and from 1983 to the present, has left more than 1.5 million southern Sudanese dead and a majority of the remaining southern Sudanese population uprooted. The massive level of often deliberate death and displacement has been one of the century's largest, yet least-recognized, tragedies. . . . The vast majority of the southern Sudanese forced from their homes are internally displaced. At the end of 1996, USCR reported that as many as 4 million Sudanese, mostly southerners, were internally displaced throughout Sudan."

Source: Liberia: Scott (1998); Sudan: Ruiz (1998, pp. 139, 141).

---

a catalyst for beneficial change, civil war typically leaves a persisting legacy of poverty and misery.

Economic and Political Legacy

Several of the adverse economic effects of civil war are highly persistent. Recall that during civil war military expenditure rises as a percentage of GDP from 2.8 to 5.0 percent; however, once the war has ended, military expenditure does not return to its former level. During the first postconflict decade the average country spends 4.5 percent of GDP on the military. The government often presents the modest reduction in military spending from its wartime level as a peace dividend, but a more accurate way of viewing postconflict military spending is to see it as a major hidden cost of conflict, hidden because abnormally inflated military spending persists long after the conflict is over. Cumulatively over the first decade of peace some 17 percent of a year's GDP is lost in increased military spending. This is far from being the only postconflict cost of war, but alone it is substantial: during the typical conflict the total income loss cumulates to around 60 percent of a year's GDP.

A second cost during conflict is capital flight. Recall that during war capital flight increases from 9 percent of private wealth to 20 percent. By the end of the first decade of postconflict peace capital flight has risen further to 26.1 percent. Far from realizing a peace dividend here, the country experiences a war overhang effect. A possible reason for this is that asset portfolios can only be adjusted gradually, so that even by the end of a war the typical portfolio may not have fully adjusted to the political uncertainty created by the war. Once a country has experienced a civil war it is much more likely to see further conflict, so that even though peace is an improvement, risk levels do not return to their preconflict level. Thus even once peace has returned, people may still wish to move more of their assets abroad. Capital repatriation requires more than just peace. The same is true, only much more powerfully, for human flight. Civil war gives a big impetus to emigration, but some of these emigrants, especially those in industrial countries, then provide a postconflict channel for further emigration.

A third persistent adverse legacy is the loss of social capital. Civil war can have the effect of switching behavior from an equilibrium in which there is an expectation of honesty to one in which there is an expectation of corruption. Once a reputation for honesty has been lost, the incentive for honest behavior in the future is greatly weakened. Clearly civil war is not the only way in which a society can become corrupted, but the point is that the costs inflicted by corruption are likely to persist long after the conflict is over.

For civil war to have some redeeming features, the most hopeful areas would be policies, political institutions, and human rights. The impact of civil war on each of these can, to an extent, be measured. With respect to policy we use a measure adopted by the World Bank, the country policy and institutional assessment (CPIA). The CPIA is an assessment on a 5-point scale of economic policy in four areas—macroeconomic, structural, social, and public sector management—with a higher score indicating better policies. While what constitutes "good" policies can be controversial, consensus on the recognition of bad policies is wider, and, unfortunately, civil war countries tend to be at this end of the spectrum. Those low-income countries that are neither at war nor in the first decade of postwar peace have, on average, a CPIA score of 2.75. For those countries that have had a civil war and re-established peace, we can track whether the war served as a catalyst for improvement. On average, during the last five years prior to war the CPIA for these countries was 2.56. During the first postconflict decade it averaged only 2.29. Although the numbers are close together, they actually reflect a substantial deterioration in policies. All four policy areas are worse in postconflict societies: their macroeconomies are less stable, their structural policies such as trade and infrastructure are less conducive to growth, their social policies are less inclusive, and their public sectors are less well managed. Civil war is thus not normally a catalyst for policy improvement, but rather for policy deterioration.

With respect to the extent to which political institutions are democratic, we use the standard political science index, polity IV. This is a 10-point scale, and as with the CPIA the bottom end of the range is probably more clear-cut than the top. The typical low-income country that is neither at war nor in postwar peace has a score of 2.11, while countries in the first decade of postwar peace average a score of only 1.49. Thus again, on average, civil war leads to a deterioration rather than an improvement in political institutions. A related measure is an index of political freedoms compiled by Freedom House. This is a 7-point scale in which, unlike the other indexes, a low score is better than a high score. The comparable numbers are 4.79 prior to conflict and 5.66 postconflict. Hence civil war again leaves a legacy of reduced freedom rather than increased freedom. A further new measure combines a democracy score and an autocracy score and ranges from 0 to 20. Countries are typically democratic if they score 15 or above. Five years after the end of the civil war the average score on this index is only 8.1 (Doyle and Sambanis 2003). Some evidence suggests that postconflict, countries tend to revert approximately to their preconflict political conditions (Sambanis 2000).

As chapter 3 shows, in reality the political legacy of civil war is far worse than these indicators imply. Once a country has had a civil war it is far more at risk of further war. This is partly because war leaves the society divided and embittered, and partly because war creates interests that favor continued violence and criminality. As a result, people's fears of a relapse into further conflict may dominate the postconflict economic landscape.

The overall economic and political legacy from civil war is thus sufficiently adverse that rapid recovery is unlikely. Collier (1999) finds some evidence for a war overhang effect, whereby after short wars the economy continues to have exceptionally low growth. This is consistent with the capital flight story, in that a short war may not give people enough time to shift their assets abroad, so they continue with capital flight even after the war is over. Chapter 5 discusses the postconflict economic recovery in detail with a focus on national and global policies. The pace of postconflict recovery is highly dependent on national policy choices and the scale and nature of international support. Recovery is not an automatic process of bouncing back. Even in successful recoveries the process is slow. Consider, for example, Uganda, where recovery was unusually rapid, yet even by the late 1990s, 10 years after the end of the civil war, per capita income had barely regained its level of the early 1970s and the retreat into subsistence had barely been reversed. At the household level, even though most respondents had been able to replace some of their assets, when interviewed 60 percent indicated that they were still worse off than before the war (Matovu and Stewart 2001).

Social Legacy

Civil War Increases Mortality Rates. Mortality rates only capture one dimension of the human consequences of conflict; however, they are a useful summary measure of the crisis and its impact. Mortality estimates can be highly inaccurate, but they are often better and more easily captured than other health indicators, which may be subject to different definitions and cultural interpretations (Keely, Reed, and Waldman 2000). Other human damage as a consequence of conflict includes morbidity and psychological effects, but mortality rates have been one of the most easily and accurately measured indicators in emergency settings.

The long-term effect of civil war on mortality can be investigated using both econometrics and case studies. A new econometric study investigates the effect on infant mortality (Hoeffler and Reynal-Querol 2003). Unsurprisingly, the mortality effect depends on the duration of the conflict. Considering a typical five-year war, the study finds that infant mortality increases by 13 percent during such a war; however, this

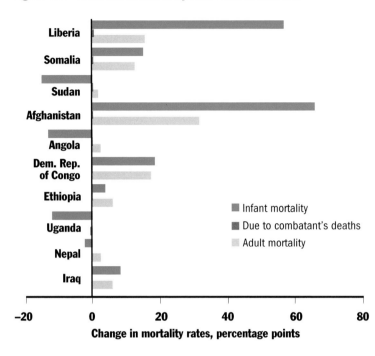

Figure 1.3   Increase in mortality rates due to civil war

Source: Guha-Sapir and Van Panhuis (2002).

effect is persistent, and in the first five years of postconflict peace the infant mortality rate remains 11 percent higher than the baseline.

Guha-Sapir and Van Panhuis (2002) collected intensive case study data on mortality rates following civil conflicts. They find that the impact on adult mortality is generally even worse than that on infant mortality (figure 1.3). The numbers indicate the percentage change in deaths per month from before the war for children under five years old and for the rest of the population. The figure compares the mortality rates of refugees and IDPs with the mortality rate of the country in the year before the conflict started (the baseline year). Among the cases listed in the table, 60 percent of the cases refer to refugees, 20 percent to IDPs, and 20 percent to residents of the country. Mortality rates were higher after conflict than before. While the rise in adult mortality might be expected to have occurred because of adults' greater exposure to the risk of combat death, few of these adult deaths are directly combat related. A comparison of these increases in mortality with the estimates of deaths as a direct result of combat reveals that the death of

Table 1.2 Mortality rates among children under five in refugee and IDP camps, selected conflicts

Population sample and year	Disease	Percentage of deaths	
		Baseline	Conflict
IDPs in Somalia, 1992	Measles	10.1	36.5
	Diarrhea	20.0	39.0
Kurdish refugees in Iraq, 1991	Diarrhea	22.9	74.0
Sudanese refugees in northern Uganda, 1994	Meningitis	0.6	0.2
Rwandan refugees in Zaire, 1994	Diarrhea	20.0	87.0
Bhutanese refugees in Nepal, 1992–93	Respiratory infections	26.2	41.4
	Diarrhea	22.9	22.9
Residents in eastern Democratic Republic of Congo, 2000	Malaria	15.5	26.0
	Diarrhea	20.0	11.0

Source: Centre for Research on the Epidemiology of Disasters (2001).

combatants is only a minor component of the overall rise in mortality. These numbers suggest that civil wars kill far more civilians even after the conflict is over than they kill combatants during the conflict.

Table 1.2 compares the preconflict baseline for mortality rates among children under five years old with postconflict rates for selected diseases and conflicts. The numbers indicate the highly mortality rates caused by infectious diseases in refugee and IDP camps after war.

Moving beyond mortality, useful summary measures are disability-adjusted life expectancy and disability-adjusted life-years (DALYs) compiled by the World Health Organization (WHO). These measures take into account both years of life lost because of disease and injury and years of healthy life lost to long-term disability. Ghobarah, Huth, and Russett (2003) find that civil wars significantly reduce these aggregate measures of national health performance. They use information on the major 23 diseases for categories of the population distinguished by gender and five different age groups. They find important effects of civil war in increasing the postconflict incidence of death and disability caused by particular infectious diseases and conditions among different population subgroups. As an example, in 1999 WHO (2000) estimates that 8.44 million DALYs were lost as a direct effect of all wars that were ongoing at that time. However, that same year a further 8.01 million DALYs were lost as a result of civil wars that had ended during 1991–97, but had increased the incidence of persistent infectious diseases. Thus the legacy effect of civil wars on DALYs was approximately as large as the effect during conflict (Ghobarah, Huth, and Russett 2003).

Why are these health effects of civil wars so persistent? They affect people through the following two main channels (Ghobarah, Huth, and Russett 2003):

- *Channel 1: "technical regress," that is, changes in living conditions make staying healthy more difficult.* Civil wars raise the exposure of the civilian population to conditions that increase the risk of disease, injury, and death.

- *Channel 2: the government has less money in the budget to spend on public health.* Civil wars produce longer-term negative consequences for public health by reducing the pool of available financial resources for expenditures on the health care system.

Table 1.3 summarizes how each of these channels affects health conditions during and after civil war ends.

Table 1.3   Effects of civil war on public health

Time	Channel 1: Technical regress	Channel 2: Budget reduction
During civil war	Civil wars destroy the infrastructure needed to maintain health care programs. Prolonged civil wars displace large populations, either internally or as refugees. Epidemic diseases are likely to emerge from crowding, bad water and poor sanitation in camps, while malnutrition and stress compromise people's immune systems.	Civil wars reduce economic growth and divert public expenditures from health care to military needs.
After civil war	Civil wars reduce the efficient use of resources that are allocated to public health, and these reductions in efficiency extend into the post–civil war period. Moreover, often refugees and internally displaced people do not return to their original homes after the war ends, but remain in makeshift camps for years. The population continues to be exposed to conditions that increase the risk of infections.	The economic legacy of civil war is to reduce the level of income for a considerable period. This squeezes all forms of public expenditure. In addition, postconflict governments typically maintain far higher levels of military expenditure than prior to the conflict, so that expenditure on health care continues to be accorded a lower priority than it would otherwise have had.

Source: Ghobarah, Huth, and Russett (2003).

Table 1.4   HIV prevalence in the military, selected countries and years
(percent)

Country and year	HIV prevalence
Angola	40.0–60.0
Cambodia (1996)	6.5
Democratic Republic of Congo	40.0–60.0
Sierra Leone (1998)	61.0
Uganda (1995/96)	27.1

Source: Elbe (2002); World Bank (1997).

Ghobarah, Huth, and Russett (2003) find that infectious diseases are the most important cause of the indirect deaths of civil war. Of these malaria is the most important, and the evidence suggests that all the age groups under 60 are affected by malaria.

As AIDS is now such a common cause of death we examine the relationship between civil war and HIV/AIDS in more detail. Military recruits are typically young, sexually active men, often unmarried. Military personnel tend to have high rates of sexually transmitted diseases (STDs), including HIV: estimates indicate that rates among military personnel are two to five times higher than among the general population, even during peacetime. When military personnel are stationed away from home, social controls in relation to engaging in sexual relationships are lower and the risk of HIV infection is likely to be higher. Prostitution around army bases also increases the spread of infection. In addition, in times of war the risk of contracting HIV or other STDs may seem low relative to the risk of death in combat.

Some figures for HIV prevalence in the military are available (table 1.4). No reliable figures are available for rebel forces, but they are likely to be at least as high as for the regular armed forces. Studies also find that the level of militarization increases the prevalence of HIV. One study finds that halving the number of men in the armed forces is associated with a reduction in the rate of seroprevalence among low-risk adults by about a quarter (Over 2003). However, HIV is not only spread through consensual intercourse, but also through gender-based violence. Regular soldiers and rebels force women to give sexual favors in exchange for "protection." Also the incidence of rape increases, often dramatically, during war, with refugees and displaced women and girls being particu-

---

Box 1.3 Angola

"THE MATERNAL AND INFANT MORTALITY RATES are the worst in Africa, estimated in 1998 at 1,854/100,000 and 166/1,000 live births, respectively. The estimated national contraceptive prevalence rate is very low (3 percent), and only 19 percent of women have assisted deliveries. IDP women are known to be at higher risk of dying from pregnancy related causes due to lack of access to health services and life in stressful conditions. A survey conducted by UNFPA and the implementing agencies in 1999 with 710 men and women in IDP camps and peri- urban areas of Matala, Chibia, Lubango, Lobito, Baia Farta and Benguela indicated that there is: (1) very poor attendance of pregnant women; (2) a lack of knowledge about child spacing and sexuality is- sues, among men and women; (3) little use of fam- ily planning methods; (4) little knowledge about STDs/AIDS; and, (5) an overall expectation of large family size. With regard to questions about forced sex, 19 percent of women indicated they knew of women who were forced to have sex." (UN 1999, pp. 42, 50).

---

larly vulnerable. Carballo and Solby (2001) estimate that more than 200,000 women refugees were raped during the Rwandan war.

Diseases have long been used as weapons of war, and AIDS is no ex- ception. HIV-infected soldiers made widespread use of rape as a system- atic tool of warfare in conflicts in Liberia, Mozambique, Rwanda, and Sierra Leone. According to Elbe (2002, p. 168): "There is documented testimony from female survivors of rape in Rwanda that the transmission of HIV was a deliberate act. According to some accounts, HIV-positive Hutu men would tell women they were raping that they would eventu- ally suffer an agonizing death from AIDS . . . some of the rapists al- legedly said 'We are not killing you. We are giving you something worse. You will die a slow death.' "

After war, the reintegration of ex-combatants into civil society poses a health problem because of their comparatively high levels of HIV prevalence (Carballo and Solby 2001). For example, a study of mass de- mobilization of Ugandan troops revealed devastating results for the rural areas where the demobilized HIV-positive soldiers retired. About 50,000 Uganda People's Defence Forces soldiers have been demobi- lized. Many of the soldiers with AIDS were retrenched to their home villages, AIDS being a major criterion for demobilization. However, hardly any counseling was undertaken to prepare such soldiers to avoid risky behavior as they reintegrated into civilian society.

The destruction of social and physical infrastructure during wartime also contributes to the spread of HIV (see box 1.3). The health system is less likely to detect the diseases associated with HIV/AIDS infection or to screen blood supplies. War also destroys the education system, which makes teaching about prevention more difficult. Finally, in most war or postconflict situations women do not have a choice regarding breastfeeding their babies, thereby increasing the risk of infecting the next generation (Machel 2000).

Psychological Damage of Civil War.   Quantitative research on the effect of civil war on mortality is feasible because mortality is easy to measure. At the other end of the spectrum of measurability is the psychological damage done by civil war. Mental health services are typically highly inadequate during conflict and postconflict situations, and so the evidence is much more fragmentary; however, the evidence that is available suggests, unsurprisingly, that the psychological effects of civil war are large and highly persistent (see box 1.4).

Box 1.4   Psychological trauma

Bosnia
"It is estimated that the recent war in Bosnia and Herzegovina caused more than 250,000 deaths, created more than 2 million refugees and internally displaced persons, and wounded 200,000 in Bosnia and Herzegovina alone. Recent epidemiologic studies have revealed that the psychiatric morbidity associated with mass violence in civilian and refugee populations is elevated when compared with non-traumatized communities. . . . Clinical reports of Bosnian refugees in treatment show rates of depressive symptoms ranging from 14 to 21% and post-traumatic stress disorder (PTSD) symptoms rates ranging from 18% to 53%."

Cambodia
"Approximately 68% of the Cambodian refugees living on the Thai border displayed symptoms of major depression and 37% showed symptoms associated with the diagnosis of posttraumatic stress disorder (PTSD). These results were anticipated by clinical studies of Cambodian refugees in the United States that revealed high rates of depression and PTSD."

Sierra Leone
"One worker from Doctors without Borders . . . in Sierra Leone asserted that the severe 'psychosocial problems . . . may ultimately threaten the prospects for long-term stability in society.' While an Interagency Appeal for the CIS region claims that psychological trauma is 'deep' and will 'probably lead to irreversible psychological consequences.' "

Source: Bosnia and Cambodia: Mollica and others (1999, p. 38); Sierra Leone: McDonald (2002, p. 6).

Civil war survivors have lost family members, friends, livelihoods, and identity. Many of them are living in refugee camps. This experience of trauma suffered on a wide scale has psychological consequences: "Intimate exposure to brutality and subsequent displacement and civil disorder leave individuals psychologically scarred and the intricate network of social interaction deeply torn" (McDonald 2002, p. 4). The experience of trauma continues after war. Moreover, living in a refugee camp or transitory settlement can constitute a "secondary wound." Most individuals will experience low-grade but long-lasting mental health problems (McDonald 2002).

During the period following displacement the threat of violence is high, as are mortality and morbidity rates. These features, together with having to live in camps, contribute to the development of a prevailing sense of hopelessness that increases the traumatic experience. Traumas are of two types, single event traumas and ongoing traumas. Life in a refugee camp is an ongoing trauma (McDonald 2002). Clinical conditions such as depression and schizophrenia are linked to premature death in refugee populations.

Ghobarah, Huth, and Russett (2003) find an indirect effect of civil wars on suicides of women of childbearing age. This probably reflects the trauma of rape. Longitudinal studies of survivors of terror, such as Holocaust survivors and survivors of the Pol Pot regime in Cambodia, show the existence of an intergenerational transmission of trauma. "The effects of massive trauma, tragically . . . do not end with deaths of survivors and may continue into the lives of their children" (box 1.4).

Landmines. A final legacy of civil war, landmines, affects both economic activity and health (this section is based on ICBL 2002). Landmines are, in effect, a negative capital stock that the society accumulates during conflict. They continue to kill and maim people long after the actual fighting has stopped. For 2001 the International Campaign to Ban Landmines recorded 7,987 landmine casualties in 70 countries, of which about 70 percent were civilians; however, as reporting is incomplete, the campaign estimates that the total number is more likely to be between 15,000 and 20,000. In comparison with previous years, when the number of casualties was estimated at around 26,000 per year, this is a considerable improvement. The decrease in the number of landmine victims is due to the international ban of antipersonnel mines in 1997,

Box 1.5 Landmines: A bitter legacy for Cambodians

CAMBODIA IS ONE OF THE MOST HEAVILY LAND-mine and unexploded ordnance (UXO) contaminated countries in the world. Although the actual fighting stopped more than a decade ago in 1991, on average more than two people are injured or killed by landmines in Cambodia every day. Even though 166 million square meters of land were cleared from 1992 through 2001 and a total of 313,586 antipersonnel mines were found and destroyed, all 24 provinces still have areas contaminated by mines and UXO. In 2001, 6,422 villages, or 46 percent of Cambodian villages, had areas contaminated with mines and/or UXO. Mine and UXO contamination restricts access to homes, agricultural land, pastures, water sources, forests, schools, dams, canals, markets, business activities, health centers, pagodas, bridges, and neighboring villages. Thus the threat of UXO and mines impedes mobility, security, economic activity, and development in several provinces, particularly in the north and northwest. With more than 80 percent of the country's population residing in rural areas, and with 40 percent of these estimated to be living below the poverty line, mine action programs continue to be of the highest priority in Cambodia's poverty reduction policy. Official reports show that 173 people were killed and 640 were injured in mine or UXO incidents during 2001. The proportion of civilian casualties was about 95 percent, with children particularly at risk (232, or 28 percent, of the casualties were children). Clearing mines, caring for the injured and disabled, and providing mine education programs place a severe strain on Cambodian public expenditure.

Source: ICBL (2002).

which resulted in the destruction of stockpiles as well as a drastic decrease in the production and trade of landmines. In addition, mine-sweeping operations have been extremely successful in detecting and destroying mines in many countries. Yet as the example of Cambodia shows (see box 1.5), landmines continue to severely disrupt normal daily activities and therefore constitute a serious obstacle to economic and social recovery.

Conclusion

THIS CHAPTER HAS FOCUSED ONLY ON THE EFFECTS OF CIVIL war within the affected country and has clearly shown that most of the suffering inflicted by civil war accrues to noncombatants who typically have no say in either whether the conflict is initiated or whether it is settled.

During the war income losses are severe and mortality and morbidity exhibit large increases. Even if a war is viewed as a costly investment for subsequent social progress, the costs during the conflict are typically so high that postconflict progress would need to be dramatic for subsequent benefits to outweigh these costs. Yet the legacy effects of civil war are usually so adverse that they cannot reasonably be viewed as social progress. Many of the costs of the war continue to accrue long after it is over. For example, the country tends to get locked into persistently high levels of military expenditure, sees capital continuing to flow out of the country at an unusually high rate, and faces a much higher incidence of infectious disease. Even economic policies, political institutions, and political freedom appear to deteriorate. Hence most modern civil wars are not remotely like the 19th century American civil war that ended slavery. Of course, finding some modern civil wars that can reasonably be seen as ushering in social progress is always possible, but these are surely the exceptions. On average, modern civil war has not been a useful force for social change, but has been development in reverse.

Let Them Fight It Out Among Themselves?

CHAPTER 1 SHOWED THAT FOR THE COUNTRIES directly affected, civil war is development in reverse, therefore preventing civil war is important for those concerned about the development of low-income countries. However, the constituency for action to prevent war is potentially much larger than this, because civil war has spillover effects for both neighboring countries and the entire international community. This chapter first considers the neighborhood effects and then turns to the global effects.

Neighborhood Effects of Civil War

PEACEFUL COUNTRIES THAT ARE ADJACENT TO COUNTRIES ENgaged in civil war suffer from direct and long-term effects caused by the civil wars of their neighbors.

Economic Spillovers

Civil wars are not only costly for the countries in which they are fought, but for the entire region. Neighboring countries must usually accommodate large numbers of refugees, because the victims of war do not usually have the means to travel to countries further away from their home country, and, in any case, arrive on foot. For example, Pakistan's burden of accommodating more than 2 million refugees from Afghanistan is considerable. However, this direct burden is probably

Box 2.1 Regional arms races

A RECENT STUDY ATTEMPTS TO MODEL WHAT level of military spending governments choose as a share of GDP. On average, governments spend 3.4 percentage points of GDP on the military, but this average varies widely and predictably. The largest increase is if a country is engaged in international warfare, when spending rises by 2.5 percentage points. Civil war raises spending almost as much, by 1.8 percentage points, that is, the military budget increases by 50 percent. The risk of war also matters. Each 10.0 percentage points on the risk of civil war raises military spending by 0.4 percentage points.

Both a past history of international war and the military expenditure of neighboring countries are highly significant. Because of these neighborhood effects military spending is, in effect, a regional public bad. Controlling for all these risks, military governments still spend more on the military, presumably because they are more susceptible to the military lobby. A wave of democratization, such as occurred in the early 1990s, is thus a regional public good. Finally, the end of the Cold War gradually, but substantially, yielded a peace dividend, as military spending fell by around 0.7 percentage points.

Source: Collier and Hoeffler (2002d).

not the most important regional economic spillover. Other effects are on the military budget, the costs of transport, and the reputation of the region in relation to investors.

An important route by which civil war affects neighbors is through regional arms races (see box 2.1). Both in response to the risk of a civil war, and especially once it has started, a government tends to increase its military expenditure sharply, typically by around two percentage points of GDP. Unfortunately, one of the strongest influences on the level of military expenditure a government chooses is the level its neighbors have chosen (Collier and Hoeffler 2002d). This may be partly because of a perceived threat, and partly because of norm setting and the emulation and rivalries of military leaderships. On average, if civil war leads a government with two neighbors to increase its military expenditure by 2.0 percentage points of GDP, by the time the arms race is back to equilibrium, the neighboring countries will each have increased their spending by around 0.7 percentage points.

In some situations war in one country directly increases the risk of war in neighboring countries. Chapter 3 discusses how the supply of armaments has sometimes spilled across borders and how rival governments can find themselves financing each other's rebel movements. Such regional increases in conflict risk are compounded by their effects on regional military expenditure. A simulation of a regionwide increase of 10 percentage points in the risk of civil war predicts that regional military expenditure would end up rising by around 1 percentage point of GDP after arms race effects.

A country's neighbors' military spending has an adverse effect on the economic growth rate. For each additional 1.0 percentage point of GDP that neighbors spend on the military, the growth rate is reduced by 0.1 percentage point.[1] Recall that during and after a civil war the government directly affected raises its military spending by around two percentage points and that this is liable to trigger a regional arms race that can persist long after the conflict is over. This alone can produce a small but widespread reduction in growth across an entire neighborhood.

Some studies have attempted to estimate the overall effect of a neighboring conflict on growth. Having a neighbor at war reduces the annual growth rate by around 0.5 percentage points.[2] Murdoch and Sandler (2002) show that civil war reduces not only the country's own growth rate, but also growth across an entire region. As most countries have several neighbors, this is a major multiplier effect of the economic cost of conflict. Recalling that the growth cost for the country itself is around 2.2 percent, a country with four neighbors is likely to inflict approximately as much economic damage on its neighbors during conflict as it does on itself.

Neighbors' growth rates may be reduced for a number of reasons. In addition to the direct burden the refugee population poses and the effect on military spending, trade is also disrupted, and this is a particularly severe problem for landlocked countries. For example, the war in Mozambique doubled Malawi's international transport costs and triggered an economic decline. Similarly, the war in the Democratic Republic of Congo closed the river route to the sea for the landlocked Central African Republic. A further effect is that the entire region is regarded as riskier, which results in a negative reputation effect with investors.

Social Spillovers

The most immediate effect of civil war on neighboring countries is the arrival of thousands of refugees and their consequences for the population of the asylum countries. As refugees stay in asylum countries for long periods after the civil war ends, the social effects of civil war on asylum countries are also persistent. Among all the long-run, indirect effects of civil war, it causes most deaths in neighboring populations through infectious diseases, especially malaria. Large-scale refugee flows put people into crowded conditions in the asylum countries without access to clean water and food, making the camps a perfect environment for the spread of infectious diseases.

Refugees and Malaria.   A global effort to eradicate malaria was undertaken in the 1950s and 1960s. By the end of the 1960s these attempts to control the disease had faded in the face of the internal problems of the countries where the incidence of malaria was the highest. The most relevant internal problem was civil war. Civil war has been a basic reason behind the observed increase in the incidence of malaria. Conflict affects the incidence of malaria both directly, when nonimmune refugees come into contact with infected individuals when they flee through rural and rainforest areas to reach a foreign country, and indirectly, when conflict impairs active control measures (Montalvo and Reynal-Querol 2002).

Figure 2.1 shows the flow and stock of refugees. Refugees stay in camps for a long time after civil wars end. Figure 2.2 shows the relationship between the stock of refugees and ongoing civil wars.

Figure 2.1   The flow and stock of refugees, 1951–2002

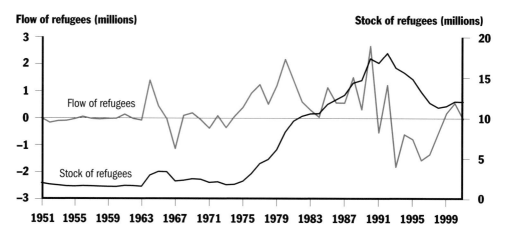

Source: UNHCR (2002).

Figure 2.2   The stock of refugees and civil wars, 1951–2001

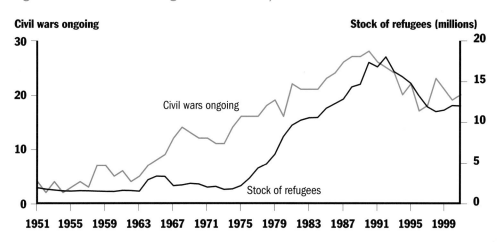

Source: Gleditsch and others (2002); UNHCR (2002).

The number of countries reporting cases of malaria varies over time. In particular, China and India have a critical influence on the number of cases. China started to report officially to WHO in 1977. Initially it reported close to 4 million cases, but then a rapid decrease took place. Meanwhile India drove the growth of cases during the 1974–77 epidemic period, when it accounted for close to 20 percent of the total cases of malaria in the world. For this reason we exclude China and India. A further reporting problem is Africa, where reporting is irregular. We use last available data before a missing period and first available figures once reporting has resumed.

Figure 2.3 shows the resulting series for cases of malaria compared with the number of refugees worldwide. The high correlation suggests that the increase in the incidence of malaria has been strongly affected by the rise in war refugees. In the Bonga refugee camp in Ethiopia in the mid-1990s: "Malaria remains clearly the main cause of morbidity accounting for 17 percent of total caseload. . . . The profile argues for an active malaria control campaign in the camps to reduce morbidity" (Guha-Sapir and Forcella 2001, p. 34).

Why might there be such a strong connection between refugees and the incidence of malaria? War leads to the movement of people. In general the anarchic situation caused by this social unrest and the military importance of paved roads force people to walk through unfamiliar rural areas and forests to avoid areas of military operations. If the civil war is

Figure 2.3   Refugees and cases of malaria, 1962–97

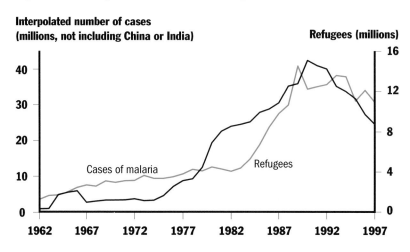

Source: UNHCR (2002); WHO (1983, 1999).

extended, this movement will end up in migration to a contiguous country as war refugees. Population movement caused by political conflicts, rural population migrations, or natural disasters is potentially the most important factor in the transmission of malaria (conditional on the dynamics between the vector, the parasite, and the environment).

While refugees move from cities to the borders, if the country has endemic malaria their probability of becoming infected by the malaria parasite increases as a result of their contact with locally immune rural populations and movement through remote areas where the vector is still predominant. The importance of contact with immune individuals is critical. Repeated infection among individuals of rural endemic areas generates an immune response in the host that controls the infection. This implies that the prevalence of malaria could be extremely high among rural populations despite a small number of reported cases.

If the migrants have contracted malaria they will probably not be diagnosed until they have arrived in the host country. These cases will therefore be counted as cases of malaria in the asylum country. The existence of many migrants infected by the malaria parasite in the asylum country increases malaria transmission to citizens of the asylum country and the contagion effect among the refugees themselves. This will happen if the asylum country has the vector, even though it may not originally be malaria endemic. In general, the concentration of refugees in camps where nonimmune and infected individuals live together increases the risk of transmission conditional on the existence of the *Anopheles* mosquito.

Research using annual data for 135 countries between 1960 and 1999 studies the effects of refugee flows from tropical countries with civil war to neighboring tropical countries (Montalvo and Reynal-Querol 2002). It finds that for each 1,000 refugees the asylum countries see 1,406 new cases of malaria. The size of the refugee population coming from tropical countries with a civil war thus has an important impact on malaria in the asylum countries. Preventing civil wars, especially in tropical countries, is therefore important for controlling malaria.

The effect of war-driven refugees on malaria is qualitatively similar to that of other refugees, an effect that is better known but is quantitatively more important. Refugees fleeing from droughts and famines do not have such a significant effect on the incidence of malaria for two reasons. First, the mechanism whereby refugees escaping from war become infected is because civil wars force people to walk through unfamiliar rural areas and forests to avoid areas of military operations, but people displaced by famines and droughts do not have to avoid paved roads, so they are less likely to be exposed to the mosquito. Second, refugees from war stay in asylum camps for long periods after the war ends, whereas once droughts and famines end refugees can quickly return home. Montalvo and Reynal-Querol (2002) find that refugees from drought who come to tropical asylum countries have no significant effect on the incidence of malaria in the asylum country.

Refugees and the Spread of HIV/AIDS. Refugees and other displaced populations are at increased risk of contracting HIV/AIDS during and after displacement because of poverty; disruption of family and social structures and of health services; increased sexual violence; and increased socioeconomic vulnerability, particularly among women and youth. Data on HIV prevalence in refugee camps are scarce; however, some examples described in box 2.2 suggest the extent of HIV infection in refugee camps in asylum countries. Ghobarah, Huth and Russett (2003) find that the most important effect of civil war on neighboring countries is caused by HIV/AIDS, with the groups that are most affected being young children (who are infected by their mothers) and young and middle-aged adults. The average loss of healthy life for these groups ranges from roughly 2 to 10 years.

Box 2.2   Eritrea

"THERE ARE CONCERNS ABOUT THE INCREASE IN the spread of HIV/AIDS, which rose from 8 in 1988 to over 13,500 cases in 2001. It is estimated that approximately 60,000–70,000 Eritreans are currently infected with HIV, which could increase significantly . . . with demobilisation and increased cross border movement" (UN 2002, pp. 10–11).

"The HIV/AIDS epidemic is perhaps the gravest health threat faced by Eritrea. The recent border conflict with Ethiopia (1998–2002) and the recur-rent drought have resulted in large-scale population movements that included internal displacement, in-flux of deportees from Ethiopia and returnees from Sudan. Mobilisation of young men and women to the military has also contributed by creating a social and economic environment that is conducive for the spread of HIV/AIDS. Intertwined with this is violence against women, including rape and other physical trauma that can be experienced during conflict and displacement" (UN 2002, p. 27).

Civil War Spillover

Civil wars are clustered in particular regions. In the 1980s there were several wars in Central America. In the 1990s there were several civil wars in, for instance, the African Great Lakes area, in Central Asia, and in the Balkans. Civil wars cluster for several reasons. They may share the same historical background: the former Yugoslavia's wars in Croatia in 1991, Bosnia in 1992–95, Croatia again in 1995, and Kosovo in 1998–99 all shared similar characteristics and were influenced by the ideology of greater Serbia and greater Croatia (Kalyvas and Sambanis 2003). In the former Soviet republics wars clustered around the Caucasus in the early 1990s, taking advantage of war- and region-specific physical and human capital (Zürcher, Kohler, and Baev 2002).

Direct contagion may occur. The civil wars in the African Great Lakes region are examples of this, as recurrent wars in Burundi and Rwanda spilled over their borders in both directions and into the Democratic Republic of Congo. The latter war also provoked interventions by Uganda and Zimbabwe. In all these wars Hutu-Tutsi antagonism was predominant (Ngaruko and Nkurunziza 2002; Prunier 1995). This recurrent ethnic conflict crossed borders and lasted over time, being at the core of around seven episodes of civil war in the two countries. Countries embroiled in civil war also often provide a safe haven for rebel groups of other countries. The wars in Liberia and Sierra Leone alternately served these purposes for the other country's rebel groups (Davies and Fofana 2002).

Refugee flows caused by civil wars may also be destabilizing to the host country. During the war in the 1990s, Burundian rebels sought refuge in neighboring Tanzania and the Democratic Republic of Congo and recruited among the Burundi refugee population in Tanzania. The provinces in the Democratic Republic of Congo neighboring those two countries had the highest incidence of fighting and displacements of people (Ngaruko and Nkurunziza 2002).

The economic spillover also increases the risk of civil war in neighboring countries (see chapters 3 and 4).

Global Effects of Civil War

CIVIL WAR IS NOT JUST BAD FOR THE NEIGHBORHOOD. DURing the past 30 years three major global social evils can reasonably be ascribed in substantial part to side effects of civil war. The global cost of these social evils has already been astronomical, and they are proving highly persistent. They are hard drugs, AIDS, and international terrorism.

The link from civil war to hard drugs is through both production and distribution. The cultivation of hard drugs, coca and opium, nowadays predominantly requires territory that is outside the control of any recognized government. Where territory is under the control of an internationally recognized government it can generally be prevailed upon to enforce anticultivation policies reasonably effectively. A by-product of civil war is that large rural areas cease to be under government control. Currently some 95 percent of the global production of opium is in civil war countries. Not only is production concentrated in civil war territory, but distribution and storage channels rely on the lawlessness civil war generates.

The link between civil war and the spread of AIDS within a nation and a region has already been discussed; however, the most far-reaching claim is that the origin of the global pandemic is a consequence of a particular civil war. The hypothesis, for which credible evidence exists, but which is far from proven, is that the conditions of war enabled what would otherwise have been a routine, localized outbreak to spiral out of control. Even if we attach only a small likelihood to this explanation being correct—say 10 percent—then one-tenth of the global cost of the AIDS pandemic should be added to the estimated global cost of civil war.

The link between civil war and international terrorism has only recently become evident. Civil war provides territory that serves as a safe haven for terrorists, and the illegal products of conflict, notably diamonds, are used both as a source of revenue and as a store of value.

Civil War and Drug Production and Trafficking

Table 2.1 shows the production of opium and coca by country from 1990 until 2001. Figures 2.4 and 2.5 group this information according to whether countries are in conflict, are postconflict, or are at peace. As the figures show, virtually all production throughout the period has been in conflict or postconflict countries. When civil war ended in Peru and intensified in Colombia production trends changed.

While production rises sharply during conflict, it is not completely eliminated in postconflict situations. This accords with the discussion in

Table 2.1 Production of opium and coca, selected countries and years, 1990–2001

(metric tons)

Country	1990	1995	2000	2001
Opium				
Afghanistan	1,570	2,335	3,276	185[a]
Colombia		71	88	88
Lao PDR	202	128	167	134
Mexico	62	53	21	71
Myanmar	1,621	1,664	1,087	1,097
Other Asian countries	45	78	38	40
Pakistan	150	112	8	5
Thailand	20	2	6	6
Vietnam	90	9	—	—
Total	3,760	4,452	4,691	1,626
Coca				
Bolivia	77,000	85,000	13,400	20,200
Colombia	45,313	80,931	266,161	236,035
Peru	196,900	183,600	46,258	49,260
Total	319,213	349,531	325,809	305,495

— Not available.

a. Opium production in Afghanistan was reported to have dropped by 95 percent from 2000 to 2001, but the UNODCCP (2003) reports that in 2002 opium production surpassed its 2000 level (3,422 metric tons).

Source: UNODCCP (2002).

Figure 2.4   Opium production, 1986–2001

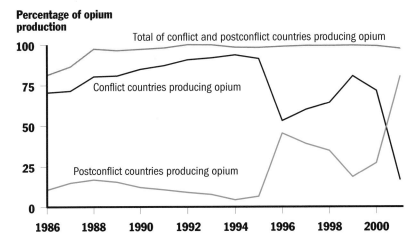

Percentage of opium
production

Source: UNODCCP (2002); Gleditsch and others (2002).

Figure 2.5   Cocaine production, 1986–2001

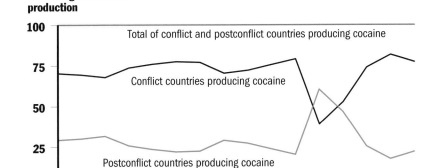

Percentage of cocaine
production

Source: UNODCCP (2002); Gleditsch and others (2002).

chapter 1 on the persistence of the loss of social capital and the criminalization of society. Production of drugs prevails long after civil war ends.

Civil war does not only affect production. The routes traffickers follow from the origin country to American, Australian, and European
markets also go through conflict and postconflict countries. "Between
70% and 90% of the heroin found in European markets (both West

and East Europe), which has traditionally been trafficked along the so called 'Balkan' route (Afghanistan – the I.R. of Iran –Turkey – Balkan countries – West Europe) with indications in recent years of the development of an alternative route through Central Asia and Russia" (UNODCCP 2002, p. 11).

Colombian trafficking organizations control the worldwide supply of cocaine, for which North America remains the principal destination. Africa, in particular, the conflict countries of West and Southern Africa, is increasingly used as a transit area for cocaine trafficking from South America to Europe. The production of hard drugs is concentrated in civil war countries for two main reasons. First, civil war creates territory outside the control of a recognized government on which drugs can be cultivated. It also creates an environment in which many people can behave opportunistically with no cost, because the normal policing institutions are weakened and are unable to control illegal activities. Second, during civil war conventional economic opportunities are severely reduced. International crime, of which drug production and trafficking are the prime example, provides a rare instance of a new economic opportunity.

Drug production affects the industrial world through two channels. First, the production of drugs in civil war countries is intimately related to their consumption in industrial countries. Not surprisingly, production and consumption trends follow the same pattern. Figure 2.6 shows the trends for opium production in Afghanistan and heroin seizures in Europe during 1980–2001. The consumption of illegal drugs results in thousands of deaths among young people in Australia, the United States, and Europe. Second, crime in the industrial world is intimately related to drugs.

The supply of drugs has social consequences for the societies of the countries where it arrives that can be divided into three groups: drug use; drug-related crime; and indirect, adverse effects of use (Reuter 2001). Drug use directly results in dependency and such risky behavior as needle sharing. Drug-related crime includes both the violation of drug laws themselves and theft and violence. The indirect, adverse effects of drug use include overdoses, suicides, abuse and discord within families, and poor school or work productivity. Moreover the government faces costs in terms of law enforcement and health expenditures.

The per capita consumption of hard drugs is highest in industrial countries (figure 2.7, table 2.2). The pattern of consumption by continent reflects production. Crossing the Atlantic is expensive and diffi-

Figure 2.6   Opium production in Afghanistan and heroin seizures in Europe, 1980–2001

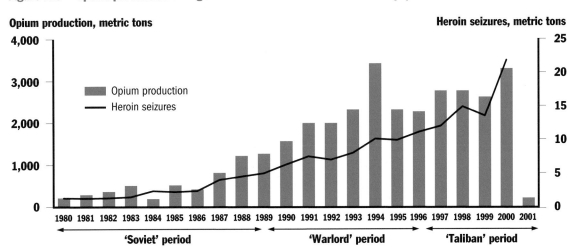

Source: UNODCCP (2002).

Figure 2.7   Estimates of annual opiate and cocaine use in the late 1990s

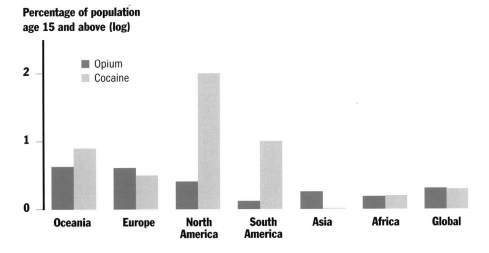

Source: UNODCCP (2002).

cult, so the main market for opium is Asia and Europe. By contrast, North America is the region that has the highest percentage of cocaine consumers (UNODCCP 2002).

Goldstein (1985) proposes three models to explain the connection between drugs and crime. The first, the psychopharmacological link,

Table 2.2   Prevalence estimates of opiate and cocaine use, selected industrial countries and years
(percentage of the population age 15 and above)

Country and year	Opiate use	Cocaine use
Australia (1998)	0.8	1.4
Belgium (1998/2000)	0.2	0.8
France (1999)	0.4	0.2
Germany (2000)	0.2	0.9
Italy (1998)	0.6	—
Italy (1998/99)	0.6	0.8
New Zealand (1999)	0.7	0.4
Spain (1998/99)	0.4	1.5
United Kingdom (2000)	0.6	1.7
United States (2000)	0.5	2.6

— Not available.
Source: UNODCCP (2002).

argues that crime is linked to the psychopharmacological effects of certain drugs. The second model, the economic-compulsive link, argues that drug users commit crimes to obtain money to buy drugs. The third model, the systematic violence link, suggests that crime among illegal drug users is linked to the drug market.

Little evidence supports the existence of a psychopharmacological link. The second explanation of the relationship between drugs and crime, the economic-compulsive link, is well supported by the literature. Statistical studies show that the rate of use of illegal drugs is much higher among people who have been in contact with the criminal justice system than among the general population (Casavant and Collin (2001). Data on drug-related crimes are scarce. The U.S. Bureau of Justice and Statistics (2002) finds that in 1997, 73 percent of federal prisoners and 83 percent of state prisoners reported prior drug use. The third model suggests that the relationship between drugs and crime goes through the illegal drug distribution market. Violence is part of this market, basically because the drug market affords no legal way of obtaining justice when rules are violated. According to Casavant and Collin (2001, p. 14): "Crime in the drug world is often caused by rivalries among individuals attempting to corner the market. This violence may involve various players—including traffickers, importers, merchants or dealers—and may be intended to control various territories, such as a neighbourhood, streets or school. Violence is then used as an organizational management strategy."

This evidence gives an idea of the impact of drugs on crime. The high proportion of convicts who are drug users indicates the potential for crime reduction in the industrial world if illegal drugs were less easily available.

Civil War as an Explanation of the Origins of the AIDS Pandemic

Epidemiological research on the spread of HIV/AIDS points out that the initial spread of HIV is closely associated with the war in Uganda in 1979. Smallman-Raynor and Cliff (1991, p. 78), geographers at Cambridge University, conclude that "the apparent geographical pattern of clinical AIDS in Uganda partially reflects the diffusion of HIV associated with civil war during the first six years of the post-Amin period." Using regression analysis they find a significant and positive correlation between the spread of HIV infections in the 1980s and 1990s and the ethnic patterns of recruitment into the Ugandan National Liberation Army. Their research supports the following hypothesis. Many rapes occurred along the borders of Tanzania and Uganda in 1979. HIV was in this region, but before 1979 contagion was sporadic and there was still no epidemic. However, because of the continuous rape, promiscuity, and dislocation during and after the war, HIV started to become an epidemic infection. The spread of AIDS from the south to the north of Uganda exhibited the same route as the one Idi Amin's soldiers followed after the war in 1979.

Civil War and International Terrorism

The link between civil war and Al Qaeda is well established. The main activists in the organization were not Afghani, yet they chose to locate in Afghanistan because it provided territory outside the control of a recognized government and under the control of the Taliban, a recently successful rebel organization. Small-scale international terrorism can hide and survive in most societies. What was distinctive about Al Qaeda when compared with other terrorist organizations was its scale. The large scale of Al Qaeda operations, such as training camps for thousands of recruits, would have been infeasible except in territory outside the control of a recognized government. Hence the safe havens produced by civil war are not just convenient for large-scale global terrorism, they are likely to be essential. Widespread civil war offers such organizations a choice of location and relocation. For example, there has been speculation that Al Qaeda might relocate in Somalia, another civil war territory with no recognized government.

Evidence indicates that Al Qaeda acquired substantial revenues from trafficking in West African conflict diamonds (Farah 2002). Recent evidence also suggests that in response to greater scrutiny in the international banking system it has shifted its assets into conflict diamonds.

As with AIDS, claiming that without civil war large-scale international terrorism would have been impossible is unnecessary. There is sufficient evidence for a reasonable inference that civil war facilitates such terrorism. If we attribute to civil war only 10 percent of the contributing factors to the September 11 attack, the cost remains enormous. The World Bank has estimated that as a result of September 11 global GDP is currently around 0.8 percent lower than it would have been (World Bank 2002a) and that about 10 more million people worldwide live in poverty than would otherwise have been the case.

Conclusion

SOMETIMES THE INTERNATIONAL COMMUNITY EXHIBITS AN understandable impatience with civil war, taking an it's-not-our-problem attitude and remarking that the participants should be left to fight it out among themselves. This chapter has tried to show why such an attitude is mistaken. Many of the costs of civil war, indeed, probably most of them, accrue outside the affected country. The active participants in conflict can be presumed to ignore these costs, as they neither bear them nor are even aware of them.

The costs of civil war can be though of as forming three ripples beyond the direct effects on combatants. The inner ripple, discussed in chapter 1, is the effect on the civilian population: the loss of income and the severe deterioration in health. Many of these losses accrue after the conflict is over, so that even if the active participants care about the effects on civilians, they are likely to be unaware of them. The second ripple, discussed in the first part of this chapter, is across the neighborhood. The economic costs of conflict suffered elsewhere in the region may be approximately as large as those suffered within the country, and severe health spillovers also occur, predominantly through refugees. The outer ripple is the global costs. In the past 30 years three devastating social shocks have been facilitated by civil war. We have not attempted to quantify the costs of these shocks, but they are clearly huge.

Our point is not to emphasize or inflate the importance of civil war among the world's problems. Rather, we wish to make the simpler point that decisions about these conflicts should not just be left to the participants. The participants bear such a small share of the costs of their actions that they will systematically indulge in civil war far beyond its likely social value.

Notes

1. Results are available on request.

2. Results are available on request.

PART II

WHAT FUELS CIVIL WAR?

PART I SHOWED THAT CIVIL WAR IS A MAJOR impediment to development and has spillovers that make it a problem of global concern. We now turn to what fuels civil war. An understanding of the factors that make civil war more or less likely is a helpful input into the formulation of policy responses, which is the subject of part III.

Chapter 3 analyzes what makes a country more or less prone to civil war and considers both the risk that a war will ignite and the factors that tend to sustain it once it has started. Although civil war is intensely political, some of the most important factors affecting proneness to conflict turn out to be closely associated with economic development: risks are much higher for the poorest countries. Furthermore, far from war resolving political struggle, countries are at risk of falling into a conflict trap whereby one civil war tends to lead to another. Chapter 4 scales this analysis up to the global level, trying to understand what has determined the global incidence of conflict and how it might change. The main statistical techniques that we use and a selective bibliography of the broader literature are set out in appendixes 1 and 2, respectively.

CHAPTER THREE

What Makes a Country Prone to Civil War?

IVIL WAR IS FUELED PARTLY BY THE CIRCUM-stances that account for the initial resort to large-scale organized violence, and partly by forces generated once violence has started and that tend to perpetuate it. We refer to the initial circumstances as the root causes and to the perpetuating forces as the conflict trap.

Most people think that they already know the root causes of civil war. Those on the political right tend to assume that it is due to long-standing ethnic and religious hatreds, those in the political center tend to assume that it is due to a lack of democracy and that violence occurs where opportunities for the peaceful resolution of political disputes are lacking, and those on the political left tend to assume that it is due to economic inequalities or to a deep-rooted legacy of colonialism. None of these explanations sits comfortably with the statistical evidence. Empirically, the most striking pattern is that civil war is heavily concentrated in the poorest countries. War causes poverty, but the more important reason for the concentration is that poverty increases the likelihood of civil war. Thus our central argument can be stated briefly: the key root cause of conflict is the failure of economic development. Countries with low, stagnant, and unequally distributed per capita incomes that have remained dependent on primary commodities for their exports face dangerously high risks of prolonged conflict. In the absence of economic development neither good political institutions, nor ethnic and religious homogeneity, nor high military spending provide significant defenses against large-scale violence. Once a country has stumbled into conflict powerful forces—the conflict trap—tend to lock it into a syndrome of further conflict.

Each war is distinctive, with its own particular personalities, events, and antecedents. Any all-embracing, general theory of civil war would therefore be patently ridiculous, and sensibly enough most analyses are country-specific, historical accounts. However, when we pan back from the particular patterns emerge, some of them surprisingly strong, which suggests that some characteristics tend to make a country more or less prone to civil war. This chapter summarizes the evidence on these statistical patterns based on global experience since the 1960s. We abstract from triggering events: the day by day political and military changes that usher in war. Our focus is on a country's longer-term social, economic, and institutional features. Recall that we are using a precise definition of civil war that excludes several other forms of violence: civil war occurs when an identifiable rebel organization challenges the government militarily and the resulting violence results in more than 1,000 combat-related deaths, with at least 5 percent on each side.

Statistical patterns are useful in that they can suggest policies that might typically work in particular situations. They can also defend us from the temptation to overgeneralize from particular conflicts and from the tendency to pick out from the multiplicity of possible causes that which conforms with the beliefs of the researcher. We will see that the large differences in proneness to conflict reflect the conjunction of several risk factors. In this sense, a conflict will usually have multiple causes.

Patterns, however, are only a supplement to analysis, not a substitute for it. Patterns come about because of behavior. Civil war occurs if a group of people forms a private military organization that attacks government forces and ordinary civilians on a large scale and with a degree of persistence. The typical such organization has between 500 and 5,000 members, although a few, such as the Sudanese People's Liberation Army, range up to 150,000 (table 3.1). Globally, such organizations are rare, but they are relatively common in extremely poor countries. To understand the root causes of civil war we need to understand the formation of these private military organizations. Why are such groups formed, that is, what are their motives? How are they formed, that is, what are their opportunities?

Table 3.1 Size of rebel organizations, selected countries and years

Country	Rebel organization	Size of group and date
Azerbaijan	Republic of Nagorno-Karabakh	1,000 in 1988; 21,000 in 1992–94
Burundi	San Echec and San Defaite	A few hundred in the mid-1990s
	National Council for the Defense of Democracy	1,000 in the mid-1990s
	Forces pour la défense de la démocratie	10,000 in the mid-1990s
	Forces nationales pour la libération	2,000–3,000 in the mid-1990s
Colombia	Fuerzas armadas revolucionarias colombianas (FARC)	850 in 1978; 6,000 in 1987; 16,000 in 2000
	Ejército popular de liberación (ELN)	30 in 1965; 270 in 1973; 350 in 1984; 4,500 in 2000
	Movimiento 19 de Abril	1,500 in 1987; disbanded in 1991 to become a political party
	United Self-Defense of Colombia	10,000 in the 1990s
Indonesia	Gerekan Aceh Merdeka (GAM)	24 to 200 in 1976–79; almost disappeared by the early 1980s; 200 in 1986–87; 200 to 750 in 1989–91; 800 in July 1999; 2,000 to 3,000 and 24,000 militia in 2001; 15,000 to 27,000 irregulars in 2001–02
	Laskar Jihad	2,000 in May 2000
Mali	Mouvement populaire de la libération de l'Azaouad	7,000 to 8,000 in 1992
Mozambique	Resistência nacional Moçambicana (RENAMO)	200 to 400 in 1976–77; 2,000 to 2,500 in 1978–79; 6,000 to 10,000 in 1980–81; 20,000 in 1984–85
Russia	Chechen fighters	1,000 in 1994; 7,000 in 1995; 9,000 in 1999; 7,000 in 2000; 4,000 in 2001
Senegal	Maquis	3,000 at the end of 1990
	Mouvement de forces démocratiques de Casamance	2,000 to 4,000 in the late 1990s

Source: Sambanis (2003).

Understanding Rebellion

R EBEL LEADERS USUALLY PROCLAIM SOME NARRATIVE OF grievances against the government, that is, they are usually at least in part leaders of political organizations pursuing objectives of political change. While this is evidently an element in their formation, political opposition to governments is not usually conducted through military organizations. The normal vehicles for political opposition are political parties and protest movements. These are quite differently structured from a private military organization.

Most political opposition is somewhat democratic and participatory, whether structured political parties, such as the African National Congress during the apartheid era in South Africa and the Movement for Democratic Change in present-day Zimbabwe, or unstructured, non-hierarchical protest movements, such as the revolutions that overthrew the communist dictatorships in Eastern Europe. By contrast, a private military organization is typically small and highly hierarchical, with power concentrated at the top of the organization, often in a single charismatic leader, with a high degree of discipline and severe punishment for dissent.

Furthermore, most political opposition does not require substantial finance for the organization to be effective. Most participation is voluntary and part-time, and activities do not require a lot of expensive inputs. By contrast, a private military organization is a costly operation. It must meet a payroll, because most members are full-time and therefore dependent on the organization for their material needs, and it must be able to purchase a good deal of imported military equipment.

Thus as well as being a political organization, a private military organization is an army and a business. Those analyzing rebel groups must always keep this triple feature—political organization, military organization, and business organization—in mind. Rebellions occur predominantly in countries where circumstances are conducive to all three features. So what are the features conducive to each aspect of a successful rebel organization?

Rebel Groups as Political Organizations

Like all political organizations, a rebellion thrives on group grievances; however, political organizations opposing the government are found in virtually all societies. Even in societies where group grievances are relatively modest, as in the high-income societies where income is equally distributed, vigorous mass opposition parties exist. Political grievances and the political conflict they generate are universal. If the main impetus for rebel groups is the representation of political grievances, then

the obvious question is why does political organization take the un-
usual form of small, hierarchical, violent rebellion rather than the more
conventional forms of mass parties or mass protest?

Why Are so Many Rebellions Ethnic?   Many rebellions have an ethnic
or religious dimension. This accords with an explanation of conflict
common on the political right that ethnic and religious hatreds are the
root cause of many wars. However, the statistical patterns are quite sur-
prising. Here we use Collier and Hoeffler's (2002c) analysis (see box 3.1).

Substantial ethnic and religious diversity significantly reduces the
risk of civil war. Controlling for other characteristics, a society is safer
if is composed of many such groups than if everyone has the same ethnicity and religion. Obviously such diverse societies are likely to be less
harmonious than homogenous societies, in that people identify more
with their own ethnic or religious group and less with the society as a
whole, and they frequently dislike other groups, but evidently a major
gulf exists between such disharmony and the resort to rebellion. An
unresolved dispute in political science concerns whether such societies
are better suited to proportional representation electoral systems, with
each group represented by its own party, or by winner take all systems,
which encourage the formation of two large, multi-ethnic parties.
Overall, however, the basic circumstances of diversity may be much less
dangerous than has popularly been thought (figure 3.1). Although ethnically diverse societies are commonly seen as fragmented, ethnicity
provides an effective basis for social networks. Such societies might
therefore be less atomistic than homogenous societies. Some evidence
indicates that ethnically diverse societies find nationwide collective action more difficult, but have an offsetting advantage in private sector
activity that can benefit from ethnic networks (Collier 2001).

More limited ethnic differentiation can, however, be a problem. If
the largest ethnic group in a multi-ethnic society forms an absolute majority, the risk of rebellion is increased by approximately 50 percent
(figure 3.2). Around half of developing societies have this characteristic
of ethnic dominance. Presumably, in such societies minorities may reasonably fear that even a democratic political process will lead to their
permanent exclusion from influence regardless of the electoral system.
Ethiopia and Sri Lanka are examples of ethnically dominant societies
with civil wars.

Box 3.1   Modeling the risk of civil war

EACH CIVIL WAR IS UNIQUE AND NEEDS TO BE studied accordingly, but investigating whether any patterns are common to many such wars is also useful. One such approach is that of Collier and Hoeffler (2002c). They adopt the conventional political science definition of a civil war, the same definition explained earlier in the chapter. Investigating all such wars that took place during 1960–99 they focus on 52 for which sufficient data are available to include in subsequent analysis. They then take all the countries in the world and divide the period 1960–99 into eight five-year subperiods. During each subperiod each country could potentially experience an outbreak of civil war, and the statistical challenge is to explain why this happened in the 52 cases but not in the others using only characteristics at the start of each subperiod. The typical developing country faced a risk of around 17 percent that rebellion would occur in each subperiod.

Collier and Hoeffler adopt an agnostic empirical approach in which, in principle, a wide range of characteristics—political, historical, geographic, economic, and social—could be significant and are introduced into a logit regression. Factors that are insignificant are gradually eliminated, and the resulting model is then tested for robustness. Three economic factors are significant: the level of per capita income, its rate of growth, and its structure, namely, the dependence on primary commodity exports. Doubling per capita income approximately halves the risk of rebellion; each additional percentage point on the growth rate reduces the risk by approximately one percentage point; and the effect of primary commodity dependence is nonlinear, peaking when such exports are around 30 percent of GDP. A country that is otherwise typical but has this high level of primary commodity exports has a 33 percent risk of conflict, whereas when such exports are only 10 percent of GDP the risk falls to 11 percent. Ethnic and religious composition also matters. Societies in which the largest ethnic group constitutes between 45 and 90 percent of the population—which Collier and Hoeffler refer to as ethnic dominance—have a risk of rebellion that is about 50 percent higher; however, other than this, ethnic and religious diversity actually reduces the risk of rebellion. Once a society has had a civil war its risk of rebellion goes up sharply, although this risk fades at about one percentage point a year.

Several other statistical models of the initiation of rebellion are available (see, for example, Elbadawi and Sambanis 2002; Fearon and Laitin 2003; Hegre and others 2001; Reynal-Querol 2002a). Approaches, and consequently results, can legitimately differ because of choices of statistical specification and of data, as this work often requires difficult judgment calls; however, all the studies agree that a link exists between poverty and civil war.

Just as dominance can cause problems, so too can polarization. Dominance occurs when one group is larger than others, polarization occurs when the society is split into two fairly equal groups. A completely polarized society, divided into two equal groups, has a risk of civil war around six times higher than a homogenous society (Montalvo and Reynal-Querol 2002). The risks polarized societies face depend on the political leadership. In normal circumstances each group tends to police its behavior toward the other group, maintaining nonviolent relations (Fearon and Laitin 1996). However, ethnicity is more easily

Figure 3.1   Ethnic fractionalization and the risk of civil war

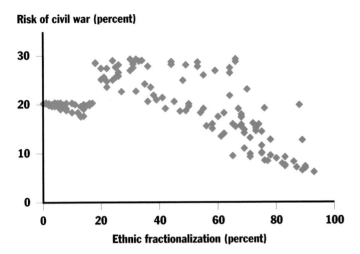

Source: Collier and Hoeffler (2002c).

Figure 3.2   Risk of civil war for the typical low-income country with and without ethnic dominance during a five-year period

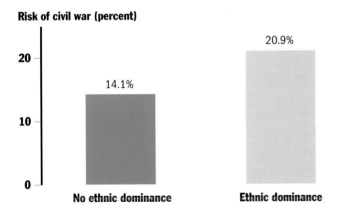

Source: Collier and Hoeffler (2002c).

manipulated by politicians than other bases for identity (Horowitz 1998). Elites can capitalize on ethnic networks to coordinate violence (Brass 1997; Gurr 2000; Hardin 1995). Thus while ethnic polarization and dominance are probably not inherently conflictual, populist politics may become disproportionately dangerous. Nationalism has often been used to counter ethnic particularity: this was how several European states were build in the 19th century (Hechter 2001). However, even nationalism can be manipulated for internal division. Irredentist nationalism attempts to extend the boundaries of a state by incorporating adjacent territory occupied by those of the same ethnicity.

An important circumstance in which ethnic differentiation can appear to be the cause of rebellion is if a country discovers a valuable natural resource such as oil. Natural resources are seldom found uniformly distributed over the entire country, but are usually concentrated in a particular part of it. The issue then arises as to who owns the resources, the whole nation or the lucky locality. The inhabitants of the lucky locality have an obvious interest in seceding from the rest of the nation and keeping the wealth for themselves. In all societies locality is one aspect of people's identity, and in ethnically differentiated societies ethnicity can be used to reinforce this sense of local identity. In most societies, wherever valuable resources are discovered some particular ethnic group is likely to be living on top of them that then has an incentive to assert its rights to secede. All ethnically differentiated societies have a few ethnic romantics who dream of creating an ethnically "pure" political entity, but resource discoveries have the potential to shift such movements from the margin of romanticism to the core agenda of economic self-interest. Take, for example, the politics of oil in the United Kingdom. Oil was discovered off the shores of Scotland during the 1960s, but it first became really valuable in 1973 when its price quadrupled. The following year the tiny Scottish Nationalist Party, which had only one seat in parliament, launched the "it's Scotland's oil" campaign, and gained 30 percent of the Scottish vote (Collier and Hoeffler 2003).

Statistically, secessionist rebellions are considerably more likely if the country has valuable natural resources, with oil being particularly potent (figure 3.3). Examples of this sort of secessionist movement are Cabinda in Angola, Katanga in the then Congo, Aceh and West Papua in Indonesia, and Biafra in Nigeria (see box 3.2). Some evidence suggests that rebel leaders massively exaggerate the likely gains from capturing ownership of the resources. Partly this exaggeration is strategic: the leaders of secessionist movements are often ethnic romantics who simply use the resource issue opportunistically to reinforce their support. Party leaders may themselves succumb to the glamour of natural resources and overestimate the likely gains. For example, leaders of the Gerekan Aceh Merdeka (the Aceh Freedom Movement or GAM) rebellion in Aceh told the local population that secession would raise

Figure 3.3   Risk of civil wars from natural resources endowment

(a) additional risk when the natural resource endowment is double the average

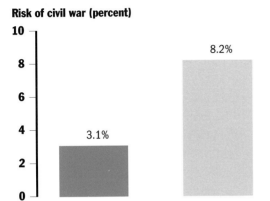

(b) the risk that the war is secessionist

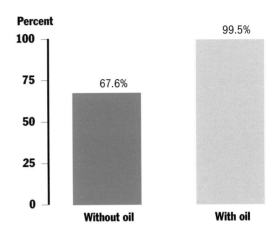

Source: Collier and Hoeffler (2002c).

Box 3.2   Oil and demands for secession in Nigeria

NIGERIA INHERITED A FEDERAL SYSTEM FROM ITS British colonial rulers in 1960. Upon independence, a British-style parliamentary democracy was created, with three semi-autonomous regions (North, East, and West). With intensifying competition over the distribution of revenues by the central government, and after the withdrawal of the British, ethno-regional conflict escalated into the Biafran war of independence in 1967 after the discovery of oil in the East. Ojukwu, the governor of the East region, de-manded that oil revenue be paid to the regional treasury, and the demand for independence grew when oil reserves were discovered. A history of political instability presaged the war: ethno-regional conflict over civil service appointments, electoral fraud allegations, a coup in 1966 followed by massacres of the Ibos, and a countercoup. Triggering the escalation in violence was the central government's decision to renege on regional autonomy arrangements after the 1967 Aburi Agreements.

Source: Zinn (2002).

---

their incomes to the level of Brunei's, a more than 10-fold exaggeration. Although such natural resource secessions are ethnically patterned and deploy the language of historic ethnic grievances, regarding their root cause as ethnicity is surely naïve (see Ross 2002b for a detailed discussion of the civil war in Indonesia).

In many developing countries the government is unwilling to meet such demands for secession, even if a majority of the locality supports it. Indeed, strong ethical arguments can be made against secession. For example, the influential theory of justice proposed by Rawls (1971) asks us to imagine making our choices behind a veil of ignorance: would the secession still be as well supported if the local population did not know in what region of the country the resources were located? The government has a legitimate interest in retaining these resources for use by the poorer majority rather than permitting them to be expropriated to create a small, rich group. The local demand may well be rational, but were such demands met, the world would become more unequal. A more legitimate demand would be that the resources should indeed be used for the poor majority rather than for a small elite. In many countries natural resources have been associated with elite corruption. For example, the International Monetary Fund (IMF) has recently reported that more than US$1 billion per year of Angolan oil revenues have been misappropriated, with large sums being paid directly into offshore bank accounts. Where a region sees a corrupt national elite stealing "its" resources, secessionist pressures are surely more likely.

Another reason why rebel leaders promote ethnic grievances so prominently is that they are a plausible and legitimate smokescreen for less reputable agendas. The discourse of grievances articulated by rebel groups cannot necessarily be trusted. As with all political movements, the rebel organization needs to emphasize grievances, and if necessary it will attempt to exaggerate them or to disguise its true interests in terms of more populist ones. For example, a violent attempted coup d'état in Fiji appeared at first sight to be motivated by the interests of the indigenous ethnic group. It turned out, however, that the leader of the coup attempt was a businessman who had been seeking a timber concession for the private American company he was representing. When the government awarded the contract to a public agency instead, he launched the coup. The coup's rallying cry of "power to indigenous people" was undoubtedly more appealing, but perhaps less accurate, than had it been "give the timber contract to the Americans." Similarly, the litany of grievances proclaimed by the Revolutionary United Front (RUF) in Sierra Leone eventually led to the offer of a settlement by the government in which the rebel leader, Foday Sankoh, would become vice president of the country. Sankoh refused this offer and instead demanded political control of the diamond trade. When he was offered this he accepted the peace settlement. As with most conflicts, that in Sierra Leone had multiple causes, including a history of clientalist politics. Natural resources are seldom the entire story behind a conflict, but they have the potential to compound other problems and make them unmanageable.

Rebel leaders often use some of the military force at their command to weaken the normal political movements whose objective is to advance the cause that the rebel group ostensibly supports. A common strategy is for a rebel organization to assassinate the moderate political leaders of the interests it purports to represent. If some of these political organizations are provoked into a military capability as a survival strategy, then one dimension of violent political conflict might be among rebel organizations with apparently similar political objectives. Civil war between rebel groups ostensibly representing the same cause or group is indeed common, for example, in Sudan (see Elbadawi, Ali, and Al Battahani 2002). Thus while the leadership may rely on a discourse of ethnic grievance and ethnic solidarity, its main energies may be devoted to a power struggle within the ethnic group.

Is the Motive Usually Greed? While political scientists and anthropologists have tended to focus on political and ethnic agendas, respectively, as the motive for civil wars, economic theorists writing on conflict have treated the motivation quite differently. Grossman's (1991, 1999) model does not distinguish between rebels or revolutionaries and bandits or pirates. Hirshleifer (2001), probably the leading economic theorist of conflict, analyzes rebellion as the use of resources to exploit others for an economic gain. The natural resource secessions discussed earlier broadly fit this economic model: political and ethnic agendas piggyback onto what is basically an attempt to expropriate resources. Is this the norm for rebellion?

Sometimes lucrative resources cannot be captured by secession, but require the capture of the state. The most obvious case of this is where the resource is foreign aid: the aid accrues to the recognized government and a rebel group can only acquire it if it overthrows and replaces that government. Grossman (1992) applies his model to aid and predicts that it will increase the risk of rebellion. For many low-income countries aid is certainly a substantial part of the government budget, and so indirectly finances many public sector jobs and contracts that are keenly contested politically. Hence a large aid inflow makes a state more attractive to capture. An empirical test of whether aid increases the risk of rebellion is thus, to an extent, a test of whether greed is an important underlying motivation for conflict. Contrary to the assumption economists commonly make, aid does not appear to increase the risk of rebellion (Collier and Hoeffler 2002b). Indirectly, as discussed later, aid affects the risk of conflict through its effects on growth, but controlling for this it has no direct effect. While the prevalence of natural resource secessions suggests that greed cannot be entirely discounted, it does not appear to be the powerful force behind rebellion that economic theorists have assumed.

Are Rebellions Responses to Political Repression?   While the political right tends to focus on ethnic and religious differences as explanations for rebellion, the political center tends to focus on the absence of political rights, maintaining that rebellion occurs where other forms of political organization are not permitted, so the big driver must be political repression or the lack of political opportunities. Surprisingly, this is not supported empirically. The evidence is muddled, but autocracies are approximately as safe as full democracies, with partial democracies having a somewhat higher risk than either (Esty and others 1998; Fearon and Laitin 2003; Hegre and others 2001). This is partly because partial democracies allow some political opposition, but do not give the opposition real influence. However, the association between partial democracy and civil war may be spurious, because partial democracies have other characteristics such as low income that increase the risk of conflict.

A much clearer empirical association is apparent between a change in political institutions and subsequent civil war: stability increases safety (Hegre and others 2001). So how does democracy affect the chances that political institutions will be stable? Unfortunately, this appears to be critically dependent on the level of economic development (Hegre 2003; figure 3.4). At low levels of per capita income, political institutions tend to be less stable in democracies than in autocracies. The average duration of a democratic political system in a low-income country is only nine years. The first four or five years are the most critical: only half survive beyond the first election (figures are calculated using the dataset developed by Gates and others 2003). As per capita income rises, democracies gradually become more stable, whereas the

Figure 3.4   The risk of civil war in democracies and nondemocracies at different levels of income

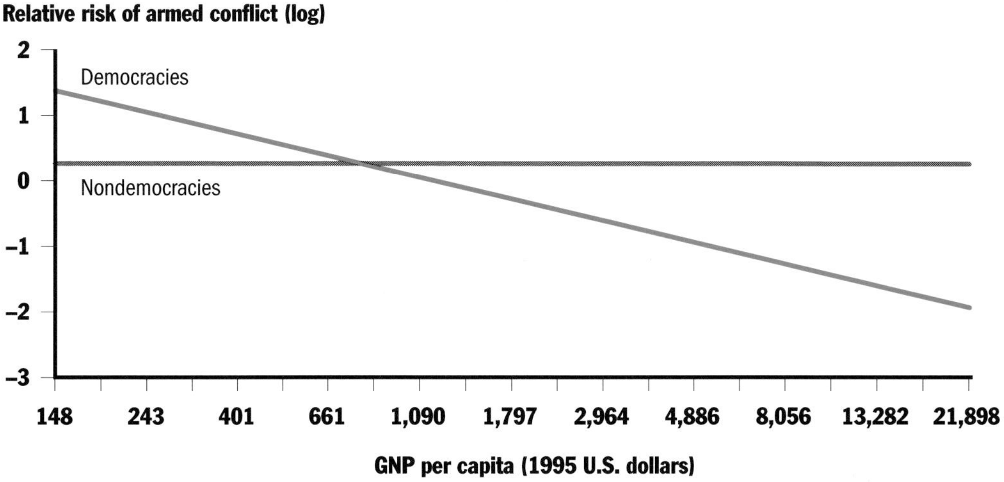

Relative risk of armed conflict (log)

Source: Hegre (2003).

stability of autocracies is unaffected. At some point, typically around US$750 annual per capita income, democracies start to become more stable than autocracies, and at high levels of income their political institutions are extremely robust (Gates and others 2003; Lipset 1959; Przeworski and others 2000).[1] Thus at higher income levels democracy indeed reduces the risk of civil war, but "one size fits all" simply is not applicable. At low income levels democracy may well be highly desirable for many reasons, but it cannot honestly be promoted as the road to peace. Historically, political institutions in low-income democracies are characterized by relatively high levels of instability, and this has probably tended to increase their risk of civil war.

While exceptions doubtless exist, in low-income countries, where rebellion is concentrated, no general tendency is apparent for it to be a strategy of last resort where other means of political expression are denied.

Are Rebellions Responses to Acute Grievances?   The interpretations of civil war popular with the political left are economic inequality and colonial legacies. In his analysis of the "paradox of power" Hirshleifer (2001) argues that poor people have more to gain from resorting to coercion than the rich. All rebel groups provide a litany of severe griev-

65

ances, many of which are undoubtedly genuine; however, for such grievances to explain rebellion they should be significantly worse than those of groups in other societies that resort to less violent political processes. Obtaining good objective measures of the intensity of grievances is difficult. Two measures that researchers have investigated are inequality of household incomes and inequality in the ownership of land. Collier and Hoeffler (2002c) find no effect of either income or land inequality on the risk of conflict, but do find that once a conflict has started it will tend to last much longer if income is unequal (Collier, Hoeffler and Söderbom 2003).

In relation to the colonial legacy, Acemoglu, Johnson, and Robinson (2001) find that colonial institutions can have long-lasting effects for good or ill. Where settlers' mortality rates were low, colonial institutions were designed for long-term growth, whereas where their mortality rates were high, colonial institutions were designed for exploitation. This legacy of institutions, as proxied by mortality rates among settlers, is highly significant in accounting for differences in recent growth performance, but turns out to have no significant explanatory power in relation to either the risk or the duration of conflict. While the colonial legacy presumably affects the risk of conflict to some degree, the connection appears to be weaker than the influence on economic performance.[2]

Whether or not acute grievances are an important driver of conflict, the evidence reviewed in chapter 1 shows clearly that civil war is a highly unreliable route to social progress. Even where the objective of correcting serious injustices motivates rebel organizations, unfortunately, the usual legacy of war is to intensify social problems.

What Are the Motives for Rebellion?   The analysis of motives for rebellion has not led us to any definitive conclusions. Although most rebel groups have public political agendas that appear reasonable, their actual agendas may be somewhat different, and in any case, similar agendas are normally promoted by mass political action rather than by rebellion. Viewed prior to a conflict, predicting which, if any, of the multiplicity of political disputes, grievances, and organizations will turn violent unless addressed is hard. To the extent that political objectives determine rebellions, the key drivers are more likely to be either a fear of the potential consequences of structural exclusion or the lure of imagined wealth, rather than the realistic prospect of rectifying acute

Figure 3.5   Improved economic performance and the risk of civil war

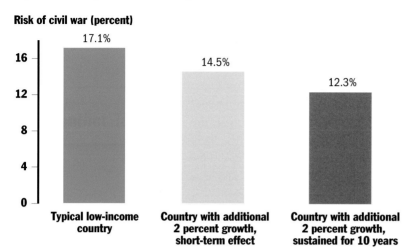

Source: Collier and Hoeffler (2002c).

grievances in the context of severe repression. This is not to deny that rebel groups have specific grievances, but rather to recognize that grievances are common, whereas private, illegal, military organizations are rare forms of political opposition.

The motive for rebellion need not be a group-specific grievance, in that rebels could be concerned about improving conditions across society. Indeed, the risk of rebellion increases substantially if average incomes are low and if the economy is in decline (figure 3.5). However, group-specific issues are more likely to motivate rebellions because the collective action problem is less acute: if rebellion is promised to improve conditions for everyone, then no one in particular has much of an incentive to fight. Generalized discontent is perhaps more likely to lead to mass protest movements than to small rebel groups. As discussed later, the association of rebellion with low incomes and economic decline may reflect other causes of rebellion.

Rebel Groups as Military Organizations

Regardless of its political agenda, a rebel group is a military organization. As such it faces problems of recruitment, cohesion, equipment, and survival.

Recruiting a Private Army   In terms of recruitment rebel groups usually look much more like an army than a political movement. First, the actual numbers of people involved in rebel activities are usually only a tiny proportion of the society. "Given the right environmental conditions, insurgencies can thrive on the basis of small numbers of rebels without strong, widespread, freely-granted, popular support rooted in grievances and, hence, even in democracies" (Fearon and Laitin 2003, p. 81). Even a relatively large rebel group such as the Fuerzas armadas revolucionarias colombianas (the People's Army or FARC) in Colombia is recruiting less than 1 Colombian in 2,000.

Second, the people who join rebel groups are overwhelmingly young, uneducated males. For this group objectively observed grievances might count for relatively little. Rather, they may be disproportionately drawn from those easily manipulated by propaganda and who find the power that comes from the possession and use of a gun alluring. Social psychologists find that around 3 percent of the population has psychopathic tendencies and actually enjoys violence against others (Pinker 2002), and this is more than is needed to equip a rebel group with recruits.[3] In Nigeria's Maitatsine region, a rebel movement was created in the 1980s by a "prophetic" leader, Marwa, who recruited 8,000 to 12,000 members. Ideological indoctrination and religious teaching were targeted on the homeless and refugees. Their insurgency caused around 5,000 deaths (Zinn 2002).

Third, as chapter 1 noted, a seemingly paradoxical, yet common, motivation for recruitment is safety. Compared with the starvation and disease facing the thousands of people displaced from their homes, the organized facilities of a rebel group provide a haven.

Fourth, many rebel movement "recruits" do not volunteer; for example, around 80 percent of Resistência Nacional Moçambicana (RENAMO) recruits were coerced. One standard technique is to kidnap recruits and then force them to commit atrocities in their home areas, thereby reducing their incentive to escape. Another technique, which the RUF in Sierra Leone adopted, was to target drug addicts on the grounds that such recruits would be easier to control. A further widespread technique is to recruit children. Children are attractive to rebel groups because they are cheap and have little regard for their own safety. For example, in Burundi rebel groups recruited children by force, purchasing Kenyan street children at the price of US$500 for

150 boys (Ngaruko and Nkurunziza 2002). Obviously children do not join rebellions because of objective social grievances.

Even where rebel groups do rely upon grievances for recruitment, they sometimes exploit them. A technique common to several groups is to target people whose parents were victims of previous government atrocities. The recruiter pretends to know who on the government side committed the atrocity and offers the opportunity for revenge (Ross, 2002b).

Recruits frequently desert. In the largest civil war of the 20th century, Russia in 1919–21, around 4 million men deserted from the Red and White Armies. The desertion rate was 10 times greater in summer than in winter, because most recruits were peasants whose time was much more valuable during the harvest season (Figes 1996).

Using Ethnicity for Cohesion   Rebel military organizations face severe difficulties of maintaining cohesion. As they operate outside the law they do not have recourse to normal contract enforcement techniques. Governments can divide a rebel movement by buying off local commanders, a technique used against the Khmer Rouge. One technique for maintaining cohesion is to have a hierarchical, dictatorial decision structure, with most power vested in a charismatic leader. A measure of this is that if such leaders are removed the rebel organization tends to collapse rapidly, examples being the eclipse of the Shining Path in Peru once Abimael Guzman had been imprisoned and the surrender of the massive União Nacional para a Independência Total de Angola (UNITA) forces in Angola following the death of Jonas Savimbi. Another common technique rebel organizations use to increase cohesion is to confine recruitment to a single ethnic group with leaders drawn from the same clan (Gates 2002). The rebellion thus uses existing ethnic "social capital." In this they resemble the solutions successful dictators favor, a spectacular example being Saddam Hussein's reliance on the Tikriti clan. In the Democratic Republic of Congo all the rebellions drew their support predominantly from particular ethnic groups, even if the conflict was resource driven. For example, the Katanga secession and the Shaba wars were led by the Lunda, Ndembu, and Yeke ethnic groups. Similarly, the Kwilu rebellion involved the Mbunda and Pende ethnic groups, while the 1996–97 rebellion led by Laurent Kabila drew its initial combatant force from among the Banyamulenge (Ndikumana and Emizet 2002).

Where the society is divided into a few large ethnic groups civil wars tend to last much longer. This is probably an indication that ethnicity is being used to maintain rebel cohesion. Recall that where societies are highly fragmented in ethnic and religious terms the risk of rebellion is actually lower than in homogenous societies, and when conflicts do occur they tend to be brief. A possible explanation for this is that in such societies large rebel groups will usually need to be multi-ethnic, but multi-ethnic groups cannot maintain cohesion. An example of a society with high ethnic fragmentation and correspondingly limited large-scale violence is Papua New Guinea. At the other end of the spectrum, Somalia is one of the most ethnically homogenous societies in Africa. Because rebel leaders actively use ethnicity to encourage cohesion, this is another reason why ethnicity is so prominent in the rebel discourse and appears to be an important root cause of conflict.

Equipping a Private Army   A private military organization needs to acquire armaments and ammunition. This is normally extremely difficult: even criminals seldom have access to armaments more powerful than handguns. Access to armaments varies enormously between countries and over time. Where rebels face large but poorly run government forces, they have occasionally been able to equip themselves by capturing government equipment, a classic case being the Eritrean People's Liberation Front versus the Derg government of Ethiopia. Similarly, in Albania and Somalia brief episodes of social disorder enabled local gangs to raid government arsenals. In Albania the looted armaments were taken across the border and became the basis for arming rebellion in the Balkans. In Somalia this set off a chain of gang militarization, destroying the possibility of central government on a long-term basis.

The breakup of the former Soviet Union established some new governments that faced acute shortages of revenue, but had huge stockpiles of armaments for which they had no use. Major illegal businesses developed, often run by former soldiers such as the Russian Victor Bout, in which stocks were air freighted to conflict zones in return for natural resource wealth. Thus the availability of military equipment for rebel groups expanded enormously during the 1990s, and its cost collapsed. AK-47s now sell for as little as US$6 in some African countries

(Graduate Institute of International Studies 2001; U.S. Department of State 1999).

Surviving and Military Viability   The sheer military viability of rebellion will differ greatly between societies, and so will influence the risk of conflict. One simple factor influencing military viability is the terrain. It is easier for large rebel groups to conceal themselves in rural areas with a low population density than in urban areas. Countries in which the population is concentrated in urban areas, but with large, scarcely populated hinterlands, are statistically more at risk of rebellion. Some evidence also suggests that rebellions are more likely to be launched in countries with extensive mountainous terrain. For example, the Eritrean People's Liberation Front was able to rely on safe havens in mountain retreats, and Nepal, one of the most mountainous countries in the world, has seen a substantial war. Countries such as Colombia, with both mountains and forests, may be geographically more prone to rebellion than countries such as Saudi Arabia (see Buhaug and Gates 2002 for an empirical study of geography and war).

A second factor influencing military viability is the capability of the government. Both good policing and military counterinsurgency operations are organizationally demanding and are much more difficult, for example, than providing basic social services.

Deterring rebellion in its early stages requires an effective local presence of government and a willingness to share information on the part of the population. Typically rebel groups kill people they suspect of being informers, and so for people to give the government information they must trust it to be effective. Local populations many neither appreciate nor trust weak states, which therefore lack the information to contain rebellion. Even highly effective governments find containing rebellion to be an arduous and complex process, although France, Germany, Spain, and the United Kingdom were eventually fairly successful in containing violent actions by, respectively, the Front de Libération Nationale de la Corse, Baader-Meinhof and its later manifestations such as the Red Army Faction, Euskadi ta azkatasuna (ETA), and the Irish Republican Army (IRA).

Less effective governments commonly attempt to prevent rebellion by substantially raising conventional military expenditure. For example, when the objective risk of rebellion is proxied by the risk estimated

Figure 3.6 Military expenditures and the risk of civil war

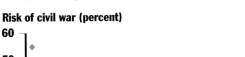

(a) how governments respond to risk

Military expenditures as a percent of GDP

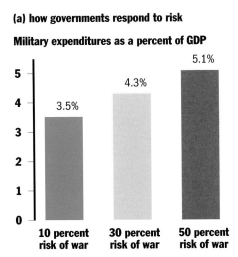

(b) how risk responds to military expenditures

Risk of civil war (percent)

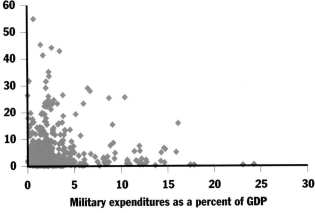

Military expenditures as a percent of GDP

Source: Collier and Hoeffler (2002d).

by the Collier-Hoeffler model (Collier and Hoeffler 2002d), an additional 10 percent risk of rebellion increases the government's preemptive military budget by more than 10 percent (figure 3.6). Yet such military expenditure is usually ineffective in deterring rebellion (see box 3.3). Controlling for this tendency of expenditure to be higher where risks are higher, high military spending has no significant deterrence effect on the risk of rebellion.

Rebel Groups as Business Organizations

Rebellion is expensive. Typically several thousand people will be full-time workers for the organization for several years. These people and their dependents must be fed, clothed, and housed. They must also be equipped. Depending on its sophistication, military equipment and ammunition can be extremely expensive and in combat conditions needs to be replaced frequently. The rebel organization faces all these costs, yet its military activities do not directly generate any revenue. As a business organization a rebellion therefore faces an acute financing problem. If it cannot overcome this financing problem the rebel group will be unviable. This is perhaps the fate of many would-be rebel movements.

> ## Box 3.3   Inefficient counterinsurgency measures in Indonesia
>
> INDONESIA HAS KNOWN MUCH POLITICAL VIO-lence in its history, including civil wars, self-determination movements, ethnic clashes, coups, and state-sponsored massacres. A civil war took place in the resource-rich province of Aceh in the early 1990s and again in 1999–2002. The war was fought between the government and GAM, an organization that had pursued autonomy since the early 1970s. For more than two decades GAM was poorly funded, had little military equipment, and few recruits. Part of the reason for GAM's growth in the 1990s was the demonstration effect in neighboring East Timor, which encouraged the Acehnese to demand independence as well. Also relevant were expectations of revenue windfalls that could result from ruling a resource-rich independent state of Aceh. But what gave GAM greater legitimacy and access to a larger pool of potential recruits than in previous years was a negative reaction by the public to the government's counterinsurgency measures of the 1980s. These actions intensified after GAM's reappearance in 1990–91. Following a period of dormancy, GAM emerged stronger in 1999 at least in part because of increased support by Acehnese public opinion, possibly resulting from the public outrage against alleged human rights abuses committed by Indonesian security forces between 1990 and 1998.
>
> *Source:* Ross (2002b).

All the rebel groups that succeed in escalating violence to the scale of civil war must therefore in part be business organizations. This does not imply that personal wealth, or indeed any other economic ambition, is the motivation for the rebellion. Rebel organizations have to be businesses because they have to cover their costs, but most are probably not run for profit. Much of the economics literature on rebellion assumes that the rebel group has economic objectives, whereas much of the political literature neglects to consider finance as a constraint, yet finance can be critical in explaining rebellion, even though it is not motivating.

Rebel groups have three broad options in raising finance: they can be initiated by someone who is already wealthy, they can seek donations, and they can operate commercial businesses. The super-rich occasionally launch their own political parties, for instance, James Goldsmith in France and the United Kingdom and Ross Perot in the United States, and occasionally they also launch rebellions. Osama Bin Laden is a spectacular current example, and when Jonas Savimbi relaunched the war in Angola in 1994 he was among the richest people in the world. As the numbers of super-rich increase, this may become more common, but historically rebel groups have usually been funded by donations or by their own commercial enterprises.

Who Donates Death?   In seeking donations, rebel groups typically do not rely heavily on voluntary contributions from the local group whose interests they promote. In this they differ markedly from normal political movements. Their main sources of donations are from foreign governments hostile to the government they oppose and from diasporas living in rich countries.

Hostile governments see several advantages in this type of military intervention. It is covert, and so avoids the normal pressures of international dispute settlement. It is containable, and does not result in domestic casualties. Until the end of the Cold War the chief sources of government finance for rebel movements were probably the two superpowers. Since the end of the Cold War regional conflicts have become more feasible, and so neighboring governments may have increased their funding of rebel groups. Obviously, obtaining clear evidence of the importance of government funding for rebel groups is difficult. One such case was the role of the government of Southern Rhodesia in funding and training RENAMO during the 1970s. Once this government collapsed, RENAMO collapsed. It was then restarted in the early 1980s by the government of South Africa. The United Nations (UN) has documented how several African governments supported UNITA. Similarly, clear evidence points to the involvement of the governments of Rwanda, Uganda, and Zimbabwe in the Democratic Republic of Congo and of the government of Liberia in Sierra Leone. Sometimes involvement is reciprocal, so that the conflict is, in effect, an international war. For example, at one stage the government of Sudan was supporting the Lord's Resistance Army fighting in northern Uganda and the government of Uganda was supporting the Sudan People's Liberation Movement fighting in southern Sudan. The rebel group probably gets significant support from a foreign government in most civil wars.

The other major source of donations for rebel groups is from diasporas in rich countries. Diasporas do not suffer the consequences of violence, nor are they in day-to-day contact and accommodation with "the enemy." Case studies suggest that diasporas tend to be more extreme than the population remaining in the country of origin: supporting extremism is a simple way of asserting continued identity with the place that has been left. A spectacular example of such financing was for the Eritrean People's Liberation Front, which levied an informal income tax on its huge diaspora. Other examples are support from the

Tamil diaspora in North America for the Tamil Tigers and support from the Albanian diaspora in Europe for the Kosovo Liberation Army.

Unlike the other sources of finance for rebellion, diaspora contributions are sensitive to the media image of the rebel group. Hence a shrewd rebel group will attempt to manage its image, playing on the concerns and memories of the relevant diaspora. After September 11 the American population became more aware of the true consequences of financing political violence, and donations to rebel groups have reputedly declined sharply. Following September 11 two rebel organizations highly dependent on diaspora contributions from North America, the IRA and the Tamil Tigers, both took unprecedented steps toward peace, with the IRA accepting "decommissioning" of its weapons and the Tamil Tigers withdrawing their demand for independence.

What Sorts of Commercial Enterprises Do Rebel Groups Engage in?

Most successful rebel organizations now rely substantially on generating finance by running businesses alongside their military and political activities. The question then becomes in what types of business activities are rebel organizations likely to be competitive? Unfortunately, the obvious answer is that rebel groups have only one competitive advantage, namely, their possession of an usually large capacity for violence. Thus the business activities to which they are well suited are various forms of extortion rackets or activities that only require military control over a limited territory. These business activities are most commonly associated with the extraction of natural resources, and civil wars occur disproportionally in countries with extensive dependence on natural resources (figure 3.7).

Recall that for military reasons rebel groups will tend to locate in rural areas. Most rural areas are poor. Obviously extortion rackets only work if there is something to extort, and this constitutes a major limitation on rebel activity: extremely poor areas are not well suited to extortion, and so tend to be unsuited for rebellion.[4] However, a minority of rural areas are well suited to extortion, namely, if they are producing primary commodities with high economic rents. Such commodities are generally for export, and the largest rents are usually from the extraction of natural resource wealth. Where such activities are under way, for rebel groups to run an extortion racket that involves charging produc-

Figure 3.7   Natural resources and the risk of civil war for low-income countries

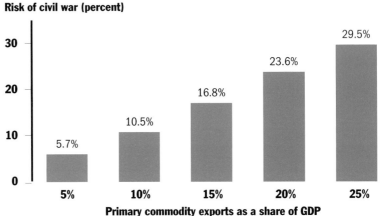

Source: Collier and Hoeffler (2002c).

ers for protection is a relatively simple matter. The best known example is diamonds in Angola and Sierra Leone. Alluvial diamonds are particularly well suited to rebel groups because the technology is so simple that the organization can directly enter the extraction process. Similarly, timber felling is a simple technology.

However, high-value agricultural exports are also sometimes a target for rebel extortion. Here the rebel group does not produce the crop itself, but levies informal taxes on production. The most spectacular example is illegal drugs, which because of their illegality are extremely valuable. Current global policy on drugs implies that drugs can only be grown on territory outside the control of a recognized government. Those rebel groups that control territory on which drugs can be grown can therefore charge large rents to producers. For example, when the U.S. government ceased to fund the mujahideen in Afghanistan, the group shifted into drug production. Similarly, estimates indicate that FARC in Colombia generates around US$500 million per year from its control of drug cultivation. Even lower-value export crops are sometimes the target of rebel extortion rackets. For example, the RUF in Sierra Leone started by levying informal taxes on coffee, and only shifted its activities to the diamond areas once it had become established.

Some extractive industries require technology that is too sophisticated for rebel groups and requires multinational corporations (MNCs), but this does not prevent extortion. Rebel groups can target MNCs by threatening expensive infrastructure. The classic infrastructure target is a pipeline: typically oil companies pay protection money to "violence entrepreneurs" in local communities. Such entrepreneurs sometimes fight among themselves for the right to extort. For example, in the delta region of Nigeria violence entrepreneurs from rival villages on either side of a new Shell pumping station recently fought it out for the extortion rights, resulting in 75 deaths. Violence in the Nigerian delta began in the mid-1990s at a modest level. It was essentially political, being directed against a military government. Despite democratization, the violence has escalated sharply, but has been transformed into something more akin to American gangland fights for control of the drug trade.

A particularly remarkable recent development is for rebel groups to raise finance by selling the advance rights to the extraction of minerals that they currently do not control, but which they propose to control by purchasing armaments financed through the sale of the extraction rights. Kabila, subsequently president of the Democratic Republic of Congo, reportedly raised several million dollars from Zimbabwean commercial interests in return for extraction contracts before launching his successful assault on Kinshasa (Graduate Institute of International Studies 2001). Similarly Denis Sassou-Nguesso, subsequently president of the Republic of Congo, reportedly sold extraction rights to help finance his military bid for power.

An alternative technique for extortion against MNCs is kidnapping followed by ransom demands. FARC generates around US$200 million annually from ransoms, disproportionately from kidnapping the employees of MNCs. Oil companies are common targets for kidnapping, and in some regions companies now suffer kidnaps as a daily occurrence. Pax Christi Netherlands (2001) estimates that during the 1990s European companies' ransoms to rebel movements amounted to US$1.2 billion, a sum that far exceeds official European aid flows to the affected governments. The Colombian rebel group Ejército de Liberación Nacional (ELN) reputedly got US$20 million in ransom from the German company Mannesmann, money that was critical for the group's purchase of sophisticated military equipment and its subsequent expansion. Rebel groups also target foreign tourists for kidnap. For example, a small rebel group in the Philippines recently ransomed a party of European tourists via Libya for US$1 million per person. Following each successful kidnapping rebel recruitment soars, presumably as young men anticipate

---

Box 3.4   Financing the Chechen rebellion

BETWEEN 1991 AND 1993 BREAKAWAY CHECHNYA controlled more than 300 kilometers of the Russian border. During this time Chechnya became an enormously profitable, illegal but tolerated, free trade zone that ensured its owners a fortune of millions in hard currency. In practice independent after 1991, Chechnya possessed an international airport and international borders with Georgia, but was still fully integrated into the Russian economic space. This meant, first, that Chechnya had access to cheap and exportable Russian natural resources; and, second, that it had access to the Russian consumer market, which was eager for all sorts of consumer goods. This made Chechnya a bonanza for the shadow economy, and its position as a hub between world markets and the Russian markets proved to be extremely lucrative. Consumer goods were imported duty free via Chechnya, while natural resources and weapons were exported to world markets without any regulation. The financial flows, which financed Dzokhar Dudaev's regime and later the war, originated in the shadow economy. Not surprisingly, Dudaev's independent Chechnya was supported and used by entrepreneurs in the shadow economy, who exploited the "free trade zone" of Chechnya for their business. These so-called patriotic businessmen were interested in an independent Chechnya, out of reach of the Russian state, but with access to the Russian space of opportunity and to the world market. They also had an interest in ensuring state weakness in Chechnya to maintain their freedom of activity.

Source: Zürcher, Koehler, and Baev (2002).

---

large payoffs. In Colombia rebel groups have combined with urban-based criminals to create a market in kidnapped people. Criminals undertake the kidnap, selling the victim on to the rebel group, which then demands a ransom. Just as markets in the victims of kidnap are arising in developing countries, so markets in ransom insurance are arising in industrial countries. Perversely, the eventual effects of kidnap insurance are to reduce the incentive to protect workers from kidnap and to increase the size of ransom payments.

Although natural resources are probably the most common target for rebel extortion in rural areas, another valuable attribute is if the area includes an international border. Physical control over a border can be valuable because of the potential for smuggling. A post-Soviet aphorism states that control over a kilometer of the Russian border sufficed to become a millionaire (see box 3.4). The potential for exploiting a border depends on the trade policies the country and its neighbors have adopted. As Russia was highly protectionist, control of the border enabled goods to be smuggled into the country. Sometimes the smuggling can go in the other direction. For example, Afghanistan is bordered by countries that have usually been highly protectionist; thus control of frontier areas in Afghanistan has enabled goods to be flown in at world prices and smuggled into these neighboring countries where they are far more valuable.

Finally, some rebel groups have used their comparative advantage in violence to capture some niche markets in extortion in industrial countries. For example, the Albanian mafia associated with the Kosovo Liberation Army reputedly now controls around 80 percent of the prostitution trade in central London (*The Observer* 2002).

So Is the Root the Loot?   We have already argued against a greed-based interpretation of rebellion. Most entrepreneurs of violence have essentially political objectives, and presumably initially undertake criminal activities only as a grim necessity to raise finance. However, over time the daily tasks involved in running a criminal business may tend inadvertently to develop a momentum of their own. The organization starts to attract more criminal types and fewer idealists, so that it may gradually change its character. Some rebel leaderships tend to do well out of war and may be quite reluctant to see it end. In some cases, such as RUF's movement from Sierra Leone to Guinea, a rebel group that finds its criminal activities thwarted in one country relocates in another country. At this point any political agenda has withered away, leaving a "roving bandit" that classic analysis tells us is the most destructive form of power (Olson 1993). Loot is not usually the root motivation for conflict, but it may become critical to its perpetuation, giving rise to the conflict trap.

The Conflict Trap

ONCE A REBELLION HAS STARTED IT APPEARS TO DEVELOP A momentum of its own. Getting back to peace is hard, and even when peace is re-established, it is often fragile.

Getting Back to Peace

The best predictor of whether a country will be in civil war next year is whether it is at civil war now (see box 3.5). Wars are highly persistent:

Box 3.5   Modeling the duration of civil war

COLLIER, HOEFFLER, AND SÖDERBOM (2003) USE A hazard regression to investigate why some wars last much longer than others. Investigating the duration of civil war is more demanding statistically than studying its onset, so the results vary considerably. Explaining the onset can use a large number of observations with a wide variation in characteristics, because the comparison is between countries with rebellions and those without. Explaining the duration of rebellions depends on the much more limited variation between countries with wars.

Other empirical studies of civil war duration include Balch-Lindsay and Enterline (2000); Buhaug, Gates, and Lujala (2002); DeRouen 2003; Elbadawi and Sambanis (2000); Fearon (2002); and Regan (2002).

---

the typical civil war lasts around seven years. As part I indicated, the costs of such wars are astronomical, and thus they are seldom forces for successful transformation. Here we are concerned with why they last so long.

Superficially, given that conflicts are so costly finding mutually beneficial agreements that end them might seem to be easy. However, consider the radical difference between rebellions against governments and strikes by workers against a company. Few unions and companies can prevent strikes altogether, but once they occur they are generally settled within days or weeks: ending strikes quickly is often easier than preventing them altogether. With rebellions it is the other way round: most governments never face a rebellion, but once one has occurred ending it is difficult. Why is rebellion so persistent?

Even where the population has significant grievances, governments are understandably reluctant to concede to violence what they have not conceded to nonviolent pressure. Clearly governments cannot afford to signal that violence is an effective political strategy, given that all societies have many groups that are willing to resort to violence to achieve their goals, so the potential is limitless. A further problem is that even if governments are willing to concede to rebels' demands, they might have no credible means of committing to the agreement, and thus the rebel group might fear that once it loses its fighting capability the government will renege, a problem known as time inconsistency. Conceding to all rebel demands may even be logically impossible. The circumstances under which one rebel group is able to thrive often also enable other groups to thrive, and sometimes these groups have opposing ob-

Figure 3.8   How chances of peace evolve worldwide

Probability of peace during the year (percent)

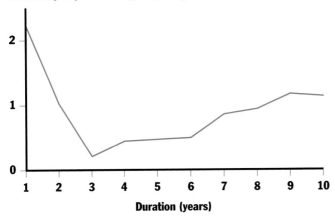

Duration (years)

Source: Collier, Hoeffler, and Söderbom (2003).

jectives. For example, in Colombia to the extent that the rebel groups have discernable political agendas, they are contradictory.

Yet significant patterns are apparent. Wars are particularly lengthy if a society has extremely unequally distributed income and a very low average income, possibly because the cost of sustaining rebellion is low if a country has many destitute people, and possibly because the governments of such countries are typically weak. Wars are particularly lengthy if the society is composed of two or three ethnic groups, perhaps because this makes creating distinct identities of support easier for both rebels and government.

Over the first four years of war the chances of peace gradually deteriorate. Presumably the conflict intensifies hatreds, and it may also gradually shift the balance of influential interests in favor of continued conflict. Criminal entrepreneurs do well out of war at the expense of other interests, and so in these early stages of conflict the criminals thrive while the honest decline. Beyond four years the chances of peace gradually improve again, perhaps reflecting the declining opportunities for extortion as the economy goes into retreat (figure 3.8).

Wars also appear to have been getting longer (figure 3.9). Note that the modest shortening of wars in the 1990s may well be temporary. As discussed in chapter 4, the end of the Cold War saw a surge in peace

Figure 3.9 Duration of civil wars over time

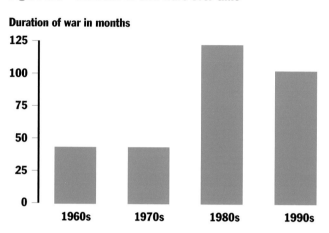

Source: Collier, Hoeffler, and Söderbom (2003).

settlements, but this was not sustained beyond the mid-1990s. The expected duration of conflict is now more than double that of conflicts that started prior to 1980 (Collier, Hoeffler, and Söderbom 2003). One possible explanation is that sustaining a conflict is easier than it used to be, because even without support from a superpower or a neighboring government, rebel groups can generate revenues and purchase armaments. Another possibility is that rebellions have gradually changed their character, becoming less political and more commercial. Violence entrepreneurs, whether primarily political or primarily commercial, may gain from war to such an extent that they cannot credibly be compensated sufficiently to accept peace. Those who see themselves as political leaders benefit from war because they can run their organizations in a hierarchical, military style with power concentrated in their own hands, something much more difficult to justify in peacetime. Those who see themselves as extortionists benefit from the absence of the rule of law in the areas they control. However leaders see themselves they will have invested in expensive military equipment that will become redundant once they agree to peace. Asking a rebel leader to accept peace may be a little like asking a champion swimmer to empty the pool.

The international community has made many efforts to shorten civil wars by means of diplomatic, economic, and military interventions. Our analysis suggests that none of these types of interventions has been systematically successful. Particular interventions might have worked, but no

Figure 3.10 The risk of civil war for a typical civil war country, just before and just after war

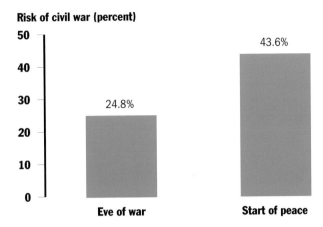

Risk of civil war (percent)

Source: Collier and Hoeffler (2002c).

general significant effect is apparent. Hence once a rebellion has started, there appears to be something of a trap: powerful forces keep a conflict going, while the international community appears almost impotent to stop it. Unfortunately this continues even once peace has been reached.

Reverting to War The typical country reaching the end of a civil war faces around a 44 percent risk of returning to conflict within five years (figure 3.10). One reason for this high risk is that the same factors that caused the initial war are usually still present. If before a war a country had low average income, rural areas well endowed with natural resources, a hostile neighbor, and a large diaspora, after the war it is still likely to have these characteristics. Some countries are intrinsically prone to civil war by virtue of their geography and economic structure, so that as the government settles with one rebel group another is likely to emerge. We would expect a country such as Colombia, with mountains, forests, and a lot of sparsely populated territory, to have a persistently higher incidence of civil war than, say, the Netherlands.

This is indeed part of the explanation for the persistence of civil war. For example, countries that go into civil war tend to have much lower incomes than other countries. This low income tends to make the conflict last a long time and to make the country more likely to have a further conflict once it has reached peace. However, another possibility is that a high degree of conflict persistence arises because of a vicious circle of civil war. We now explore various ways in which conflict in one period may increase the risks of subsequent conflict.

War Reverses Development The most obvious way in which conflict has a feedback loop is that civil war interrupts, and indeed reverses, economic development. As chapter 1 showed, during a civil war a country loses, on average, around 2.2 percentage points off its normal annual growth rate. Because the average civil war lasts around seven years, by the end of the war per capita income is around 15 percent lower than it would otherwise have been. Our previous analysis indicates that this will raise the long-term incidence of conflict for the country both by increasing its risk of further rebellion and by increasing the duration of rebellion should one occur. For the typical country experiencing a civil war, this effect of the war would increase the risk by 13.5 percent and the duration by 5.9 percent, so that the long-term incidence would rise by 16.9 percent.[5]

A related feedback loop works through the effect of conflict on the structure of the economy. Natural resource exports are relatively robust in the face of conflict, because of the high rents normally involved in their production and their relative independence of inputs from the rest of the economy. By contrast, more sophisticated exports are typically low-margin and dependent on a fragile network of business interdependencies, and these tend to get severely disrupted by the war. Furthermore, economic policy and institutions deteriorate significantly during civil war, and this takes time to put right. Studies show that diversification out of primary commodity dependence is influenced both by the level of income and by policies and institutions (Collier and Hoeffler 2002b). Thus as policies, institutions, and income all deteriorate during war and take a long time to rectify, for a much longer period than the war itself the country will find itself trapped into dependence on primary commodities. This in turn will increase the risk of further conflict.

War Triggers Emigration and Diasporas A further feedback loop is through emigration of the work force. Civil war triggers an exodus of people: some are refugees to neighboring countries, others are asylum

Figure 3.11   Diasporas and post-conflict risk

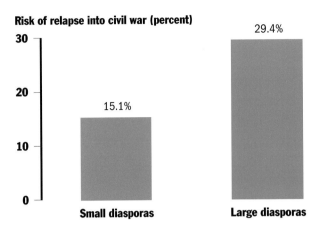

Risk of relapse into civil war (percent)

Note: Small diasporas are those of similar size to that of the United States, large as involving 10 times larger relative to the population.
Source: Collier and Hoeffler (2002c).

seekers in rich countries, and others are simply economic migrants induced to emigrate by the collapse in economic opportunities at home (Collier, Hoeffler, and Pattillo 2002). For different reasons, this emigration is also highly persistent, in that when one group of people has migrated, it tends to assist others to follow. Thus even once peace has been reached the society might continue to experience rapid emigration of workers, thereby further depressing economic growth.

Emigration not only deprives the economy of its labor force, its creates a large diaspora living in rich countries. Statistically, such diasporas increase the risk of a return to violence (Collier and Hoeffler 2002c). A potential problem is involved in interpreting this statistical association causally: to the extent that diasporas are the result of civil war, a large diaspora might simply be proxying a particularly severe war; however, when this is controlled for, the adverse effect of diasporas remains. Figure 3.11 illustrates the risk of conflict for a country with an average size diaspora in the United States versus one with a diaspora that is 10 times larger relative to the home country population. The most likely route by which diasporas increase the risk of repeat conflict is through their tendency to finance extremist organizations. To give an example, detective work has established that the massive bomb that killed 86 civilians and injured more than 1,400 in Colombo, Sri Lanka, in 1996 used 60 tons of East European explosives purchased using funds from a Singapore bank account opened by a Canadian of Sri Lankan origin (Bell 2000). As noted earlier, diasporas tend to be more extreme than the populations they have left behind.

War Leaves a Persistent and Damaging Military Lobby   During wars military spending obviously rises, and during the typical civil war the military budget increases by nearly 50 percent. Reducing this spending in the early postconflict period is not easy. There is often a widespread awareness of continued risks of conflict, and as with any powerful lobby, the military will be reluctant to see its budget cut. Furthermore, the government sometimes needs to integrate rebel forces into the army, which creates pressures for expansion.

Military spending reduces growth (Gleditsch and others 1996; Knight, Loayza, and Villanueva 1996); therefore both during and after a civil war such high military spending will be a drag on growth. However, the adverse effects of high military spending in postconflict situations can be even more serious. We have already noted that government military spending is normally ineffective as a deterrent of rebellion. Figure 3.12 shows that in postconflict situations it is actually significantly counterproductive. Statistical analysis indicates a potential problem of

Figure 3.12   Military spending and the risk of renewed conflict in postconflict countries.

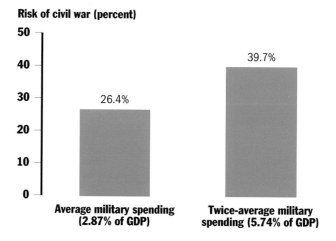

Source: Authors' calculations.

bogus causality: high spending will sometimes reflect a correct perception of an unusually high risk of further conflict, and so will simply be proxying the risk, but when this is controlled for the effect remains.

Why should high military spending in postconflict situations be so dysfunctional? A possible reason is that military spending may inadvertently be a signal of government ill-intent. Recall that one obstacle to a settlement is the low credibility of an agreement, that is, the government has more interest in promising generous peace terms than in actually delivering on them. High military spending might thus be seen as an indication that the government is likely to renege. Some indirect support for this interpretation comes from an analysis of which policies are most conducive to growth in postconflict situations. On average, countries emerge from conflict with poor policies across the board: macroeconomic, structural, and social.

Collier and Hoeffler (2002a) investigate how policy priorities should differ in such a country from one that has the same poor policies but is not postconflict. They find that simply on the criterion of maximizing short-run growth, if the country is postconflict it should give greater priority to such inclusive social policies as widening access to education and health care. Although education and health care eventually contribute to growth, they do so with long lags, so that the unusually strong effect of social policies is unlikely to be due to their direct contribution to growth. An alternative route may be that prioritizing inclusive social policies signals to the population that the government is committed to a peace settlement. On this interpretation, postconflict governments that prioritize military spending are inadvertently signaling that they will renege on the peace settlement and those that prioritize social spending are signaling that they will adhere to it. The former signal increases the risk of conflict, while the latter builds private sector confidence and thereby accelerates growth. If this interpretation is right it suggests that governments are not impotent: their policy choices can alter the risks they face. We return to this in more detail in chapter 5.

War Changes the Balance of Interests and Intensifies Hatreds   All the foregoing feedback loops work through factors that investigators have incorporated into models of conflict risk: the level, growth, and structure of income; military spending; and diasporas. However, the risk of a reversion to conflict is much higher than is accounted for by these effects. On average, only about half of the 44 percent risk of repeat conflict is due to characteristics either present before the conflict started or explicitly modeled as deteriorating as a result of conflict. The other half of the risk is due to things that happen during the conflict but are not included in the analysis. By definition, as these factors are omitted from the modeling analysis, it cannot guide us as to what they are, but we can speculate on some likely ways in which conflict increases the risk of further conflict.

One likely feedback mechanism is that violent conflict changes the balance of assets in the society, reducing the value of those that are useful during peacetime and increasing the value of those that are useful only for violence. The violence-specific assets are partly physical, such as armaments; partly human, such as the skills to use weapons and the reduced regard for human life and dignity; and partly organizational, such as the hierarchical rebel management structure and established commercial ties with arms suppliers and natural resource traders. The owners of these assets are unlikely to sit on the sidelines while their value collapses. They do well out of war and would like to get back to it.

Another likely feedback mechanism is that violent conflict leaves a legacy of atrocities. As a result, hatreds build up during periods of violence, leaving the society polarized. People of both sides want vengeance for atrocities committed during the conflict and these may supplant any prior grievances. We have already noted how rebel recruitment sometimes capitalizes on such grievances.

Conclusion

THE INTERPRETATIONS OF CIVIL WAR THAT HAVE BEEN MOST common in industrial countries either treat them as wholly an outcome of primordial ethnic and religious hatreds or force them into the familiar framework of Western politics. Rebel leaders have learnt to play up to these images of their organizations, raising money from ethnic diasporas while styling themselves as heroic political leaders. Another tempting framework, favored by economists, is to see rebel leaders as being at the apex of organized crime, enriching themselves from massive protection rackets at the expense of the wider society. The recent prominence of so-called "conflict diamonds" has increased popular awareness of this darker side of rebellion. Both these interpretations miss the reality of many rebellions; that is, even though rebel leaders are indeed violence entrepreneurs heading private military organizations that run protection rackets, they usually have some political agenda. However, they are not conventional political leaders in that they have chosen not to lead normal political movements.

Motivations—grievances and greed—are obviously part of the explanation for rebellion, but if we focus exclusively on motivation we rapidly encounter a paradox. In many situations of the most grievous injustice, both currently and historically, rebellion does not occur. Highly repressive societies often fail to trigger civil war, such as Iraq and the Democratic People's Republic of Korea. Highly unequal societies often fail to trigger civil war, such as Chile and Kenya. Extreme cases of ethnic abuses of power have often failed to trigger civil war, such as white domination in South Africa, and, delving back into history, Norman domination in England, although some forms of ethnic political exclusion do appear to increase the risk of war. Greed perhaps fares a little better as an explanation, as secessionist rebellions seem to be linked to the desire to appropriate valuable resources and some rebel leaders appear more committed to a personal than to a social agenda; however, even greed does not seem to get us very far, because states with large aid inflows are much more attractive to capture, but they do not face any greater risk of rebellion.

While the literature that tries to explain civil war has focused overwhelmingly on motivation, we also need to note that the circumstances in which rebel groups are militarily and financially viable are relatively rare. Hirshleifer (2001) has put forward a depressing proposition, the Machiavelli theorem, whereby no advantageous opportunity to exploit someone will be missed. Even though many rebellions are not motivated by the desire to exploit someone, a closely analogous proposition may be fairly accurate: no militarily and financially viable opportunity to promote a political agenda by rebellion will be missed. If a neighboring government is sufficiently hostile and the circumstances are propitious, it will seek out and promote a local violence entrepreneur. If resource-extracting MNCs offer sufficiently easy pickings in unprotected rural areas, local violence entrepreneurs will set up rudimentary protection rackets loosely linked to political demands. In such circumstances the ostensible grievance might be any of a wide range of things: grievances are not in short supply.

Globally, one of the largest mass political protests of recent years, which brought more than 400,000 people onto the streets of London, was to defend the right to hunt foxes. The typical rebel group does not need a cause that attracts anything like this level of support: a few hundred or a few thousand people will suffice to reach the level of violence that constitutes civil war. Thus most societies probably have several issues on which it is possible to find a small core of people who feel passionate and who are not averse to violence. Identifiable political groups have perpetrated violence in France (Breton separatists), the United Kingdom (animal rights activists), and the United States (anti-abortion activists), and political assassinations have occurred in Italy, the Netherlands, and Sweden. Hence most societies have the political potential for violence. Whether such violence remains peripheral, as in the foregoing examples, or becomes large enough to generate widespread death and destruction, may depend as much upon whether an illegal, private, military organization is militarily and financially viable as upon the political issue itself.

Obviously governments should address justified grievances, whether or not they are likely to lead to large-scale violence. A government that is considerate and inclusive is surely less likely to face rebellion, and, in any case, it will be a better government. However, we should be wary of vilifying those governments of low-income, natural resource–dependent countries that face rebellion. Rebellion need not be a symptom that they are markedly worse than other governments. Instead, they may be in an economic and geographic environment where rebellion is particularly easy, and perhaps even particularly attractive. A journalist interviewed Kabila when he was marching on Kinshasa. He reportedly explained that in Zaire rebellion was easy—all that was needed was ten thousand dollars and a satellite phone. The dollars were to recruit a small army, cheap because the population of Zaire was among the poorest in the world. Recall that even in Zaire the quote was an exaggeration. Kabila had received several million dollars and the support of foreign armies to launch his assault. The satellite phone was to make deals with foreign businesses in extractive industries.

Although occasionally rebellion leads to an improvement in government, more often it leads to spectacular deterioration, and therefore the presumption that rebellion should be avoided is reasonable. Partly this is a matter for governments to make greater efforts to redress reasonable grievances, but it is also a matter of making rebellion less easy. Many of the things that would make rebellion more difficult require action at the regional or global level, and the international community can actively discourage rebellion without taking sides in political disputes. This is the subject of part III.

Although political conflict is common to all societies, civil war is concentrated in the lowest-income countries. In a sense this is hopeful. It is an indication that peace does not depend on resolving all political conflict and that such conflict is normal. Rather, economic development is the critical instrument in preventing rebellion and in building the conditions in which groups engage in their conflicts through normal political means. Economic development in the lowest-income countries is not easy, but neither is it unprecedented, incredibly complex, or wildly expensive.

Once a rebellion has started, a society risks being caught in a conflict trap. Ending the conflict is difficult, and even if it ends, the risk that it will start again is high. Strong global actions can be targeted toward conflict prevention in these high-risk environments. Building a peaceful world is not just a matter of encouraging tolerance and consensus. It involves a practical agenda for economic development and the effective regulation of those markets that have come to facilitate rebellion and corrupt governance.

Notes

1. Heavy dependence on natural resources also tends to make autocracies stable and democracies unstable (Ross 2000).

2. Results available on request.

3. Mueller (2000) analyzes the wars in Bosnia and Rwanda and concludes that the number of rebels committing the atrocities was relatively small. He estimates that the genocide in Rwanda was carried out by approximately 2 percent of the male adult population.

4. A possible exception is where resources are valuable because they are locally scarce, such as water and fertile land in arid areas. Homer-Dixon (1991) has emphasized this category of conflict, but see the discussion by Gleditsch (1998).

5. The change in the long-term or self-sustaining incidence is calculated using the method explained in appendix 1. We assumed the initial probability of war initiation is 0.016 and that of termination is 0.123. We multiply the initial w probability with 1.135 (corresponding to a 13.5 percent increase) and the initial v probability with 0.9405 and recalculate the self-sustaining incidence.

CHAPTER FOUR

Why Is Civil War So Common?

THIS CHAPTER TURNS FROM A MICRO-LEVEL ANALY-
sis of what circumstances are conducive to rebellion
to a macro-level analysis of what determines the
global incidence of civil war. It looks at how the incidence of civil war has changed over time and space
and attempts to account for these changes in terms
of the underlying causes of civil war identified in chapter 3. Civil war
is increasingly concentrated in relatively few conflict-prone countries,
many of them in Africa. We use the macro-level analysis to investigate
how economic development is changing the overall incidence of civil
war. Development has not been reaching those countries most prone
to civil war. As a result, if past trends continue, the world will evolve
into a two-class system, with the majority virtually conflict free and a
minority trapped in a cycle of long internal wars interspersed with
brief, unstable periods of peace. The minority of countries caught in
the conflict trap will increasingly dominate the global incidence.

Changes in the Global Pattern of Civil War

ACTIVE WARFARE HAS CHANGED ITS CHARACTER OVER THE
past 50 years in that international wars have become rare,
whereas civil wars have become more common. In 2001 all
but one of the world's wars were civil wars. Furthermore, when international wars do occur, they tend to be short: most last less than six
months (Bennett and Stam 1996). By contrast, civil wars last a long
time, on average about seven years, and their duration has tended to
increase.

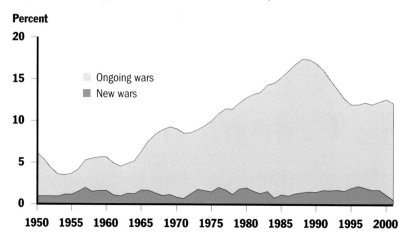

Figure 4.1 The global incidence of civil warfare, 1950–2001

Percent

Note: Proportion of countries in civil war by year. Figure shows only conflicts with at least 1,000 battle deaths over the course of the conflicts.
Source: Gleditsch and others (2002).

Figure 4.1 shows the incidence of civil war, that is, the proportion of countries that are at civil war at any one time. Between 1950 and 2000 the overall incidence rose, but this has not been a steady process: the global incidence of civil war peaked around 1990.

The global incidence of civil war at a particular time is determined by the average risk that a rebellion will ignite and by the average duration of a war once it has started. If both the risk of ignition and the duration of war were constant over a long period, the global incidence of conflict would reach a self-sustaining level: the number of wars starting would be balanced by the number of wars ending, so that the stock of active civil wars would stay constant. Throughout 1950–2001 the average annual risk that a rebellion would ignite was around 1.6 percent, while the average annual probability that an ongoing war would end was 12.0 percent, corresponding to a median duration of wars of 5.5 years. If both these probabilities turned out to be persistent, then the global incidence of conflict would eventually settle at around 12 percent, which is roughly the global incidence of conflict in the last eight years.

Fifty years ago the global incidence of civil war was clearly lower than 12 percent. This relatively peaceful period may have ended because of fundamental changes in the underlying factors that cause civil war during the 1950s and 1960s. However, in the 1950s many low-income countries were still colonies and colonialism suppressed the possibility of civil war. Independence has been bunched in two big waves, the British and French decolonizations of Africa in 1960–62 and the Russian decolonization of the early 1990s. If countries tend to be at peace during their first year of independence, there will be a long phase of adjustment after large numbers of countries have become independent. Thus for much of the period the world has had an unsustainably low incidence of civil war, and at least part of the rising incidence of civil war has been due to a movement toward the self-sustaining level. Note that a self-sustaining level need not be a desirable condition, but simply indicates the global incidence of conflict that the international community will eventually have to cope with unless it can reduce the risk of rebellion and its duration.

The observed rise in the global incidence of civil war from the 1950s to the 1970s need not of itself reflect a deterioration in the factors that cause and prolong conflict, but may simply reflect the existence of many more independent, low-income countries. To illustrate this, figure 4.2 simulates what would have happened to the global incidence of conflict since 1950 as a result of newly independent countries entering the system had all countries faced the actual average risk and duration of conflict during the period. We assume for the time being that all countries have the same risks of conflict ignition and termination and

Figure 4.2   Simulating the effects of the waves of decolonization, 1950–2020

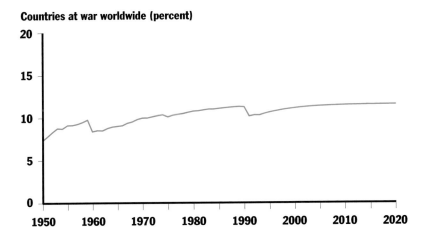

Countries at war worldwide (percent)

Source: Authors' calculations (see appendix 1).

Figure 4.3 Proportion of civil wars that end each year

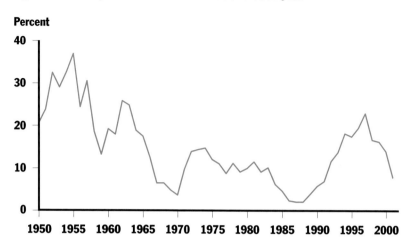

Source: Gleditsch and others (2002).

that all countries are at peace in their first year of independence.[1] The initial distribution is the actual observed incidence in 1950, around 7.5 percent. In the simulation, waves of decolonization gradually push up the global incidence of conflict to a self-sustaining level of nearly 12 percent by 2020.

The proportion of countries with new wars is shown with a darker shade in figure 4.1. No strong trend in the risk of new wars is apparent. Rather, the figure shows how wars have been steadily accumulating, as the idea of the self-sustaining level implies. However, the rate at which wars end exhibits a disturbing trend. Figure 4.3 shows the rate of war termination during 1950–2001. From 1950 to the late 1980s conflicts became steadily less likely to end. This is why we observe a peak in the incidence of conflicts around 1990, as a surge of peace settlements took place in the first half of the 1990s, but unfortunately this seems to have been a temporary phenomenon.

The most likely explanation for this surge in peace settlements is the end of the Cold War: many conflicts ended as that source of finance dried up, for example, in Mozambique. The end of the Cold War also allowed peacekeeping operations on an unprecedented scale. By contrast, other wars were made sustainable because of the inflow of weapons from the former Soviet republics (see chapter 3). This problem became important later in the 1990s, and may explain the reduction in effec-

Figure 4.4 The global self-sustaining incidence of civil war, by decades

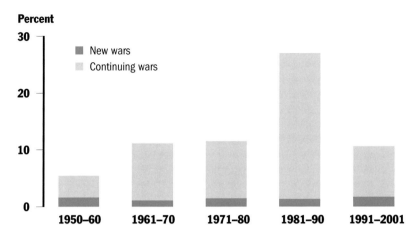

Note: Incidence of conflicts of the five decades decomposed into the share of years with wars that were new and with those that were ongoing.
Source: Based on Gleditsch and others (2002).

tive war terminations during the past five years. Overall, the net positive effect of the end of the Cold War on war duration seems to have been modest and transient.

The declining global risk of rebellion ignition and the lengthening duration of rebellion have together changed the self-sustaining global incidence of civil war. Had the risk and duration prevailing in 1971–80 persisted, the self-sustaining incidence would have been 11.5 percent, whereas had the risk and duration prevailing in 1990–2001 persisted, it would have fallen to 10.6 percent. Figure 4.4 shows the self-sustaining incidence based on the risks and termination rates for each decade. The 1980s stand out. If wars had continued to end at the same rate as in the 1980s, the incidence of war would have reached even higher levels than observed during that period. Fortunately, the improved success in ending conflicts in the 1990s prevented such a rise.

Thus while the actual global incidence of civil war has risen over the past 40 years, the underlying self-sustaining incidence may have fallen slightly. The contradictory forces have been the large increase in the number of independent, low-income countries that find themselves playing the Russian roulette of conflict risk, versus the spread of economic development that has been making the world a safer place.

Changes in the Incidence of Civil War

THIS DISCUSSION OF HOW THE UNDERLYING INCIDENCE OF civil war might itself have been changing starts by looking at changes in the risk that a rebellion will ignite. The models discussed in chapter 3 attempt a systematic, empirical analysis of the factors that underlie this risk. Here we use Collier and Hoeffler's (2002c) model. The Collier and Hoeffler model obviously omits many important things, but tests for a pure time trend find that in aggregate, these things have not tended to get significantly worse or better over time. Changes in the risk of rebellion are therefore due to changes in the variables included in the model. Whereas the end of the Cold War clearly created a surge of peace settlements, it does not appear to have had a net effect on the risk of new rebellions. Controlling for 17 new low- and middle-income states, the risk of rebellion seems to have neither increased nor decreased. The downfall of the Soviet Union definitely let loose a few civil wars that had previously been repressed,[2] but the end of the Cold War also cut off a source of finance for an unknown number of potential wars.

Hence to understand the global changes over time we need to turn to the explanatory variables included in the model. Many of these variables change only slowly or not at all, such as the ethnic and religious composition of a society and its geographic characteristics. The main factors that can change relatively rapidly are the economic variables. Recall that the three big economic drivers of rebellion are the level, growth, and structure of income.

In addition, newly independent countries have a much higher risk of conflict than other countries. The very fact that they are new countries with weak institutions and often with a legacy of decolonization wars makes them five times more war prone in their first year of independence than comparable but older countries (Hegre and others 2001). If these new countries are able to sustain peace, this history of stability itself gradually makes them safer. Moreover, most new countries are low-income, developing countries, with average income approximately half that of older countries. In sum, these two factors mean that newly independent countries face a risk that is 10 times higher than other countries.

Globally, if we compare the 1960s with the 1990s these characteristics were very different. The countries that were independent in the 1960s typically had considerably higher per capita income by the 1990s, and this tended to reduce their risk of rebellion. Also working favorably

Figure 4.5   Factors changing the global risk of conflict

Change in risk of civil war (log)

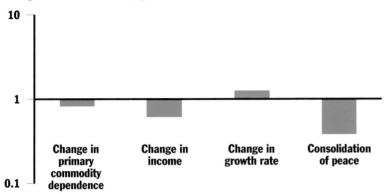

Note: Contributions to the change in risk of civil war from 1965 to 1995.
Source: Based on Collier and Hoeffler (2002c).

was a decline in the average extent of dependence on primary commodities. Offsetting this, growth rates were lower and new low-income
countries had become independent. The Collier and Hoeffler model
can be used to compare the typical risk of rebellion facing countries in
1965 and in 1995. It suggests that the typical risk declined from 9.2
percent to 6.8 percent in 1995. The main reason for this improvement
was global economic development and the consolidation of new states.

Figure 4.5 shows the overall reduction in risk and its constituent
components. The growth in average per capita income and reduction
in primary commodity dependence reduced the global average risk of
conflict by something like 30 percent from 1965 to the mid-1990s.
This reduction was offset by the lower growth rates relative to those of
the late 1960s. The increase in the average duration of postindependence peace is the factor that has made the strongest impact. This has
lead to a 50 percent decrease in risk.

What explains the trend in the duration of war? To look at this we
use a model designed to study the duration of civil war (Collier, Hoeffler, and Söderbom 2003). As with the risk of rebellion, the duration of
conflict may have changed over the past 40 years either because of
changes in the variables included in the model or because of changes in
factors that are important but are omitted. Whereas no significant time
trend in the risk of conflict ignition was apparent, its duration shows a
substantial time trend: after controlling for the explanatory variables,

Figure 4.6   The changing rates of conflict termination

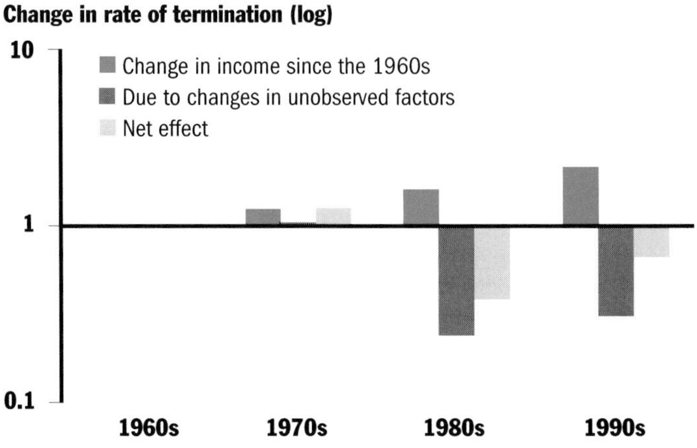

Change in rate of termination (log)

Legend:
- Change in income since the 1960s
- Due to changes in unobserved factors
- Net effect

X-axis: 1960s   1970s   1980s   1990s

Y-axis: 0.1, 1, 10

Source: Collier, Hoeffler, and Söderbom (2003).

conflicts were harder to end in the 1980s than in earlier periods. They may also have been more persistent in the 1990s. By definition, the model cannot tell us why this has happened: it is due to factors not included in the model.

In addition, some of the variables included in the model have changed. The higher per capita income is, the shorter the civil war. Recall that this might be expected for various reasons, namely, civil war is costlier at higher income levels, and thus the incentive to reach a settlement is stronger. Whatever the explanation, the strong rise in global per capita incomes has tended to shorten the duration of wars.

The overall change in the termination rate of conflict is thus the net effect of the unexplained lengthening of conflict, decade by decade, and the shortening of conflict resulting from global economic growth. Figure 4.6 shows the net effect, decade by decade. Overall, the unexplained effect has more than offset the favorable effect of global growth, therefore the duration of conflict has increased.

Unpacking the Global Incidence of Civil War

SO FAR WE HAVE FOCUSED ON GLOBAL AVERAGES. AVERAGES often conceal wide dispersions, and sometimes they also conceal important structural differences. This is the case with conflict.

Divergent Development Trends

For the past 20 years global growth has been raising incomes in much of the developing world and reducing the incidence of poverty. Much of the world's population now lives in middle-income countries, defined as those with per capita annual income above US$745. The structure of developing countries' exports has also changed dramatically. Whereas in 1980 primary commodities still accounted for three-quarters of exports, they now account for only 20 percent. Some low-income countries, including the largest, have succeeded in implementing and sustaining policy reforms conducive to rapid growth and integration into global markets. While currently they are still low-income countries, they are on track to joining China in becoming middle-income countries. Recall from chapter 3 that fast growth is not just a route to the eventual low risk that goes along with higher income levels, but also contributes directly to risk reduction. We therefore aggregate those low-income countries that have sustained reasonably good economic policies with the middle-income countries and term the combined group "successful developers." Specifically, we include all those low-income countries that over the 1990s averaged CPIA scores of 3.5 or better.[3] Some of the successful developers are still at high risk of conflict, but as a group they are already much safer than other developing countries and are on course for continuing reductions in risk.

Many developing countries have not, however, participated in these favorable trends. They have either been unable to implement reform or their reforms have not been sustained and they remain stuck in undiversified primary commodity exports. We refer to this group as the "marginalized" low-income countries. The growth rates of per capita income in the two groups of countries were dramatically different in the 1990s, negative at −1.0 percent for the marginalized countries and positive at 2.0 percent for the successful developers. The average level of income in the marginalized countries was less than a third that of the successful developers when measured on a purchasing power parity basis.

Thus in aggregate, the marginalized countries are the one group that has all three of the economic characteristics that appear to increase proneness to conflict: low income, economic decline, and dependence on primary commodities. The following section compares the risks and incidence of a civil war for a typical marginalized country with that for the typical successful developer. Figure 4.7 shows the predicted risk for

Figure 4.7 Divergent risks: marginalized countries relative to successful developers

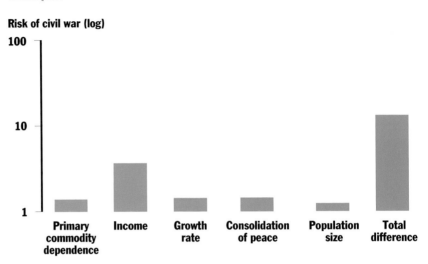

Source: Based on Collier and Hoeffler (2002c).

the typical marginalized country relative to the typical successful developer and the contribution of some important risk factors. The predicted risk is more than 10 times higher for the marginalized country. Low income has the largest impact, accounting for half the difference.

To date global development has largely missed the marginalized countries; thus, while global growth is indeed reducing the global incidence of conflict, it is doing so dramatically unevenly and cannot be relied on to secure a peaceful world. If the trends of the past 20 years continue, the successful developers will evolve into low-risk societies while the marginalized countries will face increasing risks as their per capita incomes decline. Figure 4.8 shows how the predicted risk of civil war ignition evolves for the marginalized countries and successful developers relative to the high income countries if recent growth patterns persist. Global growth is part of the process of reducing the incidence of civil war, but unless it reaches the currently marginalized countries it will progressively become less effective as a force for peace. As the successful developers evolve into a group with lower risks of rebellion, the increment to peace achieved by further growth and diversification in income becomes smaller and smaller. Global growth is not sweeping the world into peace at an accelerating rate. If present trends continue its contribution to peace will fizzle out well before global peace has been achieved.

Figure 4.8   **Development of risk of civil war for the marginalized and successful developers, 2000–2020**

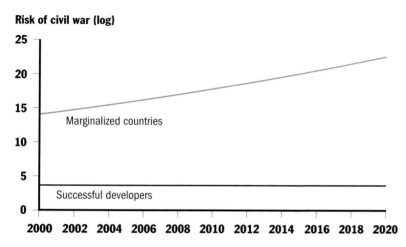

Risk of civil war (log)

Note: The contribution from growth to income per capita to the odds of war onset relative to high-income countries, with growth projections of 1.5 percent (high income), –1.0 percent (marginalized), and 2.0 percent (successful developers).
Source: Calculated from Collier and Hoeffler (2002c).

The radically different risks the successful developers and marginalized countries face imply different incidences of civil war for the two groups in the long term. As long as they remain stagnant, the marginalized countries will remain at the incidence experienced during 1990–2001, whereas the successful developers will slowly but surely reduce their incidence from their current somewhat lower level. Changes in the global incidence depend both on these two divergent trends and on the relative size of the two groups. The successful developer group is largest in terms of both number of countries and population—71 countries with around 4 billion people—versus 52 marginalized countries with around 1.1 billion people. Nevertheless, the global incidence of civil war will increasingly come to be dominated by wars in the group of poor, declining, primary-commodity exporting countries as the incidence of war in the successful developer group decreases.

Implications of the Conflict Trap

Chapter 3 introduced the concept of the conflict trap. Through various routes, once a conflict has started a society faces a greatly increased risk of further wars. Conflicts are hard to stop, and what happens during conflict increases both the risk and duration of subsequent conflict. Countries that have had a war have a two to four times higher risk of a subsequent war, even when controlling for the factors we identified earlier. Boxes 4.1 and 4.2 describe two recurrent conflicts.

Figure 4.9 indicates how the risk of war ignition is altered after a civil war compared with before a war. The risk depends on how long the country has been independent and at peace. In the first month of postindependence peace the risk of war is more than four times as high as after a decade of peace. After the first decade of consolidation, the risk does not change much as time goes by; however, if a civil war breaks out the gain from this consolidation is lost. After the war, the risk of war re-igniting is two to four times higher than the risk facing new states. This is the conflict trap: a country that first falls into the trap may have a risk of new war that is 10 times higher just after that war has ended than before the war started. If the country succeeds in maintaining postconflict peace for 10 years or so, the risk is considerably reduced, but remains at a higher level than before the conflict. This legacy of war seems to take a long time—a generation or two—before withering away (Hegre and others 2001).

Box 4.1   Recurrent conflicts example 1: Afghanistan

THE WAR IN AFGHANISTAN STARTED IN 1978 WHEN members of the Marxist-Leninist People's Democratic Party of Afghanistan captured the state; assassinated political, ethnic, and religious elites; and incited uprisings (Asia Watch 1991). After the Soviet invasion of December 1979 and the assassination of Afghan president Hafizullah Amin, the war continued with mujahideen fighting against the Soviet-installed Afghan government of Mohammad Najibullah. In 1992 the mujahideen captured power and the state changed hands, but peace negotiations among Afghanistan's many resistance factions excluded key parties. One such group was Gulbuddin Hikmatyar's Hizb-i Islami, which rejected the resulting agreement and began a series of rocket attacks on Kabul that continued into 1995 (Hiltermann 2002).

From 1992 until 1996 the war was waged by the Pashtun-dominated Taliban seeking to overthrow Burhanuddin Rabbani and his Tajik-dominated Jam'iyat-i-Islam party. After a Taliban victory in 1996 a new war started in which the Tajiks, Uzbeks, and others became the insurgents against the new "government" (Gurr, Marshall, and Khosla 2001). In 1997 the Taliban proclaimed the Islamic Emirate of Afghanistan, which was recognized by Pakistan, Saudi Arabia, and the United Arab Emirates. The Taliban never controlled all the territory of Afghanistan, and about 5 to 10 percent of that territory was controlled by the alliance known as the United Front, formed in 1996 by non-Pashtun groups opposed to the Taliban and led by Rabbani's former defense minister, Ahmad Shah Massoud.

Box 4.2   Recurrent conflicts example 2: Angola

A PATTERN OF FAILED PEACE AGREEMENTS IN Angola has checkered a history of civil war that has been ongoing since the country's independence in 1975. The war against UNITA over control of the central government from 1975 until 1994 caused approximately 345,000 deaths and ended in a stalemate that led to the Lusaka Accord and the deployment of a UN peacekeeping force. Failure to implement the agreement led to a renewal of war in late 1997. The U.S. State Department noted more than 100 ceasefire violations in a three-month period in 1996. Despite that instability, the period 1996–97 was one in which UNITA officials were becoming increasingly integrated into the government, and the annual death toll during this time was probably "only" in the low hundreds. Fighting resumed in March 1998 despite an agreement reached on January 9, 1998, for resolution of the remaining issues under the Lusaka Accord. UNITA leader Jonas Savimbi refused to move to the capital and join the government. UNITA forces quickly retook more

than 300 areas previously returned to the government, but by the end of 1999 the government, with the support of Namibian government forces, had overrun UNITA's former headquarters (Parker, Heindel, and Branch 2000). Thereafter, UNITA's military position continued to deteriorate because of a double squeeze. The government used the opportunity of high oil prices to increase military spending. At the same time the Fowler Report of the UN exposed the routes by which UNITA had been financed and supplied, as a result of which it was closed off. In February 2002 Savimbi was cornered and killed and UNITA accepted a peace settlement. The Angolan government was able to negotiate from strength. More than 10,000 people were killed in the new round of fighting, and according to the United Nations Children's Fund, nearly 75,000 people died of starvation in 1999 and at least 1.5 million people were displaced as of January 2000 because of the war (Parker, Heindel, and Branch 2000).

This increase in risk is before we account for the changes in the observable risk factors caused by the war itself. In particular, the impact of the civil war on the economy is extremely damaging (see chapter 1). Growth of GDP per capita is reduced by around 2.2 percentage points per year during war. Moreover, the effects of the war linger on after the conflict, so that the country's economic performance is hampered for several years after the conflict has ended. Only after extremely long conflicts, for example, in Mozambique, where disruption is so complete that the mere fact that large numbers of people return to work shows up as a significant improvement, will a peace agreement mean an immediate improvement in growth performance. Hence the typical conflict reduces income by some 10 to 15 percent. Such losses in income are also often associated with an increase in primary commodity dependence of roughly two percentage points (Collier and Hoeffler 2002b). These two changes imply an increase in the risk of war onset of an additional 5 percent.

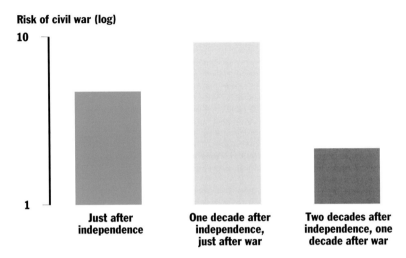

Figure 4.9   The conflict trap: risk of civil war relative to a country with no recent war

Source: Hegre and others (2001); Collier and Hoeffler (2002c).

Some risks also arise from neighbors in conflict, so to some extent the conflict trap operates at the level of a neighborhood, not just of a single country. Quantitative studies of civil war onset find no evidence that civil wars are more frequent in countries bordering on conflict countries, controlling for the explanatory variables (see, for example, Hegre and others 2001); however, civil wars spill over indirectly through their effects on the explanatory variables such as income (Murdoch and Sandler 2002). Reduced income in neighboring countries indirectly increases their risk of conflict, and as most countries have several neighbors, in aggregate, such small increases in risk can have significant effects.

The conflict trap is a tendency, not an iron law. Middle-income countries have a lower probability of falling into it. A previous conflict seems to increase the risk for middle-income countries by the same factor as for low-income countries, but as they have a lower general risk, they have better chances of maintaining peace beyond the first post-conflict decade. Figure 4.10 summarizes the predicted risks of war ignition and re-ignition for the typical country in each group.

Figure 4.11 decomposes the effect of the conflict trap into the economic factors that change as a consequence of the conflict and other unobserved factors that change during the war. Such other factors are the accumulation of weapons and military organizations and less tan-

Figure 4.10   The conflict trap by type of country

Annual probability of outbreak of war (percent)

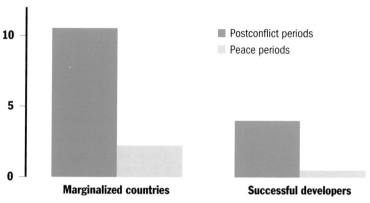

■ Postconflict periods
■ Peace periods

Source: Based on a revised version of Collier and Hoeffler (2002c).

Figure 4.11   Risk components for marginalized countries in the conflict trap, relative to the same countries preconflict

Risk of civil war (log)

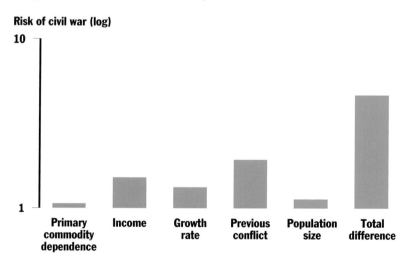

Source: Based on a revised version of Collier and Hoeffler (2002c).

gible effects of war, such as the breakdown of institutions and social po-larization. The figure compares the risk of the typical marginalized country that has not had a war for 10 years and the typical postconflict marginalized country. The postconflict country has a risk of conflict that is five times greater. Around half of that increased risk is due to negative changes in primary commodity dependence and reduced income and growth. The other half of the increased risk is unexplained and will in part be due to the selection problem: conflict countries already had unobserved characteristics that increase the risk of conflict.

The conflict trap has implications for the global incidence of conflict. The countries most prone to the trap are the marginalized low-income countries. Although poor, peaceful, stagnant economies look as if they are stuck in an equilibrium, they are, in effect, playing Russian roulette. A low-income, stagnant country that starts its independence at peace does not have a very long expected duration of that peace, although some countries, even though economically stagnant, have to date preserved peace, whether through prudent policies or good fortune, for example, Malawi, Tanzania, and Zambia. However, even long periods of peace are no guarantee of safety. Côte d'Ivoire and Nepal are recent instances of moderately democratic low-income countries with long histories of peace collapsing into civil war.

The marginalized stagnant but peaceful countries are thus living dangerously. Not only are they prone to civil war, more important, once a war has started they also face a permanently changed risk of conflict, that is, they are stuck in the conflict trap. The poor but peaceful category of countries, although currently numerous, is thus not likely to be so numerous in a global self-sustaining level. We would expect these countries either to develop, joining the successful developers, or at some stage succumb to civil war, with many then becoming trapped in conflict. In the long run poor but peaceful is not an option. The world is therefore evolving into a state in which most countries are permanently conflict free while a minority are trapped in a cycle of lengthy war, uneasy peace, and reversion to lengthy war.

This leads to a different view of the self-sustaining incidence of conflict, with radically different risks for different groups. The high-income countries have a negligible risk of civil war. A second group of countries, a majority, will be in a virtuous circle of peace, with income rising strongly and diversifying out of dependence on primary commodities. These countries will face a low and declining risk of conflict. The few civil wars that occur in this group may be long, but they will tend not to trap countries into a cycle of conflict. A third smaller group of countries will be stuck in a conflict trap. Although they may periodically reach peace, the legacy of the conflict is such that peace is not sustained. Occasionally countries will switch between these groups. Once in a while a peaceful and prosperous country might collapse into civil war and find itself subsequently stuck in a conflict trap. Similarly, once in a while a country that has been mired in repeat conflict will climb out of it. A fourth group, the poor but peaceful, will hover in between development and the conflict trap.

Figure 4.12 illustrates the trap.[4] We grouped 156 countries with adequate data coverage into the four groups of countries. Here we regard countries as in a postconflict state during the first decade after a war has ended, and as at peace if they have not had a war in the past 10 years. We estimated the predicted risks of war for a typical country in each group. The risk is a function of levels of income, primary commodity dependence, growth, and the other characteristics found to be pertinent in chapter 3. The risk changes over time after independence or war. The model was estimated for the 1960–99 period.

For the typical low-income country, the predicted probability of going to war from a state of peace is 2 percent per year, whereas the

Figure 4.12   The conflict trap in 2000: annual flows into and out of conflict

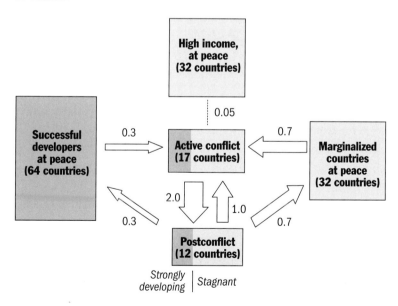

Note: Numbers next to the arrows indicate the number of countries per year that move between the different states of conflict in the self-sustaining state. Numbers in boxes indicate the self-sustaining number of countries in each conflict state. See appendix 1 for fuller coverage.
Source: Based on a revised version of Collier and Hoeffler (2002c).

probability of war from a postconflict situation is about 10 percent per year. We adopt a median duration of wars of about five years. Just as we computed a self-sustaining incidence of war from the probabilities of starting and ending wars, we can compute the self-sustaining distribution of peace, war, and the postconflict state for the typical low-income country: it is predicted to be at war 24 percent of the time, in a post-conflict state 15 percent of the time, and at peace 61 percent of the time. The corresponding predicted distribution for a typical middle-income country is 5 percent, 5 percent, and 90 percent, respectively.

Figure 4.12 simulates how this self-sustaining distribution will be reflected in global numbers of conflict onsets and fall-backs. Seventeen countries are predicted to be involved in a civil war, of which 15 are ongoing wars. Half of the conflict onsets will be from the group of post-conflict countries. In the simulation, there is one re-entry into war every year. Each year 0.7 low-income countries will go from a state of established peace to war, whereas only 0.3 peaceful middle-income countries will do so. As this pattern is self-sustaining, two wars end every year and one country leaves the postconflict period in peace.

The simulation is only an approximation, for example, it abstracts from differences within each group. However, we would expect that continued divergence in growth rates between the successful developers and the marginalized countries would gradually alter the structure of global risks. Figure 4.13 shows how given this scenario of stagnation for some and growth for others the global incidence of civil war would evolve by 2020 and by 2050.

If these projections are broadly correct they carry a disturbing message. A further 50 years of development along past trends will have little impact on the global incidence of civil war: the number of civil wars declines from around 17 to around 13. This disappointing outcome is because the outbreak of war becomes increasingly concentrated in the marginalized and postconflict countries, with their combined share of global conflict rising from 82 percent in 2000 to 94 percent by 2050.

The Changing Regional Pattern

The incidence of civil war has differed dramatically across regions. In part, this is because the countries in a region tend to have many features in common and some of these features affect the risk of conflict. In

Figure 4.13a   The conflict trap in 2020: annual flows into and out of conflict

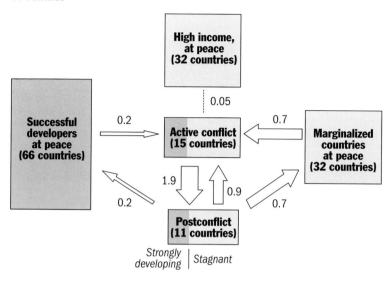

Figure 4.13b   The conflict trap in 2050: annual flows into and out of conflict

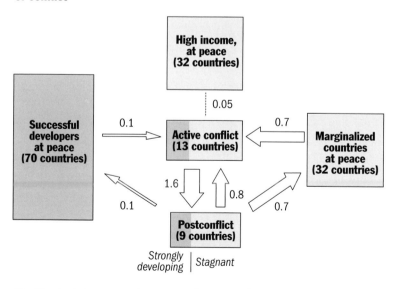

Note: The simulation assumes the same growth rates as in figure 4.8. Numbers next to the arrows indicate the number of countries per year that move between the different states of conflict in the self-sustaining state. Numbers in boxes indicate the self-sustaining number of countries in each conflict state. See appendix 1 for fuller coverage.
Source: Based on a revised version of Collier and Hoeffler (2002c).

Figure 4.14   The incidence of civil war in South and East Asia and in Oceania, 1950–2001

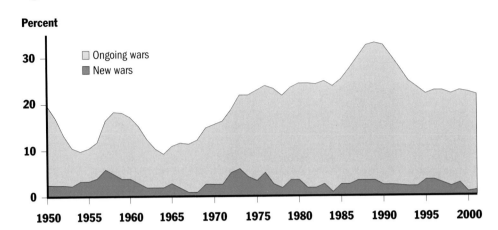

Note: Proportion of countries in civil war by year.
Source: Gleditsch and others (2002).

addition, as noted in chapter 2, civil wars generate spillover effects for neighbors. Hence if by chance a region has a relatively large number of conflicts, this will itself increase the risks facing the countries in the region that have remained at peace.

Two regions stand out over the entire 1950–2001 period. Developing Asia (figure 4.14) has had a persistently high incidence of civil war, while countries of the Organisation for Economic Co-operation and Development (OECD) have had a persistently negligible incidence. We use the previous models of conflict initiation and duration to test whether these regional effects are accounted for entirely by the factors included in the model or whether there are region-specific omitted factors. Neither model finds significant omitted effects for these regions. The radically different incidences of civil war are accounted for predominantly by the radically different levels of economic development in the countries.

Other regions have been distinctive because of either bouts or trends. Latin America had a severe bout of conflict in the 1980s, but has showed remarkably positive development since the end of the Cold War (figure 4.15). No new wars have begun since 1985, and most of the wars that began before have ended. In 2001 only the conflict in Colombia lingered on. Whether the peace in Guatemala and Peru will survive its first difficult decade remains to be seen, but according to the analy-

Figure 4.15   The incidence of civil war in Latin America and the Caribbean, 1950–2001

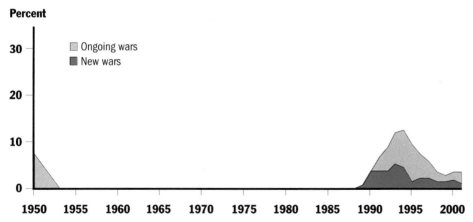

Note: Proportion of countries in civil war by year.
Source: Gleditsch and others (2002).

Figure 4.16   The incidence of civil war in Eastern Europe and Central Asia, 1950–2001

Note: Proportion of countries in civil war by year.
Source: Gleditsch and others (2002).

sis shown earlier, the prospects for these middle-income countries are good. The former Soviet bloc had a severe bout of conflict in the 1990s, but most of these conflicts were short (figure 4.16). The Middle East and North Africa region has had a stable and high incidence of civil war since the late 1960s (figure 4.17).

113

Figure 4.17   The incidence of civil war in the Middle East and North Africa, 1950–2001

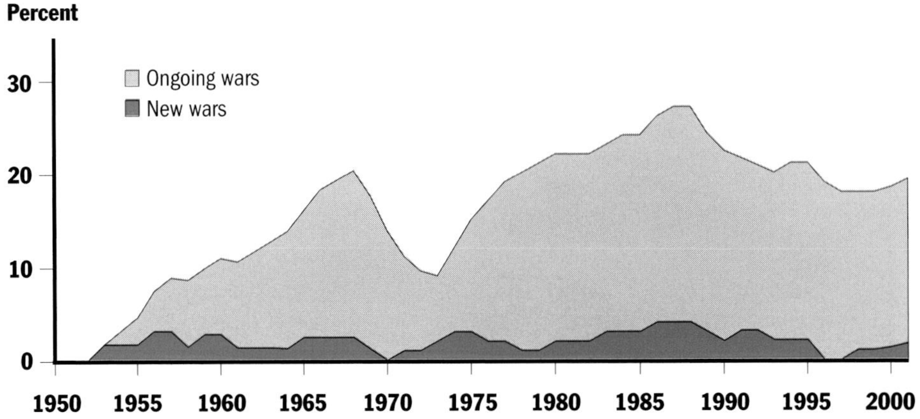

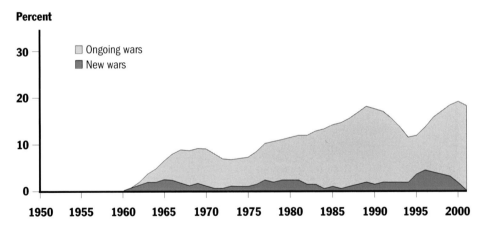

Note: Proportion of countries in civil war by year.
Source: Gleditsch and others (2002).

Figure 4.18   The incidence of civil war in Sub-Saharan Africa, 1950–2001

Note: Proportion of countries in civil war by year.
Source: Gleditsch and others (2002).

Perhaps the most disturbing trend has been the rise in the incidence of violent conflict in Sub-Saharan Africa (figure 4.18). Until the 1980s Africa had a below-average incidence, whereas now it has an incidence at par with Asia's and the Middle East's and much higher than Latin America's. It is the only region that did not see a decrease in incidence

Figure 4.19   The incidence of civil war in Africa and other developing countries, 1950–2001

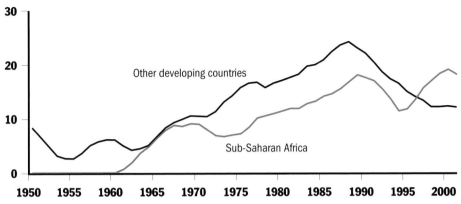

Incidence of civil war (percent)

Other developing countries

Sub-Saharan Africa

Source: Gleditsch and others (2002).

over the 1990s. Figure 4.19 shows the incidence of war in Sub-Saharan Africa compared with that in other developing countries.

The media perception of the concentration of conflict in Africa is that it is related to deep-rooted ethnic antagonisms. Africa is indeed more ethnically and religiously fractionalized than other regions of the world. It encompasses an estimated 2,000 ethnic groups, so the typical country is highly diverse. The media explanation for conflict in Africa may be right, but before one accepts it uncritically, attempting a statistically grounded analysis is worthwhile.

As with global incidence, changes in the incidence of civil war in Africa have three components: a movement to the self-sustaining level, a change in the level caused by changes in the risk of rebellion, and a change in the level caused by changes in the duration of conflict. Part of the explanation for Africa's rising incidence of conflict is indeed likely to be a gradual adjustment toward its self-sustaining level. Africa was decolonized more recently than other regions, and so its countries have been experiencing the Russian roulette of civil war risk and accumulating conflicts for a shorter period.

We first investigate whether Africa's risk of rebellion ignition is distinctive and whether it has changed over time. Africa could be distinctive either because the variables that explain the initiation of rebellion in the model are distinctive for Africa or because factors left out of the

115

model are distinctive for Africa. The latter possibility can be investigated by including a dummy variable for Africa. When this is included—both for the whole of the region and for the francophone part separately—it is insignificant; thus the distinctive behavior of the variables included within the model account for Africa's distinctive experience.

If we compare economic variables for 1970 with those for 1995, Africa appears to have changed relatively little. Per capita income had barely risen over the quarter century, and by the early 1990s growth rates had actually turned negative, whereas in the late 1960s they had been quite high. Dependence on primary commodity exports had increased slightly over the period. In combination, the Collier and Hoeffler model estimates that the risk of the initiation of rebellion in Africa increased from around 8 percent for the five-year period 1970–74 to around 12.6 percent for 1995–99. By contrast, other developing regions had, on average, experienced a substantial increase in per capita income, and even though growth rates were lower in the early 1990s than in the late 1960s, they remained positive. Furthermore, these other developing regions had sharply reduced their dependence on primary commodity exports from levels above those of Africa in 1970 to levels well below those of Africa by 1995. In combination the model estimates that these changes substantially reduced the risk that a rebellion would be initiated, from nearly 15 percent in 1970–74, a level far higher than that of Africa, to around 5 percent by 1995–99.

If the model is broadly correct it implies that the distinctively rising incidence of civil war in Africa was at least partly due to the contribution of Africa's distinctively poor economic performance to its risk of rebellion ignition. Other regions had sufficiently good economic performance to radically drive down the rate at which rebellions were initiated.

As concerns the duration of conflict, the Collier, Hoeffler, and Söderbom model does not find any distinctive Africa effect. To the extent that African conflicts last a long time it is because of factors included within the model. Here again, Africa's distinctive economic performance matters. Recall that the lower per capita income is, the longer conflicts tend to last. The divergence between Africa and other developing regions in per capita income has tended to shorten non-African conflicts relative to African conflicts. Africa has thus had no favorable offsetting effect to the unexplained global trend for conflicts to lengthen.

Africa has experienced quite different trends from other developing regions, both in the risk of conflict ignition and in its expected duration. Both of these divergences are due to its worse economic performance. As these are the two components determining the self-sustaining incidence of civil war, the implication is that the incidence rose in Africa whereas it declined substantially elsewhere.

How does this account compare with the popular media explanation of African conflict in terms of deep-rooted ethnic hatreds? Recall that the statistical analysis reported in chapter 3 agrees that ethnic and religious composition affect both the risk of conflict and its duration. Ethnic dominance is a substantial risk factor, although ethnic and religious diversity is otherwise a safety factor. Compared with other developing regions, the model considers Africa's social composition to be conducive to a low risk of conflict ignition. Its high level of diversity implies that fewer African countries (40 percent) are characterized by ethnic dominance compared with other developing regions (54 percent); however, once a conflict starts, Africa's ethnic composition is likely to lead to longer conflicts. Africa's index of ethno-linguistic fractionalization is higher than in other regions, and for the typical country this implies that conflict would be longer. The lower risk of conflict ignition and longer conflicts on the incidence of conflict offset each other, so that the effect of social composition on the incidence of conflict is ambiguous. In essence, however, the models suggest that far from Africa's conflict problem being deep-rooted in its social structure, it is a consequence of the disastrous deviation of African economic performance from that of other developing countries that set it apart during the 1970s and has proved persistent. Of course, Africa's distinctive social composition may have contributed to its poor economic performance, but this is a different issue.

Conclusion: Poverty and the Conflict Trap

INDIVIDUAL CIVIL WARS HAVE THEIR OWN IDIOSYNCRATIC causes, such as the appearance of a charismatic rebel leader coincident with government abuses of power; however, long-term changes in the global incidence of civil war are unlikely to be determined by any overall pattern in such idiosyncratic events. The behavior of two groups of countries will increasingly come to dominate the global prevalence of civil war: the marginalized countries and those in the conflict trap.

The contribution of the marginalized countries to the global incidence of conflict will depend on the size of the group and its economic performance. Thus stimulating development in the slow-growing, low-income countries is one of the two critical interventions to reduce the global incidence of conflict. The other critical intervention is to weaken the conflict trap, thereby increasing the chances of sustained peace in postconflict situations. These are not the only intervention points for enhancing global peace, but they will increasingly become the most important ones. Part III focuses on these.

Notes

1. Later in the chapter we show that newly independent countries have a particularly high risk of war. This is not accounted for in figure 4.2. A simulation including this in the specification would have had a quicker convergence to the self-sustaining incidence.

2. See Mearsheimer (1990) for an extremely pessimistic prediction just after the Cold War ended.

3. These were Armenia, Bhutan, Ghana, India, Indonesia, and Uganda.

4. The methods used to produce this figure are described in detail in appendix 1.

PART **III**

POLICIES
FOR PEACE

PART I SHOWED THAT CIVIL WAR IS DEVELOP-
ment in reverse for the countries directly affected
and that it generates huge costs both for neighbors and internationally. Those who are not the
combatants bear most of the costs of war. Modern civil war is not usually an investment in the
future: it is not a catalyst for progress. On the
contrary, even after the war ends its costs—social,
political, and economic—continue to mount. If
the international incidence of civil war could be
reduced, the world would be a better place. The
question is not whether curtailing civil war is desirable, but whether doing so is feasible. Part II
investigated the background to effective policy
formulation: what fuels war, both at the level of
an individual country and at the level of the international system. At the country level we saw

that various dimensions of economic development strongly influence the risk of war. At the international level we saw that two components of
risk dominate the overall incidence of conflict:
the risks coming from low-income, stagnant countries and the risks coming from countries in the
conflict trap.

Chapter 5 organizes the discussion of policy
interventions around each of the problems that
contribute to the international incidence of conflict. Some policies are the responsibility of the
governments of countries at risk of conflict,
while others can only be achieved by international action. Chapter 6 brings together the
most important of the policies that require an
international response, and so presents an agenda
for international action.

CHAPTER FIVE

What Works Where?

P ART I DEMONSTRATED THAT THE BULK OF THE COSTS of civil war, both social and economic, do not accrue to the active participants. A distinct possibility is that the participants will do well out of war while inflicting massive damage. Nor are the victims of civil war confined to those living in the combat-affected country. Civil war is a regional public bad: it reduces incomes and raises mortality elsewhere in the region. It is also a global public bad: through hard drugs, disease, and terrorism it inflicts death, misery, and economic loss among people who know nothing of the conflict. Many of these costs are highly persistent and outlast the civil war by many years. Because of the radical divergence between the incentives facing participants and the interests of others, conflict cannot just be left to the participants to sort out among themselves. If it is, civil wars will be too frequent and last too long. A problem with the attitude "a plague on both your houses" is that other people's houses are also affected. But what can be done?

Some of the causes of civil war are idiosyncratic and beyond the control of policy; however, as chapter 3 suggested, some combinations of characteristics make countries radically more or less prone to violent conflict. Many of these characteristics are amenable to policy: well-chosen policies can reduce the risk of civil war. Chapter 4 demonstrated that four radically different risk groups affect the global incidence of civil war. The rich countries are virtually risk free. Those that are already middle-income countries or on track to becoming middle-income countries have low and declining risks. By contrast, those countries that are poor and in economic decline and those that are stuck in the conflict trap both have much higher risks and constitute the core of the future global risk of civil war. Between them these two groups of countries have a population of around 1.1 billion people. Well-chosen policies can reduce the global incidence of civil war, but the policies that are appropriate are quite different for each group and need to take many country-specific characteristics into account. Nevertheless, focusing on the different groups facing significant risks is useful. Commonly, however, policy discussions tend either to be country specific or not to differentiate between countries based on their economic characteristics.

This chapter discusses policies that could reduce the global incidence of civil war. Some of these policies can be implemented by the government of the country at risk, some by neighbors in the region, and some by the international community. The chapter follows the country grouping developed in chapter 4.

Conflict Prevention in the Successful Developers

STATISTICALLY, THE SUCCESSFUL DEVELOPERS ARE NOT AT high risk of conflict, but neither have they reached a level of risk so low as to be able to forget about the problem. Such countries do sometimes collapse into conflict. When such conflicts do happen they are hugely costly: the country risks falling off its growth path into the conflict trap. Furthermore, in aggregate this is by far the largest group of countries, accounting for around 4 billion people. The question is not, therefore, whether to pay some attention to policies that reduce the risk of conflict for this group of countries, but rather what policies might be particularly appropriate for them.

Cushioning Adverse Shocks

Once a country is either middle-income or low-income but growing rapidly, it has relatively little scope for reducing risk by accelerating its economic performance. The exception is its greater exposure to shocks brought about by financial crashes, and so the priority is to avoid such shocks. The reduction in the risk of conflict is merely one further reason why a government should pay attention to the financial sector's health; however, to the extent that the international community is often involved in mitigating such crises, given its concern to prevent civil war because of its spillover effects, there is an enhanced reason to provide a financial cushion.

Undertaking Political Reform

The limited scope for enhancing economic performance suggests that a sensible approach would be to place greater emphasis on the reform of political institutions as a means of risk reduction. Evidence that democratic political institutions are differentially effective once a country has reached middle-income levels strengthens support for this option. Hence, as the level of income rises, economic policy becomes absolutely less important in conflict reduction, while political institutions become absolutely more important; however, as even moderate change in political institutions is a risk factor in itself, political institutions must be stable (Fearon and Laitin 2003; Hegre and others 2001).

Institutions that are internally consistent have the lowest risk of a breakdown because such institutions are self-reinforcing (Gates and others 2003; Gurr 1974). For democracies, this means a wide distribution of power and no permanent exclusions of actors from the political system. The powers of the elected executive branch of the government are balanced by a strong house of representatives, elections are open to the entire population, and multiparty competition is genuine. If one branch of government becomes too powerful, other branches will attempt to rein it in. In a consistent democracy they will succeed. In an inconsistent democracy such a contest may turn violent.

Related to this, democracy functions best as a conflict prevention mechanism when the stakes of the political contest are low (Przeworski 1991; Weingast 1997). Many of the economic policy recommendations suggested later in this chapter help to reduce the stakes by reducing the gains to narrow interests from obtaining or retaining political office. Legal and economic institutions that help achieve these aims are indispensable for a well-functioning democracy.

Most new democracies have adopted majoritarian or presidential political systems. These institutions have the advantage that they perform better in terms of accountability: placing responsibility for failed policies on a single-party government typical of these institutions is easier than placing responsibility on the minority or coalition governments that are typical of proportional systems. Moreover, governments in majoritarian or presidential political systems tend to have moderate policies, because two-party systems have a powerful incentive to adhere to the median voter's preferences and extreme parties will rarely be represented in the country's parliament. In divisive societies, however, such institutions may not offer adequate protection to minorities. This is particularly relevant to countries emerging from ethnic or religious civil wars, and systems with proportional representation may be a way to provide minority representation (Lijphart 1984; Reynal-Querol 2002a,b). Alternative ways to protect minorities are federal systems combined with two-chamber parliaments. Some evidence also suggests that among democratic political systems some designs are more effective at preventing violence than others. Both proportional representation and multiple checks and balances tend to distribute power more widely across the political spectrum, and these features are associated with a lower risk of conflict (Reynal-Querol 2002b).

Considering Faster Growth

Finally, we consider the contribution of faster economic growth for the successful developers. We can simulate the effects of such faster growth using the model underlying figure 4.12. Figure 5.1 simulates the effect of raising the growth rate of the typical country in this group by 3 percent per year between now and 2020, with a corresponding reduction in primary commodity dependence. Such an increase in growth rates

Figure 5.1   The contribution to peace of faster growth in the successful developers

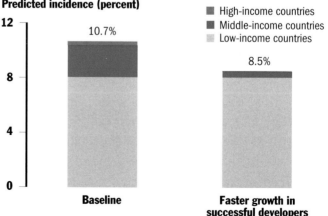

Note: The simulation is based on the model presented in figure 4.12. See appendix 1 for details.
Source: Based on a revised version of Collier and Hoeffler (2002c).

would be a massive improvement in development performance, and so is at the outer bound of what is possible. In effect, this amounts to the limits of implementing the current development strategy more successfully. As the figure shows, it offers only a modest contribution to global peace: the global incidence of civil war declines by around two percentage points. This is a relatively modest gain for a truly dramatic improvement in development.

Marginalized Countries at Peace

W E HAVE LIKENED THOSE MARGINALIZED COUNTRIES that have to date maintained peace to a group of Russian roulette players who have so far been lucky. To an extent this is unfair: poor countries that have managed to maintain peace have probably been making choices that have contributed to that peace. Nevertheless, as a class such countries are at much higher risk than the successful developers, and as chapter 4 pointed out, the risks for the two groups are not only widely different, they are also diverging: risks for the poor but peaceful have actually been rising. What can the international community do to reverse this disturbing trend?

Believing False Friends: The Military Lobby for Deterrence

Governments of poor but peaceful countries typically attempt to reduce the risk of rebellion by raising their military spending. Recall from chapter 3 that during peacetime, each additional 10 percentage points on the risk of rebellion raises military spending by around 1 percentage point of GDP. This might seem like a prudent action, and we can be sure that the military lobby will urge the government to take such action. Just like other groups, the military favors spending on itself. When the military is in political control of a country, military spending increases by two percentage points of GDP, controlling for all other influences on the military budget, such as risks and the ability to afford the expenditure.

We have also seen that military expenditure is ineffective in reducing the risk of conflict. Allowing for the potentially confusing effect of risk on spending, spending has no deterrence effect on rebellion. Hence even though governments have listened to the siren voices of their own militaries, this is not an effective way for poor but peaceful countries to reduce the risk of rebellion. Of course, governments also spend on the military to reduce the risk of international conflict. Across a neighborhood, this is obviously futile: a region is no safer if all countries have high levels of military spending. The evidence on regional arms races given in chapter 2 suggests that there is scope for regionally coordinated reductions in military spending, brokered by regional political organizations, possibly with expenditure monitored by the international financial institutions.

If military spending is not an effective instrument for peace, what else can governments do that might work better?

Reducing the Risks from Primary Commodities

Many low-income countries depend on primary commodities for their export revenue. On average, such dependence is associated with an increased risk of rebellion, poor governance, and poor economic performance; however, the average conceals extremely wide variation. In 1970 Botswana and Sierra Leone were both low-income countries with substantial diamond resources. Over the next 30 years diamonds were central to the economic and social collapse of Sierra Leone: its per capita income is now much lower than in 1970 and it has sunk to bottom place on the Human Development Index. By contrast, diamond resources were critical to Botswana's success in becoming the fastest-growing economy in the world, and it is now a middle-income country (see box 5.1). Thus even though, on average, primary commodities have been detrimental to development, they clearly have the potential to be enormously useful. The challenge, at both the national and international levels, is to adopt policies that better harness this potential.

As discussed earlier, primary commodity exports can increase the risk of conflict by four routes: financing rebels, worsening corruption in governance, increasing the incentive for secession, and increasing exposure to shocks. Each of these is amenable to policies that can make living with natural resource endowments easier.

Curbing Finance for New Rebellions   Building a rebel army is a costly undertaking; thus most small rebel groups are unable to escalate vio-

Box 5.1   A comparison of Botswana and Sierra Leone

IN 1961 DIAMOND-RICH BOTSWANA AND SIERRA Leone had approximately the same per capita income of about US$1,070; however, the countries experienced extremely different paths of economic development. Why did diamonds cause an economic miracle in Botswana and lead to a total state collapse in Sierra Leone?

In Botswana the extraction and export of diamonds came to be an engine of rapid economic growth. The country maintained a stable and well-functioning democracy since independence and enjoyed the steady leadership of three democratically elected presidents. A national development plan is the key to managing the economy, setting targets for public expenditures that are consistent with expected government revenues and the capacity of the economy.

Diamond extraction is concentrated in three large mines (kimberlite deposits). The government also encourages other industries besides diamond mining. This has allowed Botswana's economy to prosper: per capita income is currently about US$8,800 and income distribution is relatively equal. Botswana's human development record is also impressive; however, like many of its southern African neighbors, Botswana also suffers from a high HIV infection rate.

By contrast, Sierra Leone's recent history is a tragedy. Diamond wealth in combination with poor governance led to the state's collapse and created the incentive, as well as the opportunity, for a rebellion throughout the 1990s. Sierra Leone is now ranked among the poorest countries in the world, with a per capita income of about US$480. In contrast to Botswana, most diamond deposits in Sierra Leone are alluvial, that is, are found in riverbeds. Government control of extraction is difficult, because alluvial deposits are dispersed over more than one-third of the country and, unlike kimberlite deposits, can be mined using simple technology. Prospectors dig holes with shovels and sift through the dirt.

However, Sierra Leone's misfortune has been political as well as geological. Starting out as a multiparty state after independence in 1961, the country turned into a one-party state with a succession of autocratic leaders. Corruption and poor fiscal management destabilized the economy, and, from 1967 on, the government granted mining rights to individuals in return for their political support. Gradually, the government lost control over its assets, enabling private entrepreneurs and organized criminals to take charge of the diamond mining. Youths were marginalized in the economic and political collapse of the 1980s and turned increasingly to crime and drugs. For rebel leader Foday Sankoh to recruit young men for his civil war and to finance the warfare through diamond extraction was therefore relatively easy.

Sources: 1961 income figures: Heston, Summers, and Aten (2002); purchasing power parity adjusted GDI income figures for 2001: World Bank (2002a); mining information on Botswana: http://www.mbendi.co.za/indy/ming/dmnd/af/bo/p0005.htm; Davies and Fofana (2002); Harvey (1992); Hirsch (2001); Leith (2002).

lence to the level of a civil war, but the presence of primary commodities can make financing this stage of escalation easier for rebel groups. Expropriation of the commodity itself often requires a scale of violence that is beyond the capability of a rebel group in its early stages. We discuss this source of finance when we turn to policies that can shorten wars. Here we focus on two ways in which small rebel groups use primary commodities to finance their military escalation.

Some small rebel groups have been able to raise substantial finance by selling the future rights to war booty (Ross 2002a). In the 1997 civil war in the Republic of Congo the private militia of the former president, Denis Sassou-Nguesso, was funded in part by the sale of future exploitation rights to oil reserves. On the eve of the conflict Sassou-Nguesso received substantial assistance from an oil company, Elf-Aquitaine, reportedly of the order of US$150 million, and these funds were critical in enabling the defeat of the incumbent president, Pascal Lissouba. Similar uses of war booty futures occurred in Angola, the Democratic Republic of Congo, Liberia, and Sierra Leone. The phenomenon is not entirely new. In 1960 a Belgian company, Union Minière du Haut Katanga, bankrolled the Katanga rebellion in the Congo in exchange for future mineral rights. Similarly, during the Algerian war of independence, the Italian oil company Ente Nazionale Idrocarburi reportedly supplied money and arms to the National Liberation Front in exchange for future "consideration." While not new, the approach seems to have become more common in Africa during the past decade. As the supply of finance in these cases is coming from OECD-based companies it is, in principle, controllable. Such financing of political organizations in conflict with recognized governments could be made a criminal offence, analogous to the new OECD-wide legislation banning companies from bribing government officials.

Another way in which small rebel groups finance their military escalation using natural resources is by extortion of natural resource companies. Both kidnapping and sabotage of infrastructure require only modest capabilities for violence, yet the ransom payments and protection money they currently yield can be substantial. The ELN received US$20 million in ransom payments from a German company at a time when it was a weak organization, and used these funds to equip itself militarily well beyond the standard of the government forces it opposes. Currently a major oil company in West Africa is reputedly paying around US$250 million to small-scale violence entrepreneurs. The policy issue here is to discourage such payments, both by legal means and by exposure. A possible point for legal intervention is to make kidnap insurance illegal and to make all extortion payments nondeductible for tax purposes. Group of Eight governments could usefully agree that they will not provide public money to pay ransoms to rebel movements for their citizens. Currently practices differ markedly among Group of Eight governments, as revealed by their different reactions to the kidnapping of tourists and the demands for US$1 million per tourist by a small rebel group in the Philippines in 2000.

Reducing Corruption   Rebel movements, particularly those seeking to secede that part of a country endowed with natural resources, are greatly aided if the revenues from resources are embezzled by a narrow elite rather than used in a transparent manner for the common good. Governments of natural resource–abundant countries therefore have a strong interest in demonstrating that revenues deriving from natural resources are well used.

The first step here is providing trustworthy information about what the revenues actually amount to. As potential rebel groups do not trust governments, the MNCs that undertake resource extraction could provide independent information about payments. British Petroleum recently took such action in its payments to the government of Angola, but none of the other 34 oil companies active in Angola have adopted this policy. This demonstrated that the oil industry is not sufficiently concentrated for the self-regulation model to work as it did in the case of diamonds. There is therefore a case for public action to facilitate coordination in the oil industry and other extractive industries. Various approaches have been suggested. One is to make all such payments a legal reporting requirement. An alternative, proposed by Global Witness and George Soros, is to make such reporting a requirement for listing on major stock exchanges. A further alternative is for the companies to report on a confidential basis to the international financial institutions, which would then collate the information and publish aggregate revenue figures. This has the advantage of preserving the confidentiality of firm-specific information while providing a global certification system for information.

All these approaches have the advantage that by making reporting an obligation, they clearly signal that the information provided is independent of the recipient government, and thus it is more likely to be trusted. To the extent that this reduces the risk of rebellion, the chief beneficiary of this is, of course, the government itself. The principle of legally independent reporting of revenues is somewhat analogous to the increasingly accepted principle of independent central banks. In addition, obligatory revenue reporting by MNCs could be supplemented by complementary reporting on the part of recipient governments and national resource extraction companies to make the use of revenues transparent.

Finally, transparency in reporting is itself an input into scrutiny. The appropriate level for such scrutiny is within the society. Once numbers are properly provided, parliaments and the press provide the natural institutions for scrutiny, but a useful approach, especially where such institutions are recent, is to supplement this with purpose-designed scrutiny by civil society representatives. A useful model here is the Chad-Cameroon pipeline project, for which local civil society organizations, MNCs, the World Bank, and the government of Chad forged an alliance (see box 5.2). This could become a template for managing natural resources in other developing countries, a template that is needed both by the governments of low-income countries and by MNCs in the extractive sector. Many low-income developing countries are in the process of discovering natural resources and their governments keenly feel the lack of a template. For example, in 2002 the governments of both East Timor and São Tomé and Príncipe realized that they needed to learn how to manage prospective oil revenues. In the absence of a template, both chose to send a delegation to Angola, but while Angola has the advantage that communication can be in Portuguese, it is clearly not the best model for the governance of revenues. A template is also increasingly needed to encourage reputable MNCs to work in difficult environments. MNCs rate the risk that misgovernance will damage their reputations as the most important impediment to their involvement in low-income countries.

Reducing Secession   Chapter 3 showed that natural resources, especially oil, increase the risk of violent secession. How can policy reduce these risks? Transparency about the magnitude of the revenues will help to reduce the risk, because it makes exaggeration of the gains more difficult. Recall that exaggeration occurs partly because of the sheer glamour of natural resource revenues—the local population is likely to conjure up images of Bahrain and Brunei—and partly because it is a deliberate strategy of secessionist politicians. Again, only information provided independent of the government can hope to be convincing. Thus scrutiny of the effective use of revenues is an important step in defusing pressures for secession.

Box 5.2   Transparency of oil revenues in Chad

CHAD IS ONE OF THE POOREST COUNTRIES IN THE world. Oil was found in the early 1950s, but it could not be exported without a pipeline. Furthermore, civil wars from the 1960s until 1990 made it impossible to undertake the necessary investments. When Exxon tried to mobilize private financing in the 1990s, it was told that the risks would be too high unless the World Bank participated. One of the Bank's conditions was that Chad must commit itself to completely transparent management of oil revenues and that the revenues must be used for poverty reduction. The project started in October 2000. Oil revenues are projected to be around US$150 million to US$300 million per year, compared with tax revenues of less than US$200 million in 2002.

A stringent supervision mechanism was put in place: the External Compliance Monitoring Group was charged with supervising the implementation of all legal covenants regarding environmental and socioeconomic management through quarterly visits. The International Advisory Group, which visits Chad every six months, was created to advise the presidents of Chad and the Bank about maximizing the development impact of the project. Its reports are publicly available on the web. A unique feature of the Chadian model is the Petroleum Revenue Management Law of 1999. This law stipulates that all direct oil revenues have to go first to an offshore escrow account. From there, 10 percent is transferred into an account for the Future Generations Fund and the remainder is transferred to a special oil revenue account in Chad. The law specifies that 80 percent of the oil revenues must be used for additional expenditures in the four priority sectors for poverty reduction: health and social affairs, education, infrastructure, and rural development. Five percent of the royalties are to benefit the local communities in the oil producing region. The remainder can be used for general expenditures of the administration. A powerful local watchdog institution, the College de Controle et Surveillance des Ressources Petroliers, was

also created that has to authorize all commitments and disbursements from the special oil revenue account and to certify that the budget presented to parliament conforms with the Petroleum Revenue Management Law. It has nine members as follows: four from civil society, two members of parliament, one member of the Supreme Court, the national director of the central bank, and the director of the treasury.

The first oil will be pumped around July 2003, but there have already been some interesting experiences. The oil consortium was constituted in early 2000 and paid a signature bonus of US$25 million. The government treated this as off-budget income and used it without following the spirit of the Petroleum Revenue Management Law and without following its own procedures. According to the media, a large share was used to purchase weapons, because the Mouvement pour la démocratie et la justice au Tchad rebellion in the north of the country was creating many security problems. The World Bank protested, given the agreement that all oil income should be used for poverty reduction. The government agreed to freeze the remaining US$10 million and use it strictly according to the law and to have the Auditor General's Office undertake a complete audit of the money already spent. The latter was only created in 1999, and this was the first big audit it had to undertake. The full audit was published on its web site. As a result of the bonus debacle, the members of the College de Controle et Surveillance des Ressources Petroliers were nominated ahead of schedule in 2001.

There is another interesting feature about Chad: military and political power is currently held largely by people from the north of the country, while the oil fields and most agricultural land are in the south. Even though the current government is being contested, there is little talk about secession. Transparent management of oil revenues benefiting the poor majority of the population will be a key ingredient of maintaining national unity in Chad.

Source: prepared by Gregor Binkert, World Bank country manager for Chad.

A further possible strategy is to include political leaders from the locality of the discovery prominently in the government. This, fortuitously, happened in Botswana. At present, a common response is to give the locality a disproportionate share of the revenues. If this is the only strategy followed, it may even exacerbate the problem, because it appears to concede the principle that the resources belong to the locality. The government of Indonesia faced continued demands for secession from the province of Aceh even after it had conceded that 75 percent of revenues would accrue to the locality. Indeed, such generous offers may not be seen as credible in the long term. There is a good case for decentralizing some of the revenues from natural resources, but the principle of equitable division, combined with transparency, may be a more effective way of preventing secession.

Cushioning Adverse Shocks   The prices of primary commodities are highly volatile, so that countries dependent on a narrow range of commodities for their exports periodically face severe negative shocks. Recent research finds that when these shocks are large, they severely damage medium-run growth: each dollar lost in export income generates a further two dollars of output contraction (Collier and Dehn 2001). Some evidence also suggests that much of this lost growth is never recovered. Hence episodes of price crashes may induce the growth collapses that increase the risk of rebellion, and over the longer term may lead to lower levels of income. For example, in Indonesia, the East Asian financial crisis of 1998 caused income to fall by around 10 percent in Aceh. This was shortly followed by the escalation of violent conflict.

Even the governments of industrial countries with sophisticated teams of experts at their disposal would find managing such large shocks extremely difficult, but the industrial countries have not experienced such large-scale shocks since the 1930s. The governments of developing countries usually lack the expertise, and often lack the political goodwill, to implement contractionary policies effectively. There is therefore a case for international action to cushion such shocks. Donor responses to severe shocks in developing countries are currently determined by the nature of the shock. Generally, if the shock is photogenic, such as an earthquake, hurricane, or drought, aid increases rapidly and substantially, sometimes more than covering the losses incurred. Unfortunately, even though natural resource price shocks are often much larger than these calamities, they are not photogenic, and, historically, aid has shown no tendency to increase in response to such shocks: governments have been on their own.

The international community might consider three types of arrangements: risk pooling, credit facilities, and aid. The scope for risk pooling is considerable. For example, the World Bank lends to both oil exporters and oil importers. The former have an interest in repayments being low during periods of low oil prices, while the latter have an interest in repayments being low during periods of high oil prices. By structuring repayments contingent upon the oil price, the World Bank could effectively match these complementary risks and in the process reduce its own default risk. The use of derivatives markets also provides scope for risk pooling. Because these are highly technical, for developing country governments to enter directly into these markets is not usually appropriate, but the World Bank could enter into risk-bearing contracts with developing countries and then lay off these risks in derivatives markets. The Bank already manages foreign exchange positions for some developing countries, and no issue of principle would seem to be involved in the provision of such a service. The IMF has had credit facilities in the form of the Compensatory Financing Facility, but these were seldom used. In addition, for a developing country to borrow at commercial rates at the onset of a severe negative shock of uncertain duration is usually unwise. There may, however, be scope for concessional finance. Probably more important than loan finance is grant aid. Aid responses to shocks need to be set in a more rational framework, transferring resources at the margin from high-glamour natural disasters to low-profile, but more devastating, economic shocks.

Beyond cushioning price shocks, reducing them where possible also makes sense. Attempts to control commodity prices have been unsuccessful, and no basis for repeating them appears to exist; however, trade policies on the part of OECD economies can inadvertently have a sharp effect on world prices. For example, if OECD governments increase their subsidy to domestic producers when the world price of an agricultural commodity is low, then the effect will be to systematically amplify price shocks. The cushioning that such subsidies achieve for domestic producers comes at the cost of increasing the shock to producers in low-income countries. For example, the recent increase in the subsidy to American cotton producers has had the effect of further reducing the incomes of cotton farmers in the Central African Republic.

Diversifying   On average, developing country exports are no longer predominantly primary commodities, but this average is made up of continued dependence on the part of the marginalized countries and astonishingly rapid diversification by the successful developers. The success of the latter group shows that for the marginalized countries to do the same is possible, but the emergence of China and India as major exporters of labor-intensive goods makes it more difficult. In addition, diversification is not always possible; for instance, Botswana is a land-locked desert with few options other than diamonds. For such countries the priority should be to make natural resource endowments work effectively, as Botswana has indeed done, but for many countries diversification is surely feasible. For example, a country such as Ghana that has a favorable coastal location near global markets seems to have no intrinsic reason why it cannot succeed in manufacturing.

A study of the determinants of primary commodity dependence finds three factors that significantly reduce it: growth, aid, and policy (Collier and Hoeffler 2002b). On average, growth diversifies an economy, and this reduces the risk of conflict in addition to the direct contribution of growth to risk reduction. This does not imply that any policies that promote growth promote diversification, but the inducement of growth will normally assist diversification. Aid significantly reduces primary commodity dependence. This may in part be a "Dutch disease" effect, whereby the provision of foreign exchange through aid reduces the incentive to export; however, aid may also improve the infrastructure for activities that do not rely upon high, location-specific rents for their profitability. Good economic policy also significantly promotes diversification. We measure the effectiveness of policy using the World Bank's CPIAs. On average, an improvement of one point in the CPIA—roughly equivalent to the difference between African and South Asian policies—would reduce dependence on primary commodities from 15.2 percent of GDP to 13.8 percent.

Raising Economic Growth

The poor but peaceful economies are characterized, on average, by slow growth. Faster growth would reduce the risk of conflict both directly in the short term and cumulatively in the longer term by raising the level of income, and indirectly by assisting diversification. We can simulate

Figure 5.2 The contribution to peace of faster growth in the marginalized countries

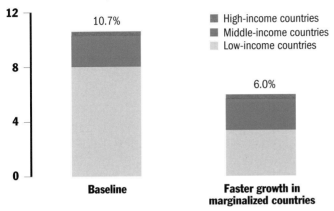

Predicted incidence (percent)

Note: The simulation is based on the model presented in figure 4.12, increasing growth by 30 percentage points. See appendix 1 for details.
Source: Based on a revised version of Collier and Hoeffler (2002c).

the effects of faster growth in the marginalized countries using the model underlying figure 4.12. Figure 5.2 simulates raising the growth of all the currently marginalized countries by 3 percent while keeping that of the successful developers unchanged. In terms of the increment to global growth this is actually much less demanding than the strategy of raising the growth rates of the successful developers: the marginalized countries are, in aggregate, a much smaller part of the world economy than the successful developers and have lower initial growth rates, yet this strategy offers a more substantial contribution to global peace. The steady-state incidence in this simulation is nearly halved, from almost 11 percent to 6 percent. Thus, the distribution of world growth is highly important in terms of the contribution of growth to peace.

This is the single biggest impact on the global incidence of conflict that we found. The primary issue is therefore how to raise growth and, following from this, whether the means of raising growth inadvertently have direct effects that worsen the risk of conflict, thereby offsetting their beneficial effects via the growth rate.

There is broad consensus that three instruments—domestic policies, international aid, and access to global markets—are all effective in raising growth. The precise way in which they interact is more controversial, but of little importance here. There is no significant disagreement about the merits of market access. Some analysts argue that aid and policies complement each other, with aid becoming more effective as policies improve, and, conversely, with policy reform being more effective with larger aid inflows. Other analysts argue that the beneficial effects of aid and policy are independent. The common ground is that where policies are reasonable, aid is effective, and that where policies are unreasonable, policy improvement will enhance growth.

Economic Policy   Controversy as to what constitutes "good" policy is considerable; for example, electorates have chosen significantly different policies in different OECD economies and periodically change their views as to what policies they want, yet all these policy environments sustain high incomes. What constitutes really bad policy is much less controversial. No reputable economist advocates high and variable inflation, high trade barriers, widespread public ownership of marketed activities other than "network industries," or use of public employment for patronage rather than for equitable service delivery. Yet this is the current reality in many of the poor but peaceful societies. A useful way of quantifying this is through the CPIA, the World Bank's policy rating system, which rates macroeconomic, structural, social, and public sector policies on a scale of 1 to 5, with a higher rating indicating more effective policy. The average rating for the marginalized countries is only 2.95, whereas that for the successful developers is 3.75. The reforms needed to effect such a change are thus considerably less controversial than policy reform in good environments. The broad technical consensus on these basic reforms reflects accumulated evidence on the consequences of bad policies. One illustrative measure is the relationship between the CPIA and growth: for the typical low-income, poor policy country, a one-point improvement in the CPIA is associated with a higher growth rate of 1.6 percentage points (Collier and Dollar 2002).

Although basic reforms are not technically particularly controversial, they can still arouse considerable opposition from within a society. Typically, bad policies are not in place by mistake, but because even though they are damaging to ordinary citizens, they favor some powerful group. Potentially, powerful groups will violently resist policy reform, therefore reform could increase the risk of conflict. In this case the favorable effects engendered by growth would be offset by this direct risk. One study investigates the effect of policy on conflict risk using the

CPIA as a measure (Collier and Hoeffler 2002b). While the CPIA has many limitations, a major advantage is that as it is constructed by World Bank operational economists working on each country, because it reflects their judgment it also proxies their advice. Thus if a country is judged to have improved its CPIA score, this is probably because changes have been broadly consistent with the advice that Bank staff have been giving. If, for example, we were to find that policy improvement increased the risk of conflict, this would indicate that Bank policy advice was exacerbating the risk of conflict.

Obviously policy deteriorates rapidly during a war; therefore to determine whether policy affects the risk of war we need to look at policies that are already in place prior to the risk period being considered. The study therefore looks at policy during the five years prior to the five-year period for which the risk of conflict is estimated. It finds no significant association between the level of economic policy, as measured by the CPIA, and the risk of subsequent conflict—that is, bad policies neither reduce the risk of conflict nor increase it, other than through their adverse effects on growth. Changes in policy do, however, have a significant effect. Improvements in the CPIA appear to reduce the risk of conflict in the subsequent period. This benign effect may well be spurious, however, reflecting nothing more than policy starting to deteriorate in the run-up to violent conflict. For example, as already noted, a higher risk of conflict induces governments to increase military expenditure.

The important point is, however, that no evidence suggests that policy improvement directly increases the risk of conflict. As long as it does not directly increase the risk of conflict, it will tend to reduce the risk indirectly through its effects on the growth rate. This does not mean that all growth-inducing policies reduce risk: there is no substitute for looking policy by policy, country by country, to see whether the potential for adverse effects exists. It simply means that there is no general presumption that where countries have implemented policy reforms as advocated by the World Bank they have systematically directly increased the risk of conflict (Collier and Hoeffler 2002b).

Aid Measuring aid entails less controversy than measuring policy. Here we use a conventional measure of aid as concessional development assistance, which excludes humanitarian assistance and military aid, neither of which is intended to raise growth. Actually quantifying the effect of aid on growth is more controversial. Applying the results of a recent study, an additional percentage point of aid as a share of GDP for the marginalized countries would raise the average growth rate of these countries by only 0.1 percentage point (Collier and Dollar 2002). Some analysts argue that aid would become more effective if combined with policy reform, but the matter that concerns us here is whether aid inadvertently increases the risk of conflict. Some economists, notably Grossman (1992), have argued this on the grounds that aid increases the honey pot to be contested.

Researchers have also investigated the effect of aid on conflict risk following the same approach as for the effect of policy. Controlling for the effect on growth, aid has no significant direct effect on the risk of conflict. Again, this does not absolve donors from the need to scrutinize their aid programs carefully to see whether particular components might increase the risks of conflict. Several case studies argue precisely this: that particular types of aid have increased the risk of conflict (see, for example, Esman and Herring 2001). Learning from such bad experiences is important: projects need to be designed with proper awareness of their potential for creating division. However, we should also be wary of generalizations from such horror stories that imply that aid is normally part of the problem. Its effects on growth imply that it is normally part of the solution.

Access to Global Markets   The poor but peaceful group of countries has largely not broken into global markets for nontraditional exports. There is a case for accelerating improvements in market access for these countries ahead of more general improvements negotiated under the development round of the World Trade Organization. Both the United States and the European Union (EU) have recently introduced such differentially favorable market access for some countries within the poor but peaceful group. The United States has introduced the Africa Growth and Opportunity Act, and early signs indicate that this is significantly facilitating African countries' entry into manufactured export markets. Similarly, for the least developed countries the EU has introduced the Anything but Arms initiative.

As with policies and aid, any favorable effects of improved market access on growth could, in principle, be offset by a direct effect on conflict risk. Indeed, we have found that exports can have a direct, adverse impact on the risk of conflict, namely, through the rents on primary commodities; however, major trade reforms are likely to diversify trade as well as to increase it.

Economic Revival: A Simulation   Each conflict has its own peculiarities; thus country knowledge always needs to supplement the group-level analysis discussed here. Models of conflict risk are not well suited for country-specific questions and are more appropriate for the sort of policy simulations of global incidence conducted in chapter 4. However, changes in global incidence are outcomes of changes in real, country-specific situations, and for illustrative purposes we take an actual conflict in a typical marginalized country and ask whether any feasible economic recovery could have helped to avert it.

The conflict episode we consider is Zaire, as it was then known, in the late 1990s. Our simulation model predicts that as of 1995 Zaire was at severe risk of a conflict. Indeed, the model estimates an 80 percent risk of a conflict during the ensuing five years. The point of using a model is not, however, to predict such risks, but rather to simulate the effect of changing a few factors that were potentially within the control of the government and the international community. The challenge set to the model was to see whether any feasible change in characteristics could have reduced the risk of conflict from 80 percent to the arbitrary target of 30 percent. The model predicts that had a package of strong economic reforms and greatly expanded aid been implemented during the first half of the 1990s, then the risk of conflict would have fallen to this level. The scale of the required policy reform is an improvement in the CPIA of 1.2 points, approximately equal to what Uganda achieved between 1986 and 1988. In conjunction with this strong reform effort, aid would have had to be tripled. While these specific results are merely illustrative, had the government and the donor community actually known and believed these figures at the time, the reforms would have been implemented and the aid would have been found.

Reducing the Risks of Ethnic Dominance

Ethnic dominance characterizes approximately half of the poor but peaceful countries; that is, the largest ethnic group accounts for a majority of the population, but the countries also have significant numbers of ethnic minorities. Recall that this increases the risk of civil war. Managing the risks of ethnic dominance calls for political solutions.

One approach is to guarantee rights to individuals so that they can challenge individual cases of ethnic discrimination. This is the approach predominantly followed in the industrial countries. A possible supplement to individual rights is to guarantee group rights to minorities. An obvious way of guaranteeing group rights is through quotas, notably on public employment. While this may sound like a radical and costly idea, the few industrial countries that are characterized by ethnic dominance have adopted it. For example, Switzerland is a classic example of ethnic dominance, with 75 percent of the population being German speaking and the rest consisting of French and Italian minorities. Switzerland guarantees minority rights by means of three devices: radical decentralization, multilingual education, and ethnic quotas. Public hiring is required to designate a certain proportion of jobs to the ethnic groups in accordance with their size. Acknowledging popular concerns about ethnic rights in this explicit fashion is often better than wishing them away.

Conversely, when the majority is significantly poorer than the minority, group rights may need to focus on the majority, but in a way that does not alarm the minority. A useful approach is to have an explicit long-term strategy for intergroup redistribution. An advantage of an explicit policy is that it contains the fears of the minority while reassuring the majority that its concerns are being addressed. The maximum pace of redistribution depends on the growth of the economy: the faster the growth, then the more that can be redistributed without threatening the absolute living standards of the minority. A good example is Malaysia, where over the course of 30 years a policy of gradual asset redistribution has helped the majority Malays to increase their share of GDP by about 15 percentage points. At the same time, GDP has grown so rapidly over the period that the redistribution has not prevented the incomes of the minority groups from rising.

Ending Conflicts

WE NOW TURN FROM THE MARGINALIZED COUNTRIES that are at peace to countries that have fallen into conflict and are stuck in it. Recall that decade-by-decade, such con-

Figure 5.3   The contribution to peace of shortening conflicts

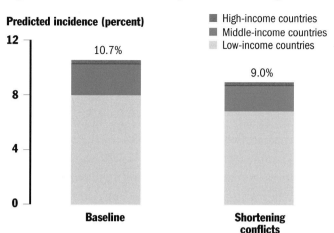

Predicted incidence (percent)

■ High-income countries
■ Middle-income countries
░ Low-income countries

Note: The simulation is based on the model presented in figure 4.12, reducing conflict duration by 20 percent. See appendix 1 for details.
Source: Estimated on the basis of a revised version of Collier and Hoeffler (2002c).

flicts appear to have been getting longer. As discussed in chapter 3, a major obstacle to reaching a settlement is that for rebel groups conflict may become a way of life, with the rebel elite doing well out of war. Furthermore, the parties to a civil war may lack the "commitment technology" that would enable them to trust an agreement. Thus shortening conflicts might seem to be the most effective way of building a more peaceful world; however, in isolation such an approach is less effective than it might appear. Unless postconflict risks are reduced, shortening the duration of conflicts is offset by a more rapid shuttle into and out of war. We can use the model underlying figure 4.12 to simulate the effects of shortening the duration of conflicts. Figure 5.3 simulates the effect of a 20 percent shortening of the duration of conflict on the global incidence and produces an overall reduction in risk of around 15 percent. This is, of course, worth achieving, but it should be seen as only part of a broader strategy for conflict reduction.

Cutting the Rebel Financial Jugular

The leadership of large rebel groups commonly does quite well out of war. Indeed, sometimes leaders amass spectacular fortunes: by the early 1990s Jonas Savimbi of UNITA was reputedly worth some US$4 billion, making him one of the world's wealthiest individuals. While fighting is so lucrative, rebels have little incentive to reach a settlement; for example, four years of negotiations with the FARC proved fruitless for the government of Colombia. Hence measures that reduce the flow of funds to rebel movements are likely to encourage them to come to the negotiating table.

Curbing Rebel Access to Commodity Markets   In the case of some commodities, rebel groups are raising substantial finance by controlling the production of the commodity in their territory and selling the output. To date the Kimberley process is the most important example of international action to reduce rebel organizations' access to commodity markets (see box 5.3). It was triggered by the Fowler Report of the UN, which drew world attention to the way in which some rebel organizations were financing their activities through the sale of diamonds and provided explicit detail about the routes involved. The Kimberley process is a private sector initiative. It was able to overcome the usual collective action problems with private sector self-regulation because the industry is unusually highly concentrated, with de Beers in a dominant position. Although the agreement itself is recent, its antecedents included de Beers' decision to cease purchasing diamonds in the open market and intensive action by the Diamonds High Council, based in Antwerp, to reduce rebel access to the market. An analysis of the initiative by Klare (2000) speculated that it might well lead to the termination of some West African conflicts. This proved percipient: over the next two years both UNITA and the RUF were defeated militarily, although both had previously been highly durable organizations. Note that in both cases other important factors were also at work: in Angola the government used the opportunity of high oil prices to massively increase its military expenditure, and in Sierra Leone the British government sent in substantial military forces. The tightening of the financial jugular complemented these changes, and probably no single component was decisive.

Establishing whether the Kimberley process is going to be effective is important, and for this a monitoring and evaluation process is needed. If the Kimberley process is ineffective, public action will probably be necessary to strengthen self-regulation. Indeed, the very existence of the

Box 5.3   The rough diamond trade and the Kimberley process

DIAMONDS HAVE LONG BEEN RECOGNIZED AS A source of conflict finance. To restrict this channel of financing, the major diamond trading countries and companies took part in the Kimberley process, which formally began in November 2002. Its primary purpose is to establish an international certification scheme for rough diamonds based mainly on internationally agreed minimum standards for certificates of origin and national certification schemes.

The participants agreed to establish internal controls to eliminate the presence of conflict diamonds from shipments of rough diamonds imported and exported from their territories. This includes designating monitoring authorities to diamond shipments and ensuring that all diamonds are imported and exported in tamper-resistant containers accompanied by Kimberley process certificates. The participants are obliged to amend or enact appropriate laws or regulations to implement and enforce the certification scheme and to maintain penalties for transgressions. They are also to collect and maintain relevant official production, import, and export data and to collate and exchange this information when necessary.

Each participating country is to ensure that a duly validated certificate accompanies each ship-

ment of rough diamonds on export and import. Importing authorities must also confirm receipt of a shipment expeditiously to the relevant exporting authority, specifying the details of the shipment. To facilitate the tracking of diamond flows, the original certificate must be readily accessible for a period of no less than three years. To further filter out conflict diamonds, the participants agreed to ensure that no shipment of rough diamonds is imported from or exported to a nonparticipant and that each shipment leaves its territory unopened and not tampered with. A degree of transparency and monitoring was integrated into the process as a result of opposition by nongovernmental organizations to proposals that the system be self-regulating.

In Ottawa in March 2002, Kimberley participants announced confidence in meeting their end of year deadline for implementing the regime, although several significant technical and operational issues remained. Success depends on whether these problems are properly resolved. One day after a resolution passed the UN Security Council in support of the Kimberley process, EU member states announced that they could not meet their obligations by the deadline of February 1, 2003.

Source: Crossin, Hayman, and Taylor (2003).

Kimberley process is an acknowledgment of the need to regulate access to the diamonds market. If the Kimberley process is effective, the question arises whether it should be replicated in a few other commodity markets, such as timber and Columbite-tantalite (usually known as coltan). Although the timber industry is much less concentrated than the diamond industry, the commodity itself is inherently easier to track while in transit.

As noted, timber is at the opposite end of the concentration spectrum from diamonds and involves many small companies. Here the most successful action to date has been at the regional level. For example, the government of Thailand increased scrutiny of the border trade in illegal timber with Cambodia that was financing the Khmer Rouge. This was so successful that it substantially accounted for the collapse of the Khmer Rouge (see box 5.4).

Realistically, the effect of better regulation of commodity markets is not literally to shut rebel organizations out of markets, but to make their activities so difficult that they can only sell their illegal booty at a deep price discount. A recent study of the duration of conflict provides some insight into the possible effects of deepening such a discount (Collier, Hoeffler, and Söderbom 2003). The study controls for all the other factors that influence the duration of a conflict and investigates the effect of world commodity prices. It finds that for countries that are heavily dependent on commodity exports, the world price of these commodities significantly affects the duration of the conflict: when prices are high the conflict is less likely to end than when prices are low. For example, for a country for which primary commodity exports account for 30 percent of GDP, a 10 percent decline in the price of its export commodities tends to shorten the expected duration of conflict by around 12 percent. The effect of targeted policies should be considerably greater than this, because they detach the price rebels receive from the world price. Potentially, creating deep price discounts and monitoring them should be feasible. An analogy is the deep discounts that are already routine for counterfeit goods.

Another activity of enormous importance to rebel groups is the production of illegal drugs for sale in rich countries. Current OECD policy toward these drugs varies, but its main thrust is to encourage the governments of developing countries to discourage production. The problem with this production-focused approach is that it makes territory outside the control of a recognized government enormously valuable, and so inadvertently helps to sustain rebellion. An alternative approach that would radically reduce the funding for rebellion would be to focus penalties on illegal consumption so as to bring down the price of illegal drugs. For example, for many years the United Kingdom had a policy that while it severely penalized trade in heroin, once heroin users were registered as addicts they were provided with supplies from official sources. This radically reduced the commercial incentive to push heroin, and under this policy regime the United Kingdom had fewer than 1,000 registered addicts. It also enabled addicts to be supplied from legal sources of production.

Box 5.4   The Khmer Rouge and the logs of war

IN 1979 THE KHMER ROUGE WERE DRIVEN INTO the jungle and waged war against the Vietnamese-installed regime led by former Khmer Rouge commander Hun Sen. The war was funded by the timber trade. The timber logged during the civil war helped create more demand for Cambodian forest products, and the exploitation of timber quickly became a sustaining factor of the war and a cause of armed conflict in its own right.

In 1992 the Security Council asked the UN Transitional Authority in Cambodia to impose a log export ban to dampen the Khmer Rouge's efforts to undermine the peace process. The Transitional Authority sent military observers to monitor Cambodia's border, but without power of arrest. The Khmer Rouge refused such monitoring in its territories, and the Thai government denied access to UN observers on its side of the border. Although Thailand eventually prohibited log exports, the Cambodian government's lifting of the ban after nine months undermined its overall impact. In the end, Thai timber imports in 1993 were only 20 percent lower than in 1992, while the gems trade, which also benefited the Khmer Rouge, continued largely unabated. The sanctions were also weakened by a 10-week delay in implementation, which led to a logging frenzy, as well as an export quota on sawn timber, which led to the proliferation of sawmills within Cambodia but did not significantly affect commercial timber harvesting rates.

After elections in 1993, the destruction of Cambodia's forests continued. Numerous logging companies dealt directly with the Khmer Rouge in a monthly cross-border timber trade worth an esti-

mated US$10 million to US$20 million. The Khmer Rouge's military decline did not end the misuse, and no revenue reached the Cambodian government. In response, the IMF froze the next US$20 million tranche of its Enhanced Structural Adjustment Facility and threatened to let its support lapse entirely if the Cambodian government failed to implement forestry reforms. In November 1996 the Enhanced Structural Adjustment Facility lapsed, and forestry went to the top of Cambodia's international agenda.

At least 1.3 million cubic meters of logs were taken between 1996 and 1997 to fuel a conflict that, in addition to lost revenues, placed additional demands on the revenues the treasury was able to raise from other sources. It effectively halted the growth of the Cambodian economy. In July 1997 a coup d'état was primarily funded by logging revenue. To pay for military backing and to reward military leaders, Hun Sen personally authorized various military regions to export logs, in contravention of Cambodian law.

The timber trade and the Khmer Rouge benefited from the support of Thai officials who used logging revenues to finance their electoral campaigning. Donors used aid conditionality on the Thai government to end the trade and stop assistance to the Khmer Rouge. The U.S. Congress threatened to end military assistance in 1996 and then all assistance in 1997. The IMF pressured Cambodia to end its acquiescence to unauthorized exports by canceling part of its Enhanced Structural Adjustment Fund loan in late 1996. The outcome was an effective ban by Thailand on Cambodian timber. These pressures contributed significantly to the demise of the Khmer Rouge.

Source: Global Witness (2002).

Curbing Diaspora Finance of Rebel Groups   Another important source of rebel finance is from diasporas in rich countries. This phenomenon is long-standing, but as the number of migrants from low-income developing countries has increased, so has the potential for diaspora finance. For instance, more Tamils live in OECD countries than live in the Jaffna peninsula of Sri Lanka, and estimates indicate that Tamil diaspora organizations raised around US$450 million per year during the 1990s, much of it used by the Tamil Tigers to buy arms. For example, a bank account opened by a Canadian of Sri Lankan origin was used to purchase the 60 tons of Eastern European explosive that killed and injured some 1,500 people in Sri Lanka in 1996. Similarly, the Kurdish Workers Party stated that it had raised around US$50 million from the Kurdish diaspora in 1992. One method of collecting money was to control the wholesale trade for Kurdish retailers and charge them inflated prices. This "tax" was then transferred to Kurdish rebels.

Only recently have the governments of industrial countries started to face up to their responsibilities to curtail the organized provision of finance from their territories. For example, the United Kingdom recently banned the activities of the Tamil Tigers. Even prior to September 11, diaspora funding for the Tamil Tigers was reportedly drying up, but the terrorist attacks brought home to North American diasporas that donating death was unacceptable (*The Economist* 2001). In 2002 the Tamil Tigers abandoned their long-standing demand for independence and entered into serious peace negotiations. At the same time the IRA, another violent organization that relied heavily on North American diaspora finance, abandoned its previous refusal to "decommission" any of its stock of armaments.

Employing International Interventions

In recent decades the international community has tried many interventions in particular civil wars with the intention of ending them. The interventions were sometimes on the side of governments and sometimes on the side of rebel organizations. Some interventions were military, and others were economic or diplomatic (see Regan (2002) for a comprehensive dataset on these interventions).

Recent studies use this dataset to investigate whether any of these types of interventions systematically shortened the duration of conflict (Collier, Hoeffler, and Söderbom 2003; Regan 2002). The results are disappointing, although such an analysis is intrinsically difficult and may have missed favorable effects. For example, one possibility is that the interventions were targeted on the most difficult conflicts, and thus the mere fact that those conflicts with interventions did not last longer than average would be evidence of modest success. The nonmilitary interventions had no significant effect. The only military intervention that was systematically effective was support for rebels: apparently external military support can defeat a government more readily than a rebel organization. This may reflect the different styles of government and rebel campaigns. Rebel forces typically withdraw into forests or mountains, whereas government forces typically withdraw into major cities where they can be subject to total defeat, such as the forces of the Derg government of Ethiopia that holed up in Asmara in 1992. Note that the findings do not imply that no international interventions have been effective, but only that no one type of intervention appears to have been systematically effective.

Negotiating Peace

Prior to a rebellion, predicting which issues and which groups have the potential to turn opposition into large-scale violence may be hard. Once a rebellion has started, who the parties to a negotiation should be becomes clearer. Nevertheless, negotiating peace is difficult. Both parties lack the means to lock into an agreement. A rebel group cannot guarantee that if it accepts peace, its more extreme members will not establish a new violent organization; for example, once the IRA had accepted a peace settlement a new group calling itself the Real IRA continued the violence. A government also finds that making commitments that rebels can trust once they disarm is difficult. In addition to this commitment problem is the danger of setting a precedent of conceding to violence what has not been conceded to normal political opposition. One of the reasons for the conflict trap may be that rebellion can appear to pay off as a strategy.

Civil wars are far less likely to end in peace agreements than international wars (Licklider 1995). Between 1940 and 1990, combatants resolved 55 percent of interstate wars at the bargaining table, whereas fewer than 30 percent of post-1945 civil wars have terminated with the signing of a peace treaty (Doyle and Sambanis 2000; Walter 1997). Furthermore, many of the treaties that end civil wars are unstable and collapse into renewed fighting. As noted earlier, the difficulty of negotiating a lasting peace is due to the parties' inability to credibly commit to the peace. In contrast to civil wars, international wars have been relatively easier to end through bargaining precisely because the parties have internationally recognized boundaries and standing armies to defend those boundaries after the war ends. Walter (1997, 2002) argues that what reduces the probability of reaching a negotiated settlement is the lack of credible guarantees offered by third parties committed to enforcing the terms of a peace treaty. In a study of modern civil wars she finds that lack of credible enforcement is the key factor explaining failures to reach a negotiated settlement.

Other authors have emphasized different causes of the long duration of civil wars. For example, secessionist conflicts tend to last longer than other civil wars because secession is perceived as a nondivisible good, and the new polity that emerges from civil war may incorporate terms of a settlement that exclude some of the parties, thereby creating incentives for new violence (Licklider 1993). Moreover, a large number of incoherent and unreconciled groups and coalitions makes negotiation harder, other things being equal, as does a rough military balance among the parties (Doyle and Sambanis 2003; Elbadawi and Sambanis 2000; Zartman 1995). Several other explanations are also possible, such as tunnel vision, organizational inertia, wishful thinking, and miscommunication. A study of 16 peace implementation episodes finds that the presence of valuable spoils of war, such as natural resources, reduces the likelihood of success, reinforcing the foregoing discussion of the need to manage natural resources effectively (Stedman 2001).

Despite the relevance of these explanations to many cases of civil war, the single most promising explanation is the lack of credible guarantees for a settlement. In effect, this argument shifts the analytical focus from the underlying causes of the long duration of civil wars to the mechanisms that explain the inability to commit to an agreement, even when the parties prefer an agreement to continued fighting.

According to Walter (1997, 2002), only parties with credible and well-established self-interest in preserving the peace, parties with sufficient military resources to engage in combat, and parties that provide costly signals of their commitment by actually deploying troops can provide credible guarantees. Without such an external commitment, the absence of a government seen as legitimate by the rebels and the history of war in the country will act as disincentives for the parties to disarm. As disarmament is typically a precondition for peace implementation, this creates a barrier to negotiation. The presence of armed rebels further undermines the government's legitimacy and sovereignty. Under these conditions, what is needed is either an external solution such as the one Walter discusses or a solution that makes the peace self-enforcing. Integrating part of the rebel forces into the national army might be one such solution.

Once the rebels demobilize, they lose their bargaining power in relation to the government. In those cases where postwar peace is based on a self-enforcing agreement, the drastic change in the parties' relative capabilities makes the agreement time inconsistent, that is, the government, which retains its military, can renege on its promise after the rebels have disarmed. The government has both the power and the incentive to renegotiate the agreement or defect from it unilaterally. This is particularly true in cases where the war had no definitive outcome, but rather the violence ended in a cease-fire, truce, or negotiated compromise. One way in which parties have attempted to insure themselves against violations of the peace agreement has been integrating parts of the rebel forces into the government's military. Similarly, in the recent settlement in Côte d'Ivoire, a leader of the rebel organization was nominated to become the minister of defense. Such solutions provide employment for the rebels and reduce their private incentives for continuing their rebellion. It also makes coordinated action by the military against rebel sympathizers more difficult.

Integration of rebels into the government army occurs only rarely. As expected, such integration is more common if the war ends in a negotiated settlement as opposed to victory; however, integrating defeated rebel forces is possible, as demonstrated by the case of Biafra, where the rebel army was integrated into the national Nigerian army after the end of the war. Where the war ends in a negotiated settlement rebel-military integration occurs in about half the cases, whereas without a treaty integration occurs in only about one-seventh of cases. While no statistical analyses of the effects of military integration on the likelihood of war recurrence are available, in several cases military integration is associated with a lowered rate of war recurrence. Examples are Nigeria after the 1966–70 Biafran war; Chad, where successive bilateral agreements with rebel groups reduced the magnitude of the insurgency in the 1980s and 1990s; the Philippines, where the government's agreement with the Moro National Liberation Front left only a fringe group, the Moro Islamic Liberation Front, fighting after 1996; and Zimbabwe, where the peace after the war of the 1970s and early 1980s has held. At the same time, integrating rebels into the government's military can threaten the interests of extreme nationalists and re-ignite civil war before the integration is completed. Examples are Rwanda, where the massacres of 1994 followed the failed Arusha Accords, and Angola, where the failure to demobilize and to reintegrate combatants within the framework of the Lusaka Accords of 1994 led to a resurgence of violence in 1996.

Reducing Postconflict Risks

AT ANY ONE TIME FEW COUNTRIES ARE IN THE FIRST DECADE of postconflict peace. For example, the global steady state depicted in figure 4.12 shows only 12 postconflict countries versus 64 successful developers currently at peace. Yet the postconflict countries have a highly disproportionate effect on the global incidence of conflict: they account for three times as many new conflicts as the entire group of successful developers. Hence in focusing development efforts on building a more peaceful world society, clearly the few postconflict countries warrant particular attention. We can use the model underlying figure 4.12 to simulate the effects of reducing postconflict risks. A wide range of policies could make the first postconflict decade safer. Furthermore, because these policies are highly focused on a few countries, they are relatively straightforward to implement. Figure 5.4 simulates how halving the risk of conflict repetition would reduce the global incidence of conflict. As the figure indicates, this would make a clear contribution to global peace, with a reduction of around a quarter in the incidence of war. Translated into the number of wars, the reduction is from 16.6 active conflicts at a time to 13, most of them in the marginalized group of countries.

Postconflict countries face two major challenges. First, as chapter 3 indicated, they have a high risk of further conflict, and so a key objective of policy must be to reduce this risk as rapidly as possible. Second, as chapter 1 noted, they inherit a severe economic and social decline from the period of conflict, and so the other key objective is to restore economic and social conditions.

The high risks of further conflict inherent to many postconflict situations reflect both risks inherited from prior to the conflict and risks caused by the conflict. The structure of the inherited risks will differ between societies, and not all risks are amenable to policy; for example, a

Figure 5.4 The contribution to peace of successful postconflict policies

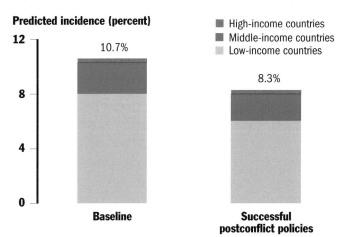

Note: The simulation is based on the model presented in figure 4.12, reducing postconflict risk of war by 50 percent. See appendix 1 for details.
Source: Based on a revised version of Collier and Hoeffler (2002c).

country that is geographically prone to conflict can probably do little about it. Nevertheless, a reasonable presumption is that if a country faces an unusually high risk from a particular source, it should devote particular attention to reducing that risk.

Going Along with False Friends: How to Spend More and Make Things Worse

Recall that the governments of poor but peaceful countries commonly respond to a heightened risk of rebellion by opting for high levels of military spending. Recall also that this is ineffective: such military spending does not alter the risk of conflict. Once the risk of civil war becomes a reality, governments further increase their military spending, though at this stage they may have little choice. During the typical civil war, military spending is around two percentage points of GDP higher than during the prior peace. In the first postconflict decade the government inherits this high level of military spending and, even though it has achieved peace, it is aware that the risk of reverting to conflict is substantial. The argument for continuing with high military spending therefore appears to be strong. This argument for deterrence will be reinforced by the special interest pleading of the military establishment, and quite possibly by rebel forces that might want to be integrated into the regular army. Thus the pressures for continued high military spending are powerful.

What are the effects of high military spending in postconflict situations? Are they simply the same as in preconflict situations, namely, ineffective? A recent study investigates this, using the same approach as for the deterrence effect of military spending in preconflict situations (Collier and Hoeffler 2003). It finds that the effect of military spending is indeed significantly different in postconflict situations. High levels of military spending postconflict significantly increase the risk of reversion to war. As with the more general study of the effect of military spending, the approach controls for the problem that a high level of military spending reflects an enhanced level of risk. Chapter 3 suggested that a possible reason why high military spending might increase the risk of reversion to conflict is that it inadvertently signals that the government lacks confidence in the persistence of peace. An important postconflict problem is that neither side trusts the other, thus the more the government spends on the military, the more the rebel organization may think that it too has to prepare for the renewal of conflict. Such mutual military escalation can easily trigger incidents that re-ignite the conflict.

Each postconflict situation is distinctive, and so any general principles are merely broad guidelines; however, one policy lesson for postconflict situations is that governments should be wary of the strong lobbying pressures for maintaining high military spending. In addition to the problems resulting from such spending, the government could forego the opportunity to realize a peace dividend from reduced spending.

Reviving Economic Growth

The level and growth of per capita income are important risk factors for conflict. Faster growth tends to reduce the risk of further conflict directly, and also cumulatively by raising the level of income. Are the effects of growth different in postconflict situations? A study that examines this finds that a given rate of growth is significantly more effective in reducing risk in postconflict situations (Bigombe, Collier, and

Sambanis 2000). Hence a sensible approach is for governments to pay considerable attention to reviving the economy.

Fortunately, on average, the first postconflict decade is a good period for growth: countries do tend to bounce back. Taking the first decade as a whole, annual per capita growth is around 1.1 percent faster than normal. This growth boom is not uniformly spread over the decade: growth is not more rapid than normal during the first two or three years, and by the end of the decade the growth spurt is fading. The growth spurt is concentrated into the middle four or five years of the decade. Some evidence suggests that the recovery is faster after longer wars, but our main concern is to understand what countries can do to accelerate the recovery (this discussion is based mainly on Collier and Hoeffler 2002a).

As with the poor but peaceful economies, the likely cocktail of interventions that might raise the growth rate combines policy reform, aid, and improved access to global markets. The issue is whether any of these should be tailored differently for a postconflict country than for an equally poor country that is not just emerging from conflict.

Economic Policy Priorities for Growth   As noted earlier, policy matters in the poor but peaceful countries. A useful broad measure of economic policy, the CPIA, helps explain variations in the growth rate among developing countries. Is the relationship between policy and growth any different for postconflict situations than in peacetime? A recent study finds that it is (Collier and Hoeffler 2002a). As measured by the CPIA, growth is more sensitive to policy during the first decade postconflict than in normal situations. For the typical postconflict country, a one-point improvement in the CPIA would raise growth by 2.5 percentage points, whereas normally its contribution to growth would be around 1.6 percentage points. Thus not only is growth more effective in risk reduction in postconflict countries, but policy reform is more effective in raising growth. But which policies matter most?

That economic policies should be distinctive in postconflict situations is indeed likely. Policies at the start of peace are usually much worse than in equally poor countries without a recent history of conflict. Hence one difference is simply that postconflict countries are at an earlier stage of reform. Related to this, the politics of reform are likely to be different: the balance between interest groups is distinctively different in postconflict situations.

Postconflict countries start with an average CPIA score of only 2.41, compared with a developing country average of 3.00, therefore much more is wrong with their policy. This is the case across the entire range of macroeconomic, structural, and social policies. The World Bank has recently developed a strategy for addressing the needs and problems of such environments known as the low-income countries under stress (LICUS) approach. The essence of the LICUS approach is that even though many policies are wrong, the capacity and appetite for reform are limited, and thus attempting reform across a broad front is not sensible. Rather, reform efforts should focus on two or three policies that are politically as easy as possible and yield rapid payoffs. The rationale for this approach is to build a constituency for reform in contexts in which the demand for reform is largely latent. Postconflict situations resemble other LICUS contexts in starting with poor policies and institutions; however, they differ in that reform may be more constrained by limited capacity than by limited appetite. The early postconflict period may politically be a relatively easy time for reform, because people expect change and old vested interests may have been weakened. This is borne out empirically by the rapid pace of reform during the first postconflict decade. By the end of the decade postconflict countries, on average, have a CPIA score of 3.05, slightly above the developing country average. Thus the greater political scope for reform may be constrained by the limited technical capacity to design and implement policies, but this is amenable to donor assistance.

In the normal LICUS environment, given that the agenda for reform has to be highly prioritized, the conventional sequence is that the top priority is to correct macroeconomic imbalances. Is there any reason to adopt a distinctive prioritization in postconflict environments? Two factors suggest that priorities should be broader in postconflict contexts than in other LICUS environments. First, the scope for rapid policy reform suggests less need to limit reform to two or three policies with rapid payoffs. Second, some evidence suggests that the relative importance of macroeconomic, social, and structural policies is distinctive in postconflict settings.

A recent study focuses on the determinants of growth in all the postconflict episodes of the 1990s (Collier and Hoeffler 2002a). For this period the CPIA can be disaggregated into three broad areas of policy—macroeconomic, social, and structural—that encompass such matters as trade and privatization. The results suggest that social policy is relatively more important and macroeconomic policy is relatively less important in postconflict situations than in normal situations. The effect seems to be quite large: if opportunities exist for modest trade-offs that improve social policies at the expense of a small deterioration in macroeconomic balances, growth is, on average, significantly augmented. The results do not in any sense imply that macroeconomic balance is unimportant, nor do they imply that it is less important than social policies. They simply suggest that relative to the strategies normally adopted, social policy should be given somewhat more weight. As the correction of macroeconomic imbalances has been accorded top priority in the normal poor policy environments, it may well be that in an absolute sense it should also be the top priority even in postconflict situations. Nevertheless, the results are important, because both governments and the teams from the international financial institutions that advise them have lacked any systematic tendency to adopt such priorities.

Why should social policies—specifically policies for social inclusion—be differentially important for the growth process in postconflict countries? As the direct effects of education and health care on growth are likely to be long term, the relatively short-term growth effects that are detected are unlikely to be due to the direct impact of these services. A more likely route by which a government priority for social inclusion might enhance growth is through its effects as a signal of government intent. We have already come across a likely signaling effect: high levels of military expenditure increase the risk of renewed conflict, perhaps because the rebel organization interprets this as a lack of government commitment to the peace settlement. Conversely, if the government attaches a high priority to inclusive social policies, this may be interpreted, not just by the rebel organization but by the wider population, as the government actively honoring the spirit of the settlement. Because the risk of conflict renewal is so high in postconflict situations, the private sector has to take this risk into account in its economic behavior, and it will obviously influence the decision of whether to invest domestically in irreversible assets or to send wealth abroad, and this decision matters for growth. Thus, by prioritizing social inclusion, the government may indirectly reassure investors. This may account for the differential contribution of socially inclusive policies to growth in post-conflict settings.

So far we have suggested that economic policy priorities should differ in postconflict situations, because both the starting point of poor policies and the politics of reform are likely to be distinctive. We now turn to a second reason: the economic inheritance is distinctive, in that civil war leaves a legacy that determines priorities for action.

As discussed in chapter 1, civil war has various economic effects beyond the overall decline in income. The most obvious is the destruction of physical assets such as the transport system. Beyond this, economic activity is disrupted. Normal business often becomes more uncertain, and so time horizons shorten. An important consequence of this uncertainty is that economic behavior tends to become more opportunistic: people have fewer incentives to build a reputation for honest dealing. In addition to destruction and disruption, assets and skilled people are diverted abroad. Finally, a retreat into subsistence activities occurs as other activities decline in response to uncertainty and predation.

These distinctive effects of conflict determine some of the postconflict policy priorities. The returns to early rehabilitation of key infrastructure destroyed during the conflict can be extremely high. For example, estimates indicate that World Bank road projects in the early postconflict phase in Uganda had a rate of return of around 40 percent. The restoration of transport connections is also important for reintegrating the rural subsistence economy into the market.

The disruption and the high level of opportunism create both priorities and constraints. For example, property rights have become confused in some postconflict situations: owners have fled and people without good title have seized or occupied their property. In these circumstances opportunistic claims flourish. Until property rights have been clarified reviving investment is difficult, and without deliberate action, the process of settling disputed claims can take many years. A priority is for the government to set up a fast-track process for resolving claims that involves setting an early time limit by which all claims must be registered in order to be considered; however, high levels of opportunism constrain what the government can realistically do.

Often the conduct of the civil service and of such professionals as lawyers and judges will have been undermined, and this limits the government's ability to collect taxes and deliver public services. Under such conditions the best approach may be to keep the government sector atypically small until reasonable practices can be reestablished.

A major potential asset of the society is wealth held abroad. A priority is therefore to induce the repatriation of these funds. All capital flight is likely to have been illegal, but it reflects two very different processes. Some capital flight will be to hide the proceeds of large-scale corruption. Other capital flight will simply reflect the prudent movement of honestly acquired assets into a safer environment. During civil war both of these occur on a significant scale, but they require quite different postconflict policies. The former should be tracked down, and with the compliance of authorities in the industrial countries the funds should be forcibly repatriated. The latter, which probably accounts for the bulk of money abroad, should be induced to return voluntarily. One way to encourage repatriation is by keeping the exchange rate competitive: a wide gap between the official exchange rate and that on the parallel market is a powerful driver of capital flight. Other significant influences on the repatriation of capital are high indebtedness, poor economic policies as measured by the CPIA, and political instability (Collier, Hoeffler, and Pattillo 2002).

Aid in Postconflict Situations   Donors typically curtail aid flows during a civil war. Various factors determine such flows, such as the economic policy of the recipient government, its per capita income, and its population. The decline in aid flows during conflict is partly a response to deteriorating policy: on average each one-point reduction in the CPIA reduces aid by around 0.3 percent of GDP. However, the deterioration in policy does not by itself account for the significant reduction in aid. In addition, the longer the war lasts, the more aid declines. By the end of a four-year war, aid will have declined by over half a percentage point of GDP simply due to this effect. How do donors respond to the restoration of peace?

In the first couple of years postconflict donors substantially increase aid; however, this is not sustained. By the third or fourth year postconflict some signs suggest that aid is below normal levels, and toward the end of the first decade it is more than one percentage point below normal levels. This overall pattern of aid allocation is readily intelligible. In the immediate postconflict period international publicity and goodwill is considerable, and so donors are keen to be seen as involved. Sometimes donors provide funds out of resources dedicated to postconflict uses, which, as new postconflict situations arise, are gradually diverted to these new needs. For the aid programs to be sustained bureaucratically, the recipient country needs to become part of the donor's normal allocation mechanism, but during the conflict the original aid programs have eroded and the donor has allocated the funds to other countries. Most donors do not have an automatic process whereby a postconflict country becomes part of its core aid allocation. Furthermore, using aid effectively during the early postconflict years is extremely difficult, and donors can easily become disillusioned with the country. For whatever reason, the pattern is that taking the first postconflict decade as a whole, aid is lower than if the country were not postconflict. Within the decade the aid profile is an initial burst followed by a gradual decline.

The pattern of donor contributions is thus distinctive in postconflict situations. Is the contribution of aid to growth also distinctive in these situations? The evidence suggests that aid during the postconflict period is more effective than normal in raising growth. The effect is not uniform: during the first two or three years of the postconflict decade aid is no more effective than in normal situations, and by the end of the decade it is also no more effective than normal. The high-impact phase is during the middle four or five years of the decade, when it is much more effective than normal. One way of expressing this is in terms of absorptive capacity. Aid, like most other resources, is subject to diminishing returns: as more aid is put into a situation the additional contribution of each dollar becomes smaller, and eventually the point of saturation is reached beyond which further aid does not raise growth and may even be damaging. During the middle phase of the postconflict decade aid absorption capacity, that is, the amount of aid that a country can absorb productively, is approximately double normal.

The phase of super-effective aid turns out to account fully for the growth spurt in postconflict economies. If a postconflict country did not receive aid during the first decade, the growth analysis suggests that it would completely miss out on the above normal growth phase. Note that the original impetus for aid was postconflict recovery. The World Bank's original name is the Bank for Reconstruction and Development, and its first task was to help restore the European economies after

World War II. Apparently this impetus was not misguided: aid has a crucial role in postconflict recovery.

Yet aid policy as it has evolved over the past half-century has evidently lost this original insight. Aid during the first postconflict decade is insufficient, and it is also mistimed, coming in when the institutional capacity to use it well is not yet in place and tapering out just as it should be surging in. The donor community can surely do better.

Postconflict aid also provides an opportunity for credible enforcement of peace agreements. Boyce (2002) argues that postconflict aid could use conditionality to encourage governments to adopt policies that secure the peace.

Reducing Risk Using Political and Military Strategies

Economic recovery helps to reduce the risk of renewed conflict, but other policies are also important.

Disarmament and Demobilization   The pace at which military forces are demobilized varies widely, as does the attention paid to reintegrating soldiers into society. What do we now know that can guide these decisions?

Disarmament, demobilization, and reintegration (DDR) involves a chain of activities that normally begins with disarmament and ends with ex-combatants (both government soldiers and members of an armed opposition group) finding new, productive roles in civilian life. The importance of this process is increasingly being recognized. The 1998 report of the UN secretary-general on "The Causes of Conflict and the Promotion of Durable Peace and Sustainable Development in Africa" cites the reintegration of ex-combatants and others into productive society as one of the priorities of postconflict peace building. DDR would help reduce conflict risk both through the direct effects of decreased military expenditure and manpower and through the indirect effects on growth and poverty reduction of budget reallocation and the return of the labor force. A structured DDR process, which demobilizes combatants in stages and emphasizes their ability to reintegrate into society, may reduce the risk of ex-combatants turning to violent crime or rejoining rebel groups in order to survive.

The starting point for the whole process is political will among the key parties: experience shows that no DDR will succeed if that is missing. In some cases the demobilized include ex-soldiers from a national army as well as ex–rebel fighters with whom they have been at war, as in Angola and Sierra Leone, while in other cases the demobilized are soldiers from two warring national armies, as in the case of Eritrea and Ethiopia. In all cases the timing of the demobilization efforts is critical: the demobilization should start as soon as possible after the parties have agreed to end the war; the different armies should be demobilized in parallel; and the quartering of combatants waiting for discharge should be as short as possible, only allowing for registration, health checks, and so on.

While disarmament and demobilization are reasonably straightforward logistical operations, reintegration is a complex and long-term process of coalescing groups with different backgrounds, experiences, norms, expectations, and capacities. The process also has psychosocial aspects, as most ex-combatants go through a process of adjusting their attitudes and expectations, and many suffer from traumatic experiences related to the war. Experience shows that successful reintegration depends to a considerable extent on the support that ex-combatants receive from their families and communities. Strengthening the absorptive capacity of the receiving communities is therefore an important part of the reintegration process. In some cases, however, ex-combatants have committed atrocities in or near their own communities and are often unable to return to these communities, for example, in Mozambique (Kingma 2002). Except under such circumstances, ex-combatants should be allowed to freely choose the community in which they settle.

DDR is a sensitive process undertaken in an environment where the sources of conflict often remain unresolved despite peace agreements, and experience has given rise to lessons that may help avoid inadvertently fueling tension (Kingma 2002). The ongoing provision of information about the process to the armed forces as well as to society at large can counter rumors and unrealistic expectations, as can the use of transparent criteria for selecting and phasing the groups to be demobilized. Efficient support for reintegration requires targeted interventions based on socioeconomic data for the ex-combatants. Knowledge of their geographic origins, family situation, education, and past occupation greatly helps the planning of realistic reintegration support, which normally includes access to training, employment opportunities, and productive assistance (for instance, micro-credit).

Support levels should, however, be in line with assistance provided to other reintegrating groups, such as the internally displaced or returning refugees, many of whom may be more vulnerable than the ex-combatants. In some conflict situations civilians view combatants as robbers and rapists rather than as fighters for a just cause, and the provision of a higher level of reintegration support for ex-combatants than for other groups is likely to provoke negative reactions. DDR activities therefore need to be designed as an integral part of the broader postwar recovery and peace-building process.

Maintaining a large army is expensive for the budget, denies the rest of the economy part of the labor force, and, as noted earlier, appears to increase the risks of further conflict. Nevertheless, governments are often hesitant to demobilize soldiers for fear that they will be disruptive. Of particular concern is the danger that demobilized soldiers will turn to violent crime. This fear has some basis, because soldiers may have lost their skills for other activities, or indeed, if they were recruited as child soldiers they may never have had any other skills. Their time in the military may have provided them with the skills and equipment for violence and desensitized them to its use. One study investigated the effects of demobilizing soldiers in Uganda during the early 1990s, a policy that the Ugandan public widely feared would lead to a crime wave (Collier 1994). Soldiers were returned to their home districts, but with large differences between districts in the number of soldiers returned, and so the study was able to determine whether any relationship existed between changes in district-level crime rates and the number of soldiers demobilized. Overall, despite the fears, the demobilization had no effect on crime; however, prior to the demobilization all soldiers had been surveyed to discover what access they had to income-earning possibilities. Around 12 percent claimed to have no access to land, and these soldiers were concentrated in a few districts. Demobilized soldiers with no access to land significantly and substantially increased local crime rates. Statistically, they were more than 100 times more likely to commit a crime than the average Ugandan. A possible implication of this is that efforts to help demobilized soldiers return to normal economic activity need to be highly targeted. Most soldiers probably do not need much assistance, but identifiable categories are likely to turn to crime.

Diasporas   Recall that the existence of a large diaspora living in rich countries is an important risk factor in postconflict societies. This is both a statistical result and is supported by evidence of how particular diasporas have tended to support and finance violent political organizations. How can policymakers respond to this risk?

One useful response is for donor agencies and postconflict governments to recognize the diasporas' potential to play a productive role in economic reconstruction. Diasporas in rich countries possess skills that are in acutely short supply in postconflict situations. Furthermore, many members of diasporas are often running businesses that could provide useful trading opportunities. They are the part of the global business community that is most knowledgeable about the country and most prepared to undertake the risks of engagement. Business people living abroad often go back to visit during early postconflict situations, combining social and business opportunities. Governments are often ineffective in harnessing this potential, and formalizing the use of the diaspora may be helpful. For example, in postconflict Afghanistan the government used the Internet to create a directory of skilled Afghans living abroad, while postconflict Eritrea had a cabinet minister dedicated to diaspora concerns. Diaspora organizations can be brought formally into business recovery strategies by organizing visits home, and can even be formally involved in the peace process. There may also be scope for recruiting second-generation diasporas into service along the lines of the Peace Corps, as Israel has effectively done for many years. A diaspora can be a wasted asset unless its members maintain family contacts. The new communications technology is well suited to this purpose, yet some postconflict governments are hesitant to permit it on security grounds. Any direct security benefits from curtailing communications may come at a high cost in terms of slowing recovery.

The donor community may also be able to encourage diasporas to play a constructive economic role. Bilateral donors can make business links with the diasporas living in their countries part of a postconflict aid program. Multilateral agencies could arrange business forums, and even design projects with an explicit role for diaspora organizations. For example, a school enrollment program could seek diaspora assistance for books, and even for volunteer teachers.

In conjunction with these greater opportunities for diasporas to play a positive role in recovery, host governments in industrial countries must recognize their responsibilities to ensure that diaspora organizations do not finance violence. For example, *The Economist* (2001) reported that diaspora remittances to the Tamil Tigers were substantially curtailed as governments tightened controls, and this may have assisted in the substantial softening of the Tamil Tigers' demands, which has greatly facilitated the peace process in Sri Lanka. September 11 has brought home to North American diasporas what the financing of violence actually means.

Political Architecture   Experience shows that democratic institutions are extremely unstable in low-income countries dependent on primary commodities. For this reason, empirical analyses fail to find any systematic risk-reducing effect of democracy in such countries. Democratic institutions are difficult to sustain unless all important actors accept that resorting to physical force is unacceptable. Where the underlying factors that predict a high risk of civil war are present, this is unlikely to be the case. In many low-income countries reducing the risk of civil war is thus a necessary precondition for democracy rather than the other way round. Outbreaks of violence often follow on the heels of reversals from democratic institutions. The external imposition of a set of unsustainable institutions without the commitment to defend them over the longer term may prove to be counterproductive; however, there may be scope for using aid conditionality to help stabilize new institutions over a longer period (Lipset 1959; Przeworski and others 2000; Ross 2000).

One attempted solution to conflict in polarized nations has been partition; however, multicultural nations are not inherently problematic. Recall from chapter 3 that highly diverse societies are much safer than polarized societies. Horowitz (1991) has proposed that instead of partition, there might be scope for regional political integration, to build larger, more complex multiethnic states (see also Sambanis 2000).

External Military Presence   In many postconflict situations the UN, a concerned neighbor, or the former colonial power provides peacekeeping troops. Given the high risks of renewed conflict in the early postconflict years, some form of military solution seems necessary. As domestic military expenditure actually appears to increase the risks, such a military presence should be external. Among external interventions various options are possible: regional or extraregional, bilateral or international. Whatever forces are deployed, however, should be seen as credible and should not be seen as a party in the conflict. Credibility depends, in part, upon rules of engagement and willingness to use force. For example, in Sierra Leone the RUF took a large UN force hostage, because the former correctly perceived that it would not meet resistance. By contrast, when a much smaller British force was deployed with clear instructions to be prepared to fight, the RUF rapidly dissolved.

In Georgia a few Russian peacekeepers have managed to bottle up the passions that fueled secessionist violence in South Ossetia and Abkhazia from 1991 to 1993, and North Atlantic Treaty Organization (NATO) military support was effective in helping the UN mission in eastern Slavonia to implement its transitional authority mandate. U.S. military intervention ended the war in Haiti, and U.S. monitors succeeded in providing legitimacy and technical assistance during the Nicaraguan elections of 1989, ending a 10-year-long war, much as international volunteers did in the case of the Cambodian elections in 1993, which installed the first publicly elected government in that country's history.

Yet every regional peacekeeping success story can be counterbalanced with a failure. Libyan intervention in Chad only exacerbated the fighting in the 1980s, Iranian intervention in Iraq only intensified Iraqi violence against the Kurds, and a multinational peace enforcement mission led by the United States in Somalia created new fault lines among previously cooperating warlords and escalated the violence in that country in the second half of the 1990s.

Regional, non-UN peacekeeping and peace building can be more effective than multilateral intervention. An important shortcoming of multilateral peacekeeping by the UN is that the participants are engaged in a coordination problem, and the possible defection from agreed action by any participants creates gaps in the collective effort. The economic costs of collective security arrangements are also substantial, and infighting occurs over the distribution of these costs and the consequences of intervention. By contrast, unilateral or regional intervention occurs only if security concerns justify the economic costs of intervention, and parties are likely to contribute to the degree to which their interests are threatened. Regional organizations can provide useful instruments for peace maintenance, and they can do so within the framework of the UN Charter. Chapter VIII of the Charter discusses the regional management of conflict. The idea behind this is that regional organizations are a better locus of activity because they are more familiar with the region, they may have greater leverage with the parties, and they are less likely to be impeded by the politics of the UN Security Council.

Security Council politics were an especially relevant consideration during the Cold War. The rule of great power unanimity that governs Council voting often paralyzed the UN's ability to intervene. Between 1946 and 1990 the great powers exercised their veto rights 279 times: the former Soviet Union did so 124 times, the United States 82 times, the United Kingdom 33 times, China 22 times, and France 18 times. However, from 1991 to 1995 they used the veto only 3 times (Russia twice and the United States once) and recorded only 20 abstentions (which need not preclude a resolution on any matter before the council). Thus in the post–Cold War period multilateral operations face fewer operational and political constraints. Since 1989 the Security Council has authorized 31 peacekeeping operations and adopted 145 resolutions under Chapter VII of the UN Charter (enforcement, non-consent-based action). By contrast, the council had authorized only 15 peacekeeping operations and adopted 22 resolutions under Chapter VII during the Cold War. In an environment of greater major power cooperation, regional organizations may lose some of their advantages in relation to the UN as an instrument for exercising collective security arrangements.

While regional organizations do have advantages and can help support the UN by constructing a network of institutions to implement the Charter, they also have shortcomings. Establishing which regional organization should intervene is often difficult because of ambiguity regarding the concept of region, that is, is geography or politics the determining factor (see Weiss 1998). An example is the public debate about NATO's involvement in the former Yugoslavia's wars. A second advantage of regional organizations may be that they can possess greater institutional resources and technical knowledge than the UN's peacekeepers; however, this is not true for all regional organizations, and the fact that their resources come directly from one or more hegemonic states may create doubts about their impartiality during peacekeeping operations. A related concern is that regional hegemons who could provide the bulk of support in a regional organization may be directly involved in the conflict. Furthermore, regional organizations' interests may be limited to regional—not global—stability, so that both their strategies and goals may be different from the global interest. Thus, while the use of regional organizations for conflict resolution has advantages, it also entails considerable limitations that perhaps account for the limited success of major regional organizations in maintaining international peace and security.

Examining Trade-Offs between Growth and Peace

The government's objectives in a postconflict situation need to be quite different from those appropriate for a peaceful situation. In particular, in view of the high risk of repeat conflict, policies for maintaining peace should receive a much higher priority in postconflict situations than in normal situations. This creates the potential for trade-offs between policies that promote growth and those that promote peace.

Policies that promote economic recovery will, on the whole, reduce risk. Recall that policy improvement, as defined by the World Bank, has no overall tendency to create risks of conflict; however, there will clearly be exceptions: some policies may raise growth but enhance either grievances or opportunities for rebellion. Growth-promoting policies will therefore need to be screened for such effects. Where a significant trade-off exists, the government may need to give priority to policies for peace building.

The most probable locations for the early stages of economic recovery are the capital city of the country and the most developed region. The most difficult regions to revive are likely to be those that the rebel organization controlled. Market forces will therefore probably agglomerate activity in a way that is disadvantageous to the rebels. The return to public economic expenditure is likely to be highest in those areas where private activity is reviving most rapidly, and so is most constrained by a lack of publicly provided goods and services. Hence there is likely to be a trade-off between the growth-maximizing geographic distribution of public expenditure and a distribution that might be regarded as fair.

The economy will need the foreign exchange from reviving export activities, but by far the easiest exports to encourage are likely to be those obtained by natural resource extraction. These activities have location-specific rents and are not as highly dependent on inputs as manufacturing. Yet an expanded resource extraction sector risks generating all the problems previously discussed: financial opportunities for rebel groups, corruption in government, and exposure to macroeconomic shocks. Indeed, the initial conflict may have been induced in part because the country was heavily dependent on primary commodities; thus a long-term strategy for diversification is desirable for peace building. A trade-off between the sector strategy that maximizes short-term growth and that which most reduces the risks of renewed conflict is therefore likely. A possible way out of this trade-off is to give priority to transparent governance of the revenues from natural resources and to establish institutions of scrutiny that are sufficiently inclusive to be credible with opposition groups.

Sequencing Postconflict Policies

We have considered two groups of policies for restoring postconflict societies: measures to revive the economy, notably aid and policy reform; and military interventions, notably demobilization and external peacekeeping. Can we say anything about the appropriate sequencing of these interventions?

The typical postconflict society begins peace with high risks of further conflict and with a weak economy. Although much can be done to revive the economy, recovery will inevitably take time. Indeed, the pace of growth tends to quicken after being modest in the first three postconflict years. Aid is not especially effective during this early period, at least in reviving growth, and any policy improvement is from a low base. Hence neither aid, nor policy reform, nor any combination of the two can reasonably be expected to deliver peace with any reliability during these early years. Of course, some situations will be inherently hopeful. Especially in middle-income countries, the risks of further conflict may sometimes be quite limited, but for low-income countries this postconflict phase will typically need a temporary intervention that goes beyond effective strategies for economic development. This is the phase during which external military intervention has a critical role to play. Currently the UN typically sees postconflict interventions as two-year operations. This may well be too short, as the economy will normally not have responded much by the end of two years.

The earliest that economic recovery can realistically hope to take over the burden of maintaining the peace is by the middle of the first postconflict decade. During this period growth rates are atypically high and, even more important, could be raised substantially more if aid were targeted to this phase. At present aid is inadequate and mistimed. The global response to postconflict situations should therefore evolve from military peacekeeping to aid during the first decade. Countries can and must graduate from postconflict status.

We can simulate the effects of a well-used first decade on the risk of conflict. Suppose that under the protection of military peacekeeping a large and well-timed aid program, combined with rapid and well-selected policy reforms, succeeds in raising the annual growth rate of the economy by two percentage points and that this is sustained over the decade. Suppose also that this enables the economy to diversify by a relatively modest two percentage points of GDP out of primary commodity dependence. By the end of the decade the risk of conflict has been halved from a 44 percent risk of conflict in the ensuing five years to a 22 percent risk, that is, the country has more or less returned to the level of risk faced by the group of marginalized countries that have enjoyed sustained peace.

Beyond the first decade the challenge of risk reduction passes to the country's government. An external military presence cannot be continued indefinitely, nor can countries that have at some prior stage had a conflict permanently preempt aid. The risks during the second decade will be substantially lower if the country has put reasonable policies, both economic and political, in place during the first decade.

Governments already tend to improve policies during the first decade. As noted earlier, policies start the decade with a CPIA rating of 2.41 and end it with a rating of 3.05, slightly above the developing country average, but this is not enough. Policy is a continuum, so no critical threshold exists that must be attained; however, recall that the dividing line between the marginalized countries and the successful developers was a sustained rating of 3.5; thus the typical postconflict country is still short of reasonable policies after a decade of reform. Some low-income postconflict countries have managed to implement much more rapid policy reform, achieving policy scores of 4.0 by the end of the first decade. A high policy score is associated with both faster growth and a more diversified economy, both of which tend to reduce risks. Suppose that by the end of the first decade the country had a policy score of 4.0. How would risks typically have evolved by the end of a second decade of peace during which the country had maintained this level of policy? The good policy environment raises the growth rate, which results in a higher income level. Both the better policy and the higher level of income in turn facilitate export diversification. Faster growth, higher income, and greater diversification all contribute to peace, reinforcing the pure effect of the passage of time, which itself lowers the risk. Twenty years after the end of the conflict the risk of renewed conflict has fallen to 12 percent over the ensuing five years: the society has effectively escaped the conflict trap.

Coping with the Health Crisis

As chapter 1 showed, civil war leaves a terrible legacy of health problems, and these require focused attention. The war destroys infrastructure, leaving the population in conditions that increase the risk of disease; squeezes the budget for the health system; and displaces people, which again increases the risk of infectious diseases. Policies to address this issue should take a long-term perspective, because refugees and IDPs may stay away from their homes for long periods after the war ends, yet current responses to humanitarian emergencies improve health conditions only in the very short term.

International assistance usually invests money in bringing doctors to devastated areas and refugees camps; however, the level of absenteeism of doctors in areas difficult to access is around 45 percent (Chadhury and Hammer 2002), and doctors stay in devastated areas only for short periods. Therefore even though the emergency actions for devastated areas are effective in the short term, the health problems remain in the long term. International assistance agencies should rethink their policies to achieve sustainable improvements in health.

Doctors need to be given an incentive to do their job, and their pay should reflect the difficulty of the job. The main problem of absenteeism has to do with incentives. Another approach could be to go outside the public sector and let nongovernmental organizations (NGOs) do this job. Doctors working for NGOs typically do not show such high levels of absenteeism; moreover, patients are more motivated and happy with NGO doctors (Reinikka and Svensson 2002). Beyond this building an infrastructure to avoid the spread of infectious diseases such as malaria and HIV is necessary that includes safe water, sanitation, and paved roads. This should occur before public medical personnel are brought into the region for long periods. Infrastructure is crucial to facilitate mobility and to ensure that professional staff will stay in the area.

IDPs should receive the same attention from the international community as refugees in asylum countries. IDPs suffer similar problems to refugees in asylum camps, but their situation is worse because they do not receive much humanitarian help. This increases mortality rates and the spread of infectious diseases. The location of camps is crucial: many have been set up far away from hospitals and safe water, which increases the risk of infectious diseases. Moreover, camps are sometimes located in areas extremely difficult to access. Before setting up any camp it should be recognized that people may stay there for long periods after the war has ended, and thus its location should be suitable for habitation in the long run; however, many camps already exist and relocating the millions of people involved is impossible. For these camps providing the basic infrastructure is important.

Another general recommendation is to have the community, whether refugees or the internally displaced, participate in the construction of public services. Services work better when the community contributes to their cost.

HIV and Other Sexually Transmitted Diseases　As discussed in chapter 1, civil wars create an environment for the spread of HIV/AIDS. Military personnel tend to have high rates of STDs, including HIV. When stationed away from home, social controls to engage in sexual relationships are lower and the risk of HIV infection is likely to be higher. Prostitution around army bases also increases the spread of infection. In addition, the incidence of rape often increases dramatically during war, with refugees and displaced women and girls being particularly vulnerable. The destruction of the social and physical infrastructure during wartime contributes to the spread of the disease. War also weakens the education system, which makes the teaching of prevention more difficult.

The basic approach used to address this problem is to combine the provision of information and support. Refugees can be provided with appropriate education programs on transmission and prevention and on the consequences of becoming infected to change their behavior. This is the strategy the UNHCR has adopted in its plan for 2002–04, and the Centre for Research on the Epidemiology of Disasters also emphasizes this approach. The refugee community can itself be used as a support group, in that associations and groups in the camp can serve as the vehicle to implement measures.

Soldiers also need targeted education programs. According to Elbe (2002, p. 176): "The armed forces themselves should be involved in combating the HIV/AIDS pandemic. In Africa these forces should be encouraged to implement education programs that discuss the illness in an open and serious manner, as well as work to reduce the stigma attached to the illness. . . . Military leaders should reevaluate military practices that expose soldiers to HIV transmission, making changes where possible."

Malaria   Civil wars increase the incidence of malaria. The existence of many migrants infected by the malaria parasite in the asylum country also increases malaria transmission to citizens of the asylum country and the contagion effect among refugees themselves.

Introducing protection measures and education programs in refugee camps is possible. "Policies to control malaria will have to include many activities that involve improving public awareness and modifying personal behavior" (Hammer 1993, p. 15). Associations and community groups can be used as vehicles to implement these measures. Simply giving bed nets directly to households is ineffective. A more effective strategy is to give them to community organizations and let them encourage households to use them. In some cases camps can be located in nonendemic areas. Sometimes discouraging people from crossing the borders of endemic areas to avoid the spread of malaria in the asylum country may also be possible.

Landmines   Chapter 1 noted the legacy of landmines and how deaths and injuries from them have recently been substantially curtailed. This is an example of successful international public action. The decrease in the number of landmine victims is due to the international ban of antipersonnel mines in 1997, which resulted in the destruction of stockpiles and a drastic decrease in the production of landmines and trade in them. In addition, minesweeping operations have been extremely successful in detecting and destroying mines in many countries.

Conclusion

FOR 40 YEARS THE GLOBAL COMMUNITY HAS LARGELY IGNORED civil war. Two attitudes underlie this neglect: "it's not our problem" and "nothing can be done."

It's Not Our Problem

Civil war does not just affect the participants. Through displacement and disruption it affects the entire society; through spillovers such as refugees and arms races it affects the entire region; and through drugs, disease, and terrorism it affects rich countries. Behind the it's-not-our-problem response is a sense that both parties to a war are probably to blame, and that they might as well come to their senses by fighting it out among themselves. Such a view is seriously misguided, in that sometimes the active participants in a civil war do well out of it. This is one reason why civil wars last so long: the people whose decisions determine events are not the ones who are hurting. Furthermore, while in retrospect governments could always have done more to avert conflict, in poor, stagnant, and natural resource–abundant economies even democratic and egalitarian governments face a high risk of rebellion. Civil war *is* our problem.

Nothing Can Be Done

Civil war may be our problem, but if we can't do anything about it, so what? Underlying the nothing can be done view is an interpretation of the causes of conflict that is both patronizing and misleading, that is, that civil wars are caused by ancestral ethnic and religious hatreds. As we have seen, whether a country is prone to civil war is related to more mundane factors, such as the level of income, its structure, and its rate of growth. A country's ethnic and religious composition plays a part, but its effect is ambiguous: highly diverse societies actually have a lower risk of conflict than homogenous societies. While no single magic bullet policy will drastically reduce the global incidence of civil war, many relatively simple policies would have significant effects and together would have a major impact. The instruments of economic development, properly combined and targeted, are an important part of the quest for a more peaceful world.

CHAPTER SIX

An Agenda for International Action

WITHOUT PURPOSIVE INTERNATIONAL action the incidence of civil war will remain high. Based on past trends, global growth will contribute little to a more peaceful world. The rationale for international action is that more widespread peace would confer global benefits. Civil wars inflict immense social costs, but these costs are largely incidental to the combatants and leaders who determine whether they start and end. For the countries directly affected, civil war is development in reverse. Hence a core part of the international constituency for action to reduce the incidence of civil war consists of those who support a reduction in global poverty; however, the potential coalition for action is far larger than this core group. Spillovers from civil wars adversely affect both the regions in which they occur and, through drugs, disease, and terrorism, high-income societies. Given these spillovers, the direct participants in a conflict do not have the moral right to exclude consideration of its effects on the regional and global communities. Yet when Jonas Savimbi, leader of the UNITA rebel group in Angola, decided to go back to war in 1998, neither the adverse economic consequences for neighboring countries, nor the role of Angolan territory as a transit point for coca trafficking to Europe, is likely to have weighed heavily on his mind. Likewise, when President Laurent Gbagbo of Côte d'Ivoire decided to reject the peace settlement that had been agreed on between his government and rebels in January 2003, the likely health repercussions for neighboring countries and the potential for engendering a haven for global crime probably did not feature prominently in his calculations. But they should in ours.

The question is thus not whether the international community has the right to intervene, but whether interventions are available that are likely to be effective at a reasonable cost. Inaction is also expensive. Several civil wars reached the point at which international military intervention became unavoidable. For example, Bosnia, Cambodia, El Salvador, Haiti, Rwanda, and Somalia cost outside powers a total of US$85 billion (Brown and Rosecrance 1999). Other strategies do not need to be cheap to be more cost-effective than this military option. Chapter 5 reviewed both national and international policies organized around the different categories of countries that were at risk of conflict. This chapter assembles the most salient of the interventions that require some degree of international action.

Precedents for International Action

THE BACKGROUND FOR CONSIDERING INTERNATIONAL ACtion is the UN's Monterrey Conference on Development Finance held in 2002, which produced consensus around the principle of shared responsibilities. To substantially reduce the global incidence of conflict, policy changes are critical both in the OECD countries and in the marginalized, low-income, developing countries. Monterrey is not just crying in the wind: the international community has recently demonstrated an unprecedented capacity for collective action. The Kimberley process, begun in 2000, has introduced regulation into the diamonds trade, making it harder for rebel groups to obtain financing from the extortion of diamond producers, and so has helped to bring peace in Angola and Sierra Leone. The OECD-wide criminalization of bribery of government officials has reduced the corrupting effect of natural resource rents upon governments. At a military level, the international ban on antipersonnel landmines, adopted in 1997, has already more than halved the number of casualties.

These three international initiatives are each significant changes in the right direction. They demonstrate that international action is possible, and that it need not take an inordinate amount of time—for example, the Kimberley process took only two years. The task now is to identify a short list of feasible international actions that would cumulatively make a substantial difference. This chapter makes a start at such an agenda. No single "magic bullet" policy will deliver global peace, but several policies are reasonably effective and mutually supporting. For example, policies to reduce the risk of postconflict reversals complement policies to shorten conflicts. Yet even though policies make sense as a complementary package, they do not need to be promoted as a package. Different groups are already promoting particular component reforms, and this is a realistic process of change. The rationale for presenting policies as a package is that it can be helpful for each group to see how its efforts can contribute to the bigger picture. As no one policy has magical effects, each individually is open to the charge that it will not address the core of the conflict problem. While the simulations in chapter 5 support the view that no single policy is decisive, this chapter simulates a policy package and finds that it would more than halve the global incidence of civil wars.

International Policies for Peace

WE NOW FOCUS ON THREE OPPORTUNITIES FOR INTERnational collective action: aid, the governance of natural resources, and military interventions.

Aid

The World Bank is an aid agency, and so beginning our discussion of an international agenda with the role of aid is appropriate. From the perspective of reducing the global incidence of civil war, has the international community got aid right?

Providing Aid in Postconflict Situations   One important respect in which the international community has probably not got aid right is during the first postconflict decade. Historically, aid has come in a rush during the first couple of years of peace and then evaporated. Taking the postconflict decade as a whole, aid has usually been lower than in non-conflict situations. The latest evidence suggests that aid is particularly effective in raising growth during the postconflict decade, but that it is more effective in the middle of the decade than at the beginning. Aid in postconflict situations should be much larger than it has usually been, but it should be phased in gradually. This would require significant, but not impossible, changes in donors' practices. The most straightforward change would be to lengthen the period between the political commitment of postconflict aid and its disbursement.

Retargeting Aid to Low-Income Countries   A second respect in which the international community has probably got aid wrong is in its allocation between countries. The risk of conflict is much higher in low-income countries than in middle-income countries, but historically the international community has allocated much aid to countries that are not particularly poor. The motivations for this have been partly commercial and geopolitical and partly an outcome of bureaucratic inertia. As chapter 5 showed, growth is far more effective in reducing the global incidence of civil war if it occurs in low-income countries. Here the concern for a more peaceful world leads to the same conclusion as a concern for more effective poverty reduction. The World Bank has led the way here: its allocation of concessional development assistance (through International Development Association funds) is much better targeted on low-income countries than most bilateral programs. Fortunately, bilateral programs are improving; for example, the new American Millennium Challenge Account promises to be far more poverty-focused than past U.S. Agency for International Development allocations.

Providing Aid in Environments of Poor Policies and Weak Governance   A third respect in which the international community has probably got aid wrong is in its composition. The countries most at risk of civil war are those with both extremely low incomes and poor policies, institutions, and governance. In these environments conventional aid programs have historically not been very successful. While policies, institutions, and governance must be improved, the attempt to induce reform through conditionality has largely failed to overcome the powerful forces of inertia.

The World Bank, the United Nations Development Programme, and the Development Assistance Committee of the OECD are currently piloting an alternative approach, LICUS, which emphasizes a more informed approach to the political economy of reform (World Bank 2002b). This approach initially targets aid for capacity building at a few relatively uncontentious reforms with quick payoffs, so that the latent constituency for reform can gradually be built. Whereas in most situations donor coordination means that donors should each do different things, in LICUS situations donors should do the same thing, that is, reinforce efforts to break out of low-level equilibrium traps.

In postconflict situations, the LICUS approach is different. Postconflict situations are often politically ripe for rapid and extensive reforms, but what is acutely lacking is the technical capacity to design and implement them. Hence part of the donor response should be to strengthen technical capacity, for example, by financing the return of skilled members of the diaspora.

Expanding Aid   A fourth respect in which the international community has probably not got aid right is in its overall scale. Even accepting the argument that aid is relatively ineffective in environments of poor policies, institutions, and governance, in many low-income countries facing significant risks of conflict additional aid would significantly raise growth and cumulatively make them safer societies.

Using Aid to Reinforce Existing Democratic Institutions   A final respect in which the international community has probably not got aid right is its treatment of political change. Recall that in low-income countries democracy is typically quite fragile, and that the very fragility of political institutions is an important source of conflict risk. Historically, to the extent that bilateral donors have included political institutions in their conditions, the focus has been on encouraging political change. Understandable as this is, it may also be quite dangerous, as well as being highly intrusive. An alternative approach is to attempt to reinforce existing democratic institutions, where they exist, by conditioning aid upon adherence to the country's constitution. Conditioning aid upon constitutionality is potentially stabilizing and is nonintrusive. It mirrors attempts by some regional organizations to discourage unconstitutional political change by withholding membership.

International Governance of Natural Resources

Natural resource endowments offer the potential for poverty reduction, but historically have often been associated with conflict, poor governance, and economic decline. The adverse effects of natural resource endowments flow through several channels, and so several distinct global interventions could all be helpful. The options discussed here are explored more fully in World Bank (2003).

Shutting Rebel Organizations Out of Markets   The Kimberley process is designed to shut rebel organizations out of the global market for rough diamonds. It will have been effective even if rebels are still able to sell the diamonds they extort from local producers, as long as the price the rebels can get on the illicit market is driven to a deep discount. It is too early to judge whether the Kimberley process will be a sustainable success. If it proves ineffective, intergovernmental legislation will have to reinforce the current private, voluntary agreement. Nevertheless, the existence of such a private agreement demonstrates that all parties have recognized the need for effective action. If, however, the Kimberley process succeeds, then it could provide a model for the governance of other commodities that inadvertently fund conflict, notably timber and coltan. In this respect key international actions that will be needed over the next year are to monitor and evaluate the Kimberley process. Parallel to this, certification and tracking procedures can be prepared for timber and coltan (Crossin, Hayman and Taylor 2003; Sherman 2002).

Each commodity transaction has a financial counterpart. Just as at some point in the chain of physical transactions a conflict diamond switches from being illicit to licit, so at some point in the chain of financial transactions money is laundered. Monitoring and investigating the financial transactions may often be easier than tracking the physical transactions. Requiring official scrutiny of physical transactions at some points, notably customs, in relation to information about counterpart financial transactions may also be useful. Left to its own devices, the international banking system is unlikely to provide the necessary degree of scrutiny, as the pressures of competition encourage secrecy and complicity rather than active scrutiny. By the early 1990s UNITA reputedly held some US$4 billion on the New York financial market.

In the wake of the September 11 terrorist attacks on the United States significant moves are under way to require banks to know their clients and to report doubtful transactions. The weakest links in this effort are the offshore havens, which often lack both the will and the capacity to police the banks that they register. Such havens are analogous to territory outside the control of a recognized government, but they are easily dealt with by the withdrawal of recognition as banking authorities. Thus a key global action is to place an enforceable requirement of client knowledge and reporting upon banks, coupled with a de-recognition process for banks and banking authorities that do not comply (Winer and Roule 2003).

One practice that financed several rebel organizations during the 1990s was the sale of "war booty futures," whereby a rebel organization received finance up front in return for an entitlement to natural resource extraction in the future if the rebel organization succeeded in securing territory (Ross 2002a, 2003). Reputable companies rightly view this practice as unacceptable, but it nevertheless occurs on the fringes of the corporate world. There is a strong case for making such transactions criminal in the country in which the company is registered, analogous to the OECD agreement criminalizing international bribery.

A further way in which rebel organizations gain access to revenues from natural resources is to threaten the companies involved in extraction with extortion and kidnapping. The financial flows from companies to rebel movements from these activities are considerable, and both governments and civil society should discourage companies from operating in such conditions. The insurance industry has recently developed products offering ransom insurance. The overall effect will obviously be to increase the ransom payments demanded, and thus there is a good case for banning ransom insurance. OECD governments should also put their own house in order: they could undertake that they would not use public money to pay ransoms to rebel movements, and correspondingly, they could mandate that companies could not treat extortion payments as tax deductible costs of doing business.

A final important source of rebel finance is from illicit primary commodities, notably opium and coca. As discussed earlier, the current regulatory environment makes territory outside the control of a recognized government hugely profitable to the rebel group that controls it. Just as the participants in civil wars have ignored the spillover effects on other societies, so have national drug policies in OECD societies. Antidrug policies could be redesigned in a number of ways that would reduce financial flows to rebel groups. For example, a combination of increased penalties for illegal consumption and the creation of a legalized supply for registered addicts would reduce the profitability of illegal production.

Reducing Countries' Exposure to Price Shocks   A distinct reason why countries dependent on natural resources and other primary commodities for their exports tend to have a record of conflict and poverty is that they are exposed to shocks. The prices of primary commodities are highly volatile, and periodically such countries face a crash in export prices. Such large declines in export income in turn tend to produce a contraction in aggregate output and severe pressure on the budget. Episodes of rapid economic decline increase the risk of conflict, and some evidence indicates that the output losses are persistent.

Governments of low-income, shock-prone countries face macroeconomic management problems of a scale that the governments of industrial countries have not seen since the 1930s, yet they have basically been left to cope on their own. "Photogenic" shocks, such as earthquakes or droughts, typically result in a massive donor response that is sometimes even larger than the cost of the shock itself. Yet even though price shocks are often much more devastating, they have not tended to trigger any significant donor response. Until recently, the international community had two instruments to address the problem: the Compensatory Financing Facility of the IMF and the Stabex Facility of the EU. For different reasons neither of these worked well, and both are currently in abeyance. The Compensatory Financing Facility was a nonconcessional borrowing facility, but for a country to borrow commercially at the onset of a severe negative shock is usually unwise. Meanwhile Stabex disbursements were so slow that they tended to arrive during the subsequent price upturn.

The international community might consider three approaches to cushioning shocks. First, the IMF could consider the case for a more concessional facility triggered at times of severe price crashes. Second, once the IMF had a system in place that signaled eligibility for such a facility, it could function as a guide to the provision of grant finance by bilateral donors, grants probably being the most appropriate cushion for large adverse shocks. Third, the World Bank could develop both risk-pooling and risk-bearing facilities. For example, pooling the risks oil exporters and oil importers face might be possible, because their price risk is precisely offsetting. The Bank might also be able to act as an intermediary between low-income governments and the derivatives markets, basically taking on the burden of staff supervision to avoid the maverick trader problem, which could otherwise be ruinous (Guillaumont 2003).

In addition to these means of cushioning shocks, the OECD countries should eliminate those features of their commercial policies that inadvertently accentuate global price crashes. When domestic farmers receive increased price subsidies in response to a crash in world prices— such as the recent increase in the subsidy to American cotton farmers— this depresses the price to cotton farmers in low-income countries. Nobody wants this to happen, and low-income farmers in OECD countries do not wish to feel that they are profiting at the expense of their even poorer counterparts. It is simply the consequence of a lazy and incompetently designed approach to social protection. Similarly, tariff escalation is typical of the barriers that developing countries' exports face. Tariffs on processed commodities are higher than on raw materials, tending to lock exports into undiversified resource extraction. President Jacques Chirac has recently taken up the theme of reducing exposure to price shocks, urging the international financial institutions to devise effective price cushioning instruments and proposing a moratorium on commercial policies such as agricultural subsidies that increase price volatility.

Increasing the Transparency of Natural Resource Revenues   The governments of low-income, resource-abundant countries have a strong interest in the various proposals for international action. They are often under threat from rebel organizations that receive finance from natural resources and would be helped if such financing were curtailed, and they are periodically hit by export price crashes and would benefit from instruments that reduced and cushioned these shocks. As in the Monterrey consensus, however, they have counterpart responsibilities to demonstrate that their revenues from natural resources are well used. As seen earlier, one of the major threats such governments face is from the violent secession of resource-rich regions, and the best defense against this is likely to be credible scrutiny of how revenues are used. In addition, for resources to be well used is not enough in the many situations where the government is not fully trusted, and so it will need to convince doubters by establishing a credible, independent process of verification.

In essence, what is required is an international template for the acceptable governance of natural resource revenues to which a government with significant revenues could chose to subscribe (Lunde and Swanson 2003). Such a template would have five elements. First, host governments should require international companies in the extractive industries operating in the country to report payments in sufficient detail to permit internationally comparable accounting of natural resource revenue payments to governments. Such reporting could be either to the general public, as envisaged in the "publish what you pay" campaign launched by Global Witness and George Soros, or to a trusted independent authority such as the international financial institutions. Second, the government should require that national resource extraction companies, whether private or government owned, should report on the same basis. Third, the government should undertake to report its receipts from all the foregoing sources. Fourth, an independent authority, such as the international financial institutions, should collate the reported information, attempt to reconcile payments and receipts, integrate the net government revenue figure with standard budget information on revenues and expenditures, and publish the results on an annual basis. A possible division of labor here would be for the World Bank to collate, reconcile, and aggregate the data from companies, while the IMF would integrate the net revenue figure into the budget data it already scrutinizes under its routine annual consultations with governments as mandated under its Article IV. Fifth, the government should designate, and if necessary establish, credible domestic institutions of scrutiny, such as parliamentary committees, or ad hoc entities that include civil society as in Chad, to which the international financial institutions could report the information. Such reports should avoid obscurantist, technocratic jargon. Prime Minister Tony Blair has launched an initiative along these lines.

Attracting More Reputable Resource Extraction Companies   Some low-income countries are facing severe difficulties in attracting reputable resource extraction companies. If the effect of greater international public scrutiny on resource extraction was that reputable companies withdrew from difficult environments to be replaced by fly-by-night operations, then global efforts would have been counterproductive. Survey evidence suggests that the two main impediments deterring good companies are the risk to their reputations and the political risk of unreasonable treatment. The template concept described earlier has the potential to address both these risks (Bray 2003).

One success of the Chad-Cameroon pipeline model of improved governance of natural resource revenues was that it provided international companies with a degree of reputational protection. The international financial institutions in effect certified the governance structure as acceptable. The introduction of a more standardized template for appropriate governance, and its adoption by governments interested in attracting reputable companies, would provide a much higher degree of reputational cover. Such a template also has the potential to address political risk. At present, the insurance entities that supply cover for political risks, notably the Multilateral Investment Guarantee Agency (MIGA), which is part of the World Bank Group, have to assess each governance situation on an ad hoc basis. If governments subscribed to the good governance template, this would be pertinent information for MIGA and other insurers. MIGA might be able to provide a formal undertaking that proposals for investment in signatory countries would receive more favorable treatment in relation to risk assessment than proposals for investment in other countries.

Tightening Scrutiny of Illicit Payments   The proposed template is intended to provide convincing evidence that legitimate payments from companies to governments are properly used. Illicit payments by natural resource extraction companies to bribe people of influence are a different problem. The OECD agreement to criminalize such payments is a start toward curbing them; however, bribes to officials can be disguised as "facilitation payments" to companies controlled by their relatives, and so complementary efforts are required. Some resource extraction companies have now unilaterally undertaken not to make such facilitation payments.

For the industry to determine the precise boundary between legitimate and illegitimate payments and embed this in corporate rules of behavior is surely desirable; however, the international banking system also has an important role. The family of President Sani Abacha was able to deposit sums absurdly in excess of his presidential salary, evidently corruptly siphoned off from Nigerian oil revenues, in reputable international banks. Banks now have somewhat greater responsibility to know their clients and to report suspect receipts. Cooperation is also beginning to increase in repatriating corrupt money. Nevertheless, there is scope for much tighter reinforcement of antibribery legislation on the part of the international banking system.

In some cases increased scrutiny will reveal information about incumbent officials and politicians. In a few cases such politicians may be so elevated as to be above their own national law. Consider, for example, the limited options available to Nigerian society had the scale of President Abacha's corruption been publicly exposed while he was still in power. In such cases the international community has some responsibility to impose penalties that inconvenience the guilty party without inflicting suffering upon the society. The UN has been developing sanctions that offer some scope for such a targeted approach toward penalties (Cortright and Lopez 2002; Le Billon 2003).

Military Expenditures and Interventions

Coordinating Reductions in Military Spending
One of the important routes by which a conflict in one country adversely affects neighboring countries is through neighborhood arms races. In response to the risk of civil war, and even more in response to its actual occurrence, the concerned government sharply increases its military expenditure. Neighbors tend to copy this increase for various reasons. Postconflict, countries tend to get locked into this high level of expenditure for many years. The research underlying this report has found that high military expenditure is normally ineffective in deterring rebellion, and that in postconflict situations it is significantly counterproductive and actually increases the risk of renewed conflict. Hence all concerned parties have an interest in curtailing military spending; however, because one motive for military spending is protection from neighbors, reducing spending in an uncoordinated way is difficult.

A possible solution to this coordination problem is for regional political organizations to join forces with the international financial institutions to offer their services as honest brokers. The regional organizations can facilitate the necessary political cooperation between neighbors, while the international financial institutions can provide an impartial scrutiny process to ensure that agreed spending reductions actually occur. In the past the World Bank's routine public expenditure reviews have politely skirted round military spending, but there is a robust, non-political case for thorough scrutiny. In the absence of such coordinated efforts, the continuing postconflict military burden can come to exceed the costs incurred during the war itself.

Sequencing Military Interventions with Aid and Reform   This report has placed considerable emphasis upon the conflict trap: postconflict situations carry high risks of further conflict. In the first few years after conflict the risks are often so high, and the scope for accelerated economic recovery so modest, that external military peacekeeping is probably essential. International relations experts emphasize that such interventions are most credible if they are by parties that have a direct and long-term interest in sustaining peace in the country.

The most challenging task is to sequence such military intervention with development strategies in a way that avoids gap periods of exceptionally high risk. Obviously each situation must be evaluated individually, but as an approximate guide, even a large and well-timed aid program will not produce a substantial growth spurt until around the fifth postconflict year. Rapid policy and institutional reform should be started immediately after peace has been established, and capacity-building aid will probably be needed for this. However, given the typical poor starting point, reform is unlikely to deliver an environment that can sustain rapid growth without aid until around the end of the postconflict decade. In particular, evidence indicates that democratic institutions are fragile in low-income countries and that this fragility increases the risk of conflict. This suggests that the international community should be wary of imposing an apparently "appropriate" constitutional design during a peace settlement, sending in troops and big aid for the first two years of peace, and then withdrawing militarily and financially and hoping for the best. The military commitment should be for longer. The aid commitment should be later and larger and conditioned upon the maintenance of political institutions. A critical postconflict stage is the first election, typically in the fourth or fifth year of peace. This is a further reason why aid should be peaking around this time, rather than being in steep decline as has often been the case. The emphasis on policy reform should be continuous over the decade and give priority to policies for social inclusion.

Conclusion: A New Goal for 2015?

THE PROPOSED AGENDA FOR INTERNATIONAL ACTION HAS three building blocks: better use of aid, improved governance of natural resources, and enhanced coordination of military and developmental strategies during the postconflict period. This is by no means an exhaustive agenda, and chapter 5 discussed several other policies; however, being comprehensive and being focused involves a trade-off.

If the proposed package were implemented, how would it help to reduce the global incidence of civil war? First, fewer of the low-income, weak policy countries that we have referred to as marginalized would fall into conflict. These are a minority of the developing world, and account for only around 1.1 billion people, but they are an important part of the conflict problem. Providing a larger amount of aid, focusing more strongly on policy reform, cushioning large external shocks, reducing military spending, and increasing the transparency of natural resource revenues would all raise growth. Faster growth, combined with more credible scrutiny of how revenue is used, would reduce disaffection. Other measures to improve the governance of global markets in natural resources would make acquiring finance more difficult for rebel movements.

Second, conflicts would be shorter. Rebel organizations would be weaker because of reduced finance, and socially inclusive policies would have a similar effect: more equal societies tend to have shorter conflicts.

Third, once out of a conflict, countries would be less likely to relapse. Better aid, better coordination with military intervention, and faster policy reform would improve opportunities for reconstruction during the first postconflict decade. Greater attention would be paid to the stability of political institutions, to the transparent governance of natural resource revenues, and to the regional de-escalation of military spending.

Between them these three consequences of the proposed package would probably have a major impact on the global incidence of civil war. Around 85 percent of new civil wars are either the marginalized countries falling into conflict or postconflict countries relapsing. This is why global growth alone is insufficient to tackle the problem: these are the countries that have largely missed out on global growth. How big an effect could we hope for? Any estimates are speculative, but the simulations in chapter 5 started from a baseline incidence of civil war of 10.7 percent: at any one time, roughly 1 country in 10 is embroiled in a civil war. The analysis of the effect of an additional and sustained 3 percent growth in the marginalized countries predicted a reduction in the incidence of war by 4.7 percentage points. During the 1990s the aggregate per capita GDP of this group declined by around 1 percent per year, so that an additional 3 percent would be a dramatic turn-around, but would not imply growth rates that are spectacularly high in absolute terms. If the duration of conflict could be shortened by about a year, the incidence would fall by around 1.7 percentage points. If the risk of postconflict relapse could be halved, this would reduce the incidence by 2.4 percentage points. As a package the three effects would more than halve the global incidence of civil war (Figure 6.1).

As with most developmental policies, realizing their full effects takes time; however, by 2015—the timetable for the Millennium Development Goals—the global incidence of conflict could at least be halved,

Figure 6.1   The contribution of the policy package to peace

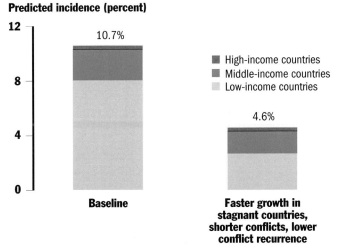

Predicted incidence (percent)

Baseline: 10.7%

High-income countries
Middle-income countries
Low-income countries

Faster growth in stagnant countries, shorter conflicts, lower conflict recurrence: 4.6%

Note: The simulation is based on the model presented in figure 4.12. See appendix 1 for details.
Source: Based on a revised version of Collier and Hoeffler (2002c).

analogous to the overarching Millennium Development Goal of halving poverty. Peace is not officially included as a Millennium Development Goal, yet at the minimum it is important as an instrument for attaining these goals. More reasonably, and in view of the spillover effects of conflict, peace can be seen as a core objective of the international community. Potentially, the international community could adopt the same approach to reducing the incidence of civil war as it has to the objective of reducing world poverty. It could set a target, such as halving the incidence of civil war by 2015; adopt a strategy; and monitor the outcomes. Monitoring the incidence of civil war is easier than monitoring global poverty. Feasible strategies are available that if implemented are likely to make the target attainable.

International cooperation is always difficult, but since the mid-1990s the international community has achieved cooperation for related policies. Given the terrible global cost of civil war we may wish that it had pursued such efforts more vigorously.

Methods and Data

Data Set and Model

T HE FIGURES AND PROBABILITY ESTIMATES PRESENTED IN chapters 3–5 are based mainly on the logistic regression analysis reported in tables 3 and 5 in Collier and Hoeffler (2002c). The data set used is global, spans the years 1960–99, and covers 161 countries. We divide the data series into eight subperiods, 1960–64, 1965–69, …, 1995–99.

In our regressions we estimate the probability of a war breaking out during a five-year period, and the model can be written in the following general form:

$$Y_{it} = a + bX_{it} + cM_{i,t-1} + dZ_i + u_{it}, \tag{A1.1}$$

where t and i are time and country indicators. The dependent variable is a dummy variable indicating whether a war broke out during the five-year period, so that Y_{it} is the log odds of war. The explanatory variables are either measured at the beginning of the period (the X variables in equation (A1.1), for example, income per capita, primary commodity exports/gross domestic product [GDP], population), or during the previous five-year period (the M variables, for instance, per capita income growth), or are time invariant or changing slowly over time (the Z variables, for example, social fractionalization).

The expected probability $\hat{p}_{it}$ of a war breaking out can be calculated by using the estimated coefficients obtained from equation (A1.1):

$$\hat{a} + \hat{b}X_{it} + \hat{c}M_{i,t-1} + \hat{d}Z_i = \hat{W}_{it} \tag{A1.2}$$

$$\hat{p}_{it} = \frac{e^{\hat{W}_{it}}}{(1 + e^{\hat{W}_{it}})} \cdot 100 \qquad (A1.3)$$

We calculate probabilities for hypothetical observations. For example, we find the average values for $\bar{X}_{it}$, $\bar{M}_{i,t-1}$, $\bar{Z}_i$ for a subgroup of countries and take this to be a typical country within the subgroup. We then calculate $\hat{p}_{it}$ by applying equation (A1.3). For the policy simulations in chapter 3 we used the probability for the average developing country as a baseline.

For figure 3.1 we used the actual values of social fractionalization and ethnic dominance and the average values for each observation to predict the risk of civil war.

Figures 3.3(a) and 3.3(b) are based on a model extending the analysis in Collier and Hoeffler (2002c). Details are available on request.

Figure 3.6 is based on a military expenditure function where the risk of civil war breaking out is one of the explanatory variables. Details are presented in Collier and Hoeffler (2002d). Details are available on request.

Figure 3.7 uses the formula for calculating expected probabilities shown above, based on model 11, table 5, in Collier and Hoeffler (2002c). In the typical low-income country, primary commodity exports have a value of 15 percent of GDP. Such a country is represented in the middle column in the figure. The other columns represent calculations made using different values for primary commodity exports/GDP ratios.

The chances of peace depicted in figures 3.8 and 3.9 show the probability of a war ending in the first, second, and so on year, as estimated in an exponential regression model with period and time dummies as the only explanatory variables. For details see Collier, Hoeffler, and Söderbom (2003).

For figure 3.10 we used the average values for the five-year observations during which a war broke out and the average values for the five-year observations during which a war ended.

In figure 3.11 we use a model presented in Collier and Hoeffler (2002c) in which the diaspora is an explanatory variable (table 3, model 6). In the first column we use the average value of the diaspora (1.3 percent), and in the second column we assume a diaspora 10 times as large.

Figure 3.12 uses a regression model presented in Collier and Hoeffler (2002a) showing that military expenditure increases the risk of renewed conflict in postconflict societies.

The self-sustaining level of civil war is the steady-state distribution of a first-order Markov chain. Denote the annual probability of war initiation as w and the annual probability of war termination as v. These two probabilities form the following transition matrix:

$$T = \begin{vmatrix} 1-w & w \\ v & 1-v \end{vmatrix}$$

The distribution vector d_{t+1} of countries in war and in peace at time $t + 1$ is the product of this transition matrix and the distribution vector d_t at t:

$$d_{t+1} = \begin{vmatrix} 1-w & w \\ v & 1-v \end{vmatrix} \begin{vmatrix} i_t \\ 1-i_t \end{vmatrix}$$

where the incidence or level i_t is the number I_t of countries at war divided by all countries N_t. If the annual probabilities are constant, the incidence of war will converge to a self-sustaining level, $s = w/(w + v)$ (Taylor and Karlin 1998), where the number of countries exiting war equals the number entering war. In the Gleditsch and others (2002) dataset, the annual probability of war initiation is 0.016 and the average annual probability of war termination is 0.1233, giving a self-sustaining level of $s = 0.115$.

Figure 4.2 plots the incidence of war at t = 1950, 1951, …, 2020 obtained by subsequent multiplications of the transition vector and the incidence for the previous year. The incidence in 1950 was 0.075, and the figure simulates the convergence toward the steady-state incidence. If M_t countries become independent countries at year t, they are assumed to be at peace the first year, and the simulated incidence is adjusted to $i'_i = I_t/N_t + M_t$, where I_t is the number of countries estimated to be at war at t.

Figure 4.4 shows the self-sustaining incidence for each decade based on the transition probabilities observed in each of these decades. The observed incidence (figure 4.1) does not correspond to the self-sustaining levels, because the convergence takes many years.

Figures 4.5 decomposes the log odds of civil war for a typical country in 1995 (expressed as a ratio to the log odds of a typical country in 1965) into the effect of individual variables by computing $\beta_k(X_{k,1995} - X_{k,1965})$ for each variable. A version of model 5–11 presented in Collier and Hoeffler (2002c) with a decaying function of peacetime was used for this figure and figures 4.10–4.12.

Figure 4.7 compares the average marginalized country with the average successful developer in the same manner.

Figure 4.8 sets the estimated log odds of civil war for high-income countries as the baseline, and plots the log odds of the average marginalized country and the average successful developer assuming that income changes at the specified annual rates.

Figure 4.6 does the same for the income and period dummies in the duration model (Collier, Hoeffler, and Söderbom, 2003), setting the estimated hazard of war termination in the 1960s as 1.

Figure 4.9 shows the estimated log odds of civil war outbreak for the specified categories relative to the estimated log odds for a country with no recent war.

Figure 4.11 decomposes the ratio of the odds of the typical post-conflict marginalized country to the typical no conflict marginalized country in the same way as Figure 4.5.

To produce figures 4.10, 4.12, 4.13, and the figures in chapter 5 and 6, we divided countries into three categories: Those at war (denoted with w); peace countries, defined as countries that had not been at war for the last 10 years (p); and postconflict countries, defined as countries that had ended a civil war less than 10 years before the year of observation (z). With three states the transition matrix has nine transition probabilities: the probability p_{ww} of going from a state of war to war, the probability p_{wz} of going from a state of war to a postconflict state, and so on. The transition matrix is then

$$T = \begin{vmatrix} p_{ww} & p_{wz} & 0 \\ p_{zw} & p_{zz} & p_{zp} \\ p_{pw} & 0 & p_{pp} \end{vmatrix}$$

Two of these transition probabilities are by definition 0: countries cannot go directly from war to peace and from peace to postconflict. We estimated each of these transition probabilities for the typical marginalized country, the typical successful developer, and for high-income countries. We assumed the probability of reversion to war from the postconflict state to be constant over the 10 years even if model 4 assumes this probability to be steadily decreasing over time. We used the estimated probability for the average time since the end of the war for the postconflict group. The probability of transition from postconflict to peace was assumed to be $0.1(1 - p_{zw})$ if a country does not revert to war. The probability that the year of observation is the last year of the postconflict period is 0.1.

Based on these transition probabilities, we estimated the steady-state distribution over these three states for each of these three subgroups. The box in figure 4.12 labeled "successful developers at peace" shows the number of successful developers at peace in equilibrium (93 percent of 71 countries). The boxes labeled "active conflict" and "postconflict" show the total number of countries at war and in the postconflict state in all three country groups. The arrows show the number of countries transiting from one state to another. These figures are computed as the transition probability times the number of countries in the initial state. For instance, the probability for marginalized countries of going from peace to active conflict is estimated to be 0.022. In the estimated steady state, 32 of the 52 marginalized countries are at peace, and 0.022*32 = 0.7 countries are going into conflict per year. The arrows between the active conflict and postconflict boxes add the estimated number of transitions of countries of all three groups.

Given the estimated steady-state distributions, we obtained the estimated incidence of (active) war. Figures 5.1–5.5 and 6.1 show the incidence for the baseline (based on predicted probabilities for the average country in each group in 1990–99) compared with the incidence predicted when the underlying variables are altered as specified.

Data Sources

Diaspora

We used data on the foreign-born population from the U.S. Bureau of the Census and divided these numbers by the total population in the country of origin (see http://www.census.gov/population/).

Ethnic Dominance

Using ethno-linguistic data from the original data source (USSR 1964) we calculated an indicator of ethnic dominance. This variable takes the value of 1 if a single ethno-linguistic group makes up 45 to 90 percent of the total population and 0 otherwise. We would like to thank Tomila Lankina for the translation of the original data source.

GDP Per Capita

We measure income as real purchasing power parity-adjusted GDP per capita. The primary dataset is the *Penn World Tables 5.6* (Summers and Heston 1991). Since the data are only available for 1960–92, we used the growth rates of real purchasing power parity-adjusted GDP per capita data from the *World Development Indicators* (World Bank 2002a) to obtain income data for the 1990s.

Geographic Dispersion of the Population

We constructed a dispersion index of the population on a country-by-country basis. Based on population data for cells of 400 square kilometers we generated a Gini coefficient of population dispersion for each country. A value of 0 indicates that the population is evenly distributed across the country and a value of 1 indicates that the total population is concentrated in one area. Data are available for 1990 and 1995. For years prior to 1990 we used the 1990 data. We would like to thank Uwe Deichman of the World Bank's Geographic Information System Unit for generating these data. He used data from the Center for International Earth Science Information Network, Columbia University; the International Food Policy Research Institute; the World Resources Institute; and Gridded Population of the World.

Peace Duration

This variable measures the length of the peace period (in months) since the end of the previous civil war. For countries that never experienced a civil war we measure the peace period since the end of World War II. In chapter 4 we used a decaying function of peacetime: exp(–peace duration/24).

Population

Population measures the total population. The data source is the *World Development Indicators* (World Bank 2002a).

Primary Commodity Exports/GDP

The ratio of primary commodity exports to GDP proxies the abundance of natural resources. The data on primary commodity exports and GDP were obtained from the World Bank. Export and GDP data are measured in current U.S. dollars.

Social, Ethno-linguistic, and Religious Fractionalization

We proxy social fractionalization in a combined measure of ethnic and religious fractionalization. Ethnic fractionalization is measured by the ethno-linguistic fractionalization index. It measures the probability that two randomly drawn individuals from a given country do not speak the same language. Data are only available for 1960. In the economics literature this measure was first used by Mauro (1995). Using data from Barrett (1982) on religious affiliations we constructed an analogous religious fractionalization index. Following Barro (1997) we aggregated the various religious affiliations into nine categories: Catholic, Protestant, Muslim, Jew, Hindu, Buddhist, Eastern religions (other than Buddhist), indigenous religions, and no religious affiliation.

The fractionalization indexes range from 0 to 100. A value of 0 indicates that the society is completely homogenous, whereas a value of 100 characterizes a completely heterogeneous society.

We calculated our social fractionalization index as the product of the ethno-linguistic fractionalization and the religious fractionalization indexes plus the ethno-linguistic or the religious fractionalization index, whichever is the greater. By adding either index we avoid classifying a country as homogenous (a value of 0) if the country is ethnically homogenous but religiously diverse or vice versa.

War Start

We use mainly the data collected by Small and Singer (1982) and Singer and Small (1994). War start is a dummy variable. It takes a value of 1 if the country was at peace at the beginning of the period and war broke out during the following five years. If the country remained at peace during the entire period we record a value of 0. A missing value is recorded if the country was at war at the beginning of the period. We record 78 outbreaks of civil war, but cannot use all these observations in our regressions because of missing data for some of the explanatory variables.

A Selected Bibliography of Studies of Civil War and Rebellion

THE LITERATURE ON CIVIL WAR IS EXTENSIVE AND dates back at least to Hobbes (1660) and Hutcheson (1755). In the modern economics literature Tullock (1974) made the seminal contribution. Below is a collection of central contributions and broad literature reviews grouped into core topics. Many of the works listed are also relevant to other subjects.

Economic Factors

Economic Motives

Blomberg and Hess 2002; Brough and Elliott 1989, 1999; Collier 1998, 2000; Collier and Hoeffler 2002c; Collier and Sambanis 2002; De Soto 1989; Garfinkel and Skaperdas 1996; Grossman 1991, 1995; Hirshleifer 1978, 1987, 1988, 1991a,b, 1995a,b, 2001; Kuran 1989, 1995; Lichbach 1995; Mehlum, Moene, and Torvik 2002; Olson 1982; Sandler 2000; Silver 1974; Skaperdas 2002; Tullock 1971, 1974.

Economic Effects of Civil War

Blomberg and Hess 2002; Brogan 1951; Brown and Rosecrance 1999; Collier 1999; Murdoch and Sandler 2002a,b.

Foreign Aid and Conflict

Anderson 1990; Collier and Hoeffler 2002a,b; Grossman 1992; Prendergast 1996.

Inequality and Conflict

Hegre, Gissinger, and Gleditsch 2003; Lichbach 1989; Muller 1985; Muller and Seligson 1987.

Resource Scarcity and Abundance

Bächler and Spillmann 1996; Buhaug and Gates 2002; Collier and Hoeffler 2002c; de Soysa 2002a,b; Hauge and Ellingsen 1998; Homer-Dixon 1991; Klare 2001; Le Billon 2001; Le Billon, Sherman, and Hartwell 2002; Reynal-Querol 2002a; Ross 2003.

Role of Ethnicity and Nationalism

Ethnic Conflict

Bates 2001; Brass 1997; Brubaker and Laitin 1998; Elbadawi and Sambanis 2002; Ellingsen 2000; Fearon and Laitin 1996; Gurr 1995; Horowitz 1985; Mason 1984; Newman 1991; Olzak and Nagel 1986; Vanhanen 1999; Varshney 2002.

Nationalism and Ethnicity

Anderson 1983; Connor 1994; Deutsch 1953; Gellner 1983; Hechter 2001; Ignatieff 1993; Smith 1991.

Secession and Self-Determination

Alesina and Spolaore 1997; Buchanan and Faith 1987; Horowitz 1991; Kaufmann 1996; Marcouiller and Young 1995; Muller and Opp 1986; Sambanis 2000; Tullock 1985.

Anatomy of Rebellion

Strategic Logic of Rebellion and Repression

Davenport 1999; DeNardo 1995; Gates 2002; Gottschalk 1944; Grossman 1991, 1995; Hardin 1995; Hopper 1950; Kuran 1989; Lichbach 1995; Moore 1998; Muller and Weede 1990; Neumann 1949; Odom 1992; Posen 1993; Skaperdas 2001; Wintrobe 1998.

Form and Magnitude of Political Violence

Brass 1985; Brito and Intriligator 1988, 1990; Cartwright, Delorme, and Wood 1985; Deutscher 1952; Kalyvas 2001; Palmer 1954.

Emotional Roots of Conflict

Ellwood 1905; Le Bon 1913; Petersen 2002; Riezler 1943.

Social Protest and Rebellion

Arendt 1965; Davies 1962; Gurr 1970; Hibbs 1973; Huntington 1968; Johnson 1964; McAdam, Tarrow, and Tilly 2000; Olson 1971, 1982; Tilly 1978; Tullock 1971, 1974.

Sociology of Revolution

Goldstone 2002; Goldstone, Gurr, and Moshiri 1991; Lasswell and Kaplan 1955; Moore 1966; Skocpol 1987; Sorokin 1925.

Role of the State

State Weakness and Insurgency

Bates 2001; Brough and Elliott 1989, 1999; Esty and others 1995, 1998; Fearon and Laitin 2003; Herbst 2000; Leites and Wolf 1970; Lichbach 1984; Odom 1992; Olson 1971, 1982; Tullock 1987.

Democracy, Democratization, and Civil War

Esty and others 1998; Fearon and Laitin 2003; Hegre and others 2001; Huntington 1968; Muller and Weede 1990; Reynal-Querol 2002b; Snyder 2000; Wood 2000.

Development and Democratization

Burkhart and Lewis-Beck 1994; Dahl 1989; Huntington 1968; Lipset 1959; Muller 1995; Przeworski and others 2000; Ross 2000; Vanhanen 1990.

Legitimacy

Schutz and Slater 1990; Zartman 1995.

International Dimensions of Civil War

Betts 1994; Brown 1996; Carment and James 1997; Lake and Rothschild 1998; Midlarsky 2000; Regan 2000, 2002.

Negotiation and Implementation of Peace

Azam 1995; Doyle and Sambanis 2000; Doyle, Johnstone, and Orr 1997; Fearon 2001; Licklider 1993, 1995; Mason and Fett 1996; Paris 1997; Stedman, Rothschild, and Cousens 2002; Walter 2002; Zartman 1985.

Bibliography

The word "processed" describes informally reproduced works that may not be commonly available through libraries.

Alesina, A., and E. Spolaore. 1997. "On the Number and Size of Nations." *Quarterly Journal of Economics* 112(4):1027–56.

Anderson, B. 1983. *Imagined Communities: Reflections on the Origins and Spread of Nationalism.* London: Verso.

Anderson, M. B. 1990. *Do No Harm. How Aid Can Support Peace—Or War.* Boulder, Colo.: Lynne Rienner.

Arendt, H. 1965. *On Revolution.* New York: Penguin.

Azam, J. P. 1995. "How to Pay for Peace." *Public Choice* 83(1/2): 173–84.

Bächler, G., and K. R. Spillmann, eds. 1996. *Environmental Degradation as a Cause of War—Kriegsursache Umweltzerstörung.* Chur, Switzerland: Ruegger.

Bates, R. H. 2001. *Prosperity and Violence. The Political Economy of Development.* New York and London: Norton.

Betts, R. K. 1994. "The Delusions of Partial Intervention." *Foreign Affairs* 73(6): 20–33.

Blomberg, B., and G. Hess. 2002. "The Temporal Links between Conflict and Economic Activity." *Journal of Conflict Resolution* 46(1): 74–90.

Brass, P. 1985. *Ethnic Groups and the State.* London: Croom-Helm Brown.

———. 1997. *Theft of an Idol.* Princeton, N.J.: Princeton University Press.

Brito, D. L., and M. D. Intriligator. 1988. "A Predator-Prey Model of Guerrilla Warfare." *Synthese* 6(2): 235–44.

———. 1990. "An Economic Model of Guerilla Warfare." *International Interactions* 15(3/4): 319–29.

Brogan, D. W. 1951. *The Price of Revolution.* London: Hamish Hamilton.

Brough, W. T., and V. L. Elliott. 1989. "The Economics of Insurgency." Paper presented at the Public Choice Society Annual Meeting, March 17–19, Agency for International Development, Washington, D.C. Processed.

———. 1999. "The Economics of Insurgency." In Mwangi S. Kimenyi and John Mukum Mbaku, eds., *Institutions and Collective Choice in Developing Countries: Applications of the Theory of Public Choice.* Burlington, Vt.: Ashgate.

Brown, M. 1996. *International Dimensional of Internal Conflict.* Cambridge, Mass.: MIT Press.

Brown, M. E., and R. Rosecrance, eds. 1999. *The Costs of Conflict.* Boulder, Colo.: Rowman & Littlefield.

Brubaker, R., and D. D. Laitin. 1998. "Ethnic and Nationalist Violence." *Annual Review of Sociology* 24: 243–52.

Buchanan, James M., and Roger Faith. 1987. "Secession and the Limits of Taxation." *American Economic Review* 77(5): 1023–31.

Buhaug, H., and S. Gates. 2002. "The Geography of Civil War." *Journal of Peace Research* 39(4): 417–33.

Burkhart, R. E., and M. S. Lewis-Beck. 1994. "Comparative Democracy: The Economic Development Thesis." *American Political Science Review* 88(4): 903–10.

Carment, D., and P. James, eds. 1997. *Wars in the Midst of Peace.* Pittsburgh, Pa.: University of Pittsburgh Press.

Cartwright, P. A., C. D. Delorme, Jr., and N. J. Wood. 1985. "The By-Product Theory of Revolution: Some Empirical Evidence." *Public Choice* 46(3): 265–74.

Collier, P. 1998. "On Economic Causes of Civil War." *Oxford Economic Papers* 50(4): 563–73.

_____. 1999. "On the Economic Consequences of Civil War." *Oxford Economic Papers* 51: 168–83.

_____. 2000. "Rebellion as a Quasi-Criminal Activity." *Journal of Conflict Resolution* 44(6): 839–53.

Collier, P., and A. Hoeffler. 2002a. "Aid, Policy, and Growth in Post-Conflict Societies." Policy Research Working Paper no. 2902. World Bank, Washington, D.C.

_____. 2002b. "Aid, Policy, and Peace: Reducing the Risks of Civil Conflict." *Defence and Peace Economics* 13(6): 435–50.

_____. 2002c. "Greed and Grievance in Civil Wars." Working Paper Series 2002–01. Centre for the Study of African Economies, Oxford, U.K. Available on: http://www.csae.ox.ac.uk.

Collier, P., and N. Sambanis. 2002. "Understanding Civil War: A New Agenda." *Journal of Conflict Resolution* 46(1): 3–12.

Connor, W. 1994. *Ethno-nationalism: The Quest for Understanding.* Princeton, N.J.: Princeton University Press.

Dahl, R. 1989. *Democracy and Its Critics.* New Haven, Conn., and London: Yale University Press.

Davenport, C. 1999. "Human Rights and the Democratic Proposition." *Journal of Conflict Resolution* 43(1): 92–116.

Davies, J. C. 1962. "Toward a Theory of Revolution." *American Sociological Review* 27(1): 5–19.

DeNardo, J. 1985. *Power in Numbers: The Political Strategy of Protest and Rebellion.* Princeton, N.J.: Princeton University Press.

De Soto, H. 1989. *The Other Path: The Invisible Revolution in the Third World.* Translated by June Abbot. New York: Harper and Row.

de Soysa, I. 2002a. "Ecoviolence: Shrinking Pie or Honey Pot?" *Global Environmental Politics* 2(4): 1–27.

_____. 2002b. "Paradise Is a Bazaar? Greed, Creed, and Governance in Civil War, 1989–99." *Journal of Peace Research* 39(4): 395–416.

Deutsch, K. W. 1953. *Nationalism and Social Communication: An Inquiry into the Foundations of Nationality.* Cambridge, Mass., and New York: Technology Press of the Massachusetts Institute of Technology and Wiley.

Deutscher, I. 1952. "The French Revolution and the Russian Revolution: Some Suggestive Analogies." *World Politics* 4: 369–81.

Doyle, M. W., and N. Sambanis. 2000. "International Peacebuilding: A Theoretical and Quantitative Analysis." *American Political Science Review* 94(4): 779–801.

Doyle M. W., I. Johnstone, and R. O. Orr, eds. 1997. *Keeping the Peace: Multidimensional UN Operations in Cambodia and El Salvador.* Cambridge, U.K.: Cambridge University Press.

Elbadawi, I., and N. Sambanis. 2002. "How Much Civil War Will We See? Explaining the Prevalence of Civil War." *Journal of Conflict Resolution* 46(3): 307–34.

Ellingsen, T. 2000. "Colorful Community or Ethnic Witches' Brew? Multiethnicity and Domestic Conflict during and after the Cold War." *Journal of Conflict Resolution* 44(2): 228–49.

Ellwood, C. A. 1905. "A Psychological Theory of Revolutions." *American Journal of Sociology* 11: 49–59.

Esty, D. C., J. Goldstone, T. R. Gurr, P. T. Surko, and A. N. Unger. 1995. "Working Papers: State Failure Task Force Report." Science Applications International Corporation, McLean, Va.

Esty, D. C., J. A. Goldstone, T. R. Gurr, B. Harff, M. Levy, G. D. Dabelko, P. T. Surko, and A. N. Unger. 1998. *State Failure Task Force Report: Phase II Findings.* McLean, Va.: Science Applications International Corporation.

Fearon, J. D. 2001. "Why Do Some Civil Wars Last So Much Longer Than Others?" Paper prepared for the World Bank-University of California at Irvine Conference on Civil War Duration and Post-conflict Peace Building, May 18–20, Irvine, Calif.

Fearon, J. D., and D. D. Laitin. 1996. "Explaining Interethnic Cooperation." *American Political Science Review* 90(4): 715–35.

_____. 2003. "Ethnicity, Insurgency, and Civil War." *American Political Science Review* 97(1): 75–90.

Garfinkel, M. R., and S. Skaperdas, eds. 1996. *The Political Economy of Conflict and Appropriation.* New York: Cambridge University Press.

Gates, S. 2002. "Recruitment and Allegiance: The Microfoundations of Rebellion." *Journal of Conflict Resolution* 46(1): 111–30.

Gellner, E. 1983. *Nations and Nationalism.* Ithaca, N.Y.: Cornell University Press.

Goldstone, J. A., ed. 2002. *Revolutions: Theoretical, Comparative, and Historical Studies,* 3d ed. Fort Worth, Tex.: Harcourt Brace College Publishers.

Goldstone, J. A., T. R. Gurr, and F. Moshiri. 1991. *Revolutions in the Late 20th Century.* Boulder, Colo.: Westview Press.

Gottschalk, L. 1944. "Causes of Revolution." *American Journal of Sociology* 50: 1–8.

Grossman, H. I. 1991. "A General Equilibrium Model of Insurrections." *American Economic Review* 81(4): 912–921.

_____. 1992. "Foreign Aid and Insurrection." *Defence Economics* 3(4): 275–88.

_____. 1995. "Insurrections." In K. Hartley and T. Sandler, eds., *Handbook of Defense Economics,* vol. 1. Amsterdam: Elsevier Science BV.

Gurr, T. R. 1970. *Why Men Rebel.* Princeton, N.J.: Princeton University Press.

_____. 1995. *Minorities at Risk: A Global View of Ethno-political Conflicts.* Washington, D.C.: United States Institute for Peace.

Hardin, R. 1995. *One for All: The Logic of Group Conflict.* Princeton, N.J.: Princeton University Press.

Hauge, W., and T. Ellingsen. 1998. "Beyond Environmental Scarcity: Causal Pathways to Conflict." *Journal of Peace Research* 35(3): 299–317.

Hechter, M. 2001. *Containing Nationalism.* Oxford, U.K.: Oxford University Press.

Hegre, H., R. Gissinger, and N. P. Gleditsch. 2003. "Globalization and Internal Conflic." In G. Schneider, K. Barbieri, and N. P. Gleditsch, eds., *Globalization and Conflict.* Boulder, Colo.: Rowman & Littlefield.

Hegre, H., T. Ellingsen, S. Gates, and N. P. Gleditsch. 2001. "Toward a Democratic Civil Peace? Democracy, Political Change, and Civil War, 1816–1992." *American Political Science Review* 95(1): 33–48.

Herbst, J. 2000. *States and Power in Africa: Comparative Lessons in Authority and Control.* Princeton, N.J.: Princeton University Press.

Hibbs, D. 1973. *Mass Political Violence: A Cross-National Causal Analysis.* New York: Wiley.

Hirshleifer, J. 1978. "Competition, Cooperation, and Conflict in Economics and Biology." *American Economic Review* 68(2): 238–45.

_____. 1987. *Economic Behavior in Adversity.* Chicago: University of Chicago Press.

_____. 1988. "The Analytics of Continuing Conflict." *Synthese* 76(2): 201–33.

_____. 1991a. "The Paradox of Power." *Economics and Politics* 3(3): 177–200.

_____. 1991b. "The Technology of Conflict." *American Economic Review Papers and Proceedings* 81(2): 130–134.

_____. 1995a. "Anarchy and Its Breakdown." *Journal of Political Economy* 103(1): 26–52.

_____. 1995b. "Theorizing about Conflict." In K. Hartley and T. Sandler, eds., *The Handbook of Defense Economics.* Amsterdam: Elsevier Science BV.

_____. 2001. *The Dark Side of the Force. Economic Foundations of Conflict Theory.* Cambridge, U.K.: Cambridge University Press.

Hobbes, T. 1660. *Leviathan or the Matter, Forme, and Power of a Commonwealth, Ecclesiastical and Civil.* Reprint 1991. Cambridge Texts in the History of Political Thought Series. Richard Tuck, ed. Cambridge, U.K.: Cambridge University Press.

Homer-Dixon, T. F. 1991. "On the Threshold: Environmental Changes as Causes of Acute Conflict." *International Security* 19(1): 5–40.

Hopper, R. D. 1950. "The Revolutionary Process." *Social Forces* 28: 270–79.

Horowitz, D. L. 1985. *Ethnic Groups in Conflict.* Berkeley, Calif.: University of California Press.

_____. 1991. "Self-Determination: Politics, Philosophy, and Law." *NOMOS* 39: 421–63.

Huntington, S. P. 1968. *Political Order in Changing Societies.* New Haven, Conn.: Yale University Press.

Hutcheson, Frances. 1755. *A System of Moral Philosophy.* Reprint 1968. New York: Augustus M. Kelley.

Ignatieff, M. 1993. *Blood and Belonging: Journeys into the New Nationalism.* New York: Farrar, Straus, and Giroux.

Johnson, C. 1964. *Revolution and the Social System.* Stanford, Calif.: Hoover Institution on War, Revolution, and Peace.

Kalyvas, S. 2001. "The Logic of Violence in Civil War: Theory and Preliminary Empirical Results." University of Chicago, Chicago. Processed.

Kaufmann, C. 1996. "Possible and Impossible Solutions to Ethnic Civil Wars." *International Security* 20(4): 136–75.

Klare, M. 2001. Natural Resource Wars: The New Landscape of Global Conflict. New York: Metropolitan Books.

Kuran, T. 1989. "Sparks and Prairie Fires: A Theory of Unanticipated Political Revolution." *Public Choice* 61(1): 41–74.

_____. 1995. *Private Truths, Public Lies: The Social Consequences of Preference Falsification.* Cambridge, Mass.: Harvard University Press.

Lake, D. A., and D. Rothschild, eds. 1998. *The International Spread of Ethnic Conflict: Fear, Diffusion, and Escalation.* Princeton, N.J.: Princeton University Press.

Lasswell, H., and A. Kaplan. 1955. *Power and Society.* New Haven, Conn.: Yale University Press.

Le Billon, P. 2001. "The Political Ecology of War: Natural Resources and Armed Conflicts." *Political Geography* 20(5): 561–84.

Le Billon, P., J. Sherman, and M. Hartwell. 2002. "Controlling Resource Flows to Civil Wars: A Review and Analysis of Current Policies and Legal Instruments." Background Paper for the Conference on Policies and Practices for Regulating Resource Flows to Armed Conflicts, May 20–24, Bellagio Study and Conference Center, Bellagio, Italy. Available on: http://www.ipacademy.org.

Le Bon, G. 1913. *The Psychology of Revolution.* New York: Putnam.

Leites, N., and C. Wolf, Jr. 1970. *Rebellion and Authority: An Analytic Essay on Insurgent Conflicts.* Chicago: Markham.

Lichbach, M. I. 1984. "An Economic Theory of Governability: Choosing Policy and Optimizing Performance." *Public Choice* 44(2): 307–37.

_____. 1989. "An Evaluation of Does Economic-Inequality Breed Political-Conflict Studies." *World Politics* 41(4): 431–70.

_____. 1995. *The Rebel's Dilemma. Economics, Cognition, and Society Series.* Ann Arbor, Mich.: University of Michigan Press.

Licklider, R. 1993. *Stopping the Killing.* New York: New York University Press.

_____. 1995. "The Consequences of Negotiated Settlements in Civil Wars, 1945–1993." *American Political Science Review* 89(3): 681–90.

Lipset, S. M. 1959. "Some Social Requisites of Democracy: Economic Development and Political Legitimacy." *American Political Science Review* 53(1): 69–106.

Marcouiller, D., and L. Young. 1995. "The Black Hole of Graft: The Predatory State and the Informal Economy." *American Economic Review* 85(3): 630–46.

Mason, T. D., 1984. "Individual Participation in Collective Racial Violence: A Rational Choice Synthesis." *American Political Science Review* 78(4): 1040–56.

Mason, T. D., and P. J. Fett. 1996. "How Civil Wars End: A Rational Choice Approach." *Journal of Conflict Resolution* 40(4): 546–68.

McAdam, D., S. Tarrow, and C. Tilly. 2000. *Dynamics of Contention.* Cambridge, U.K.: Cambridge University Press.

Mehlum, H., K. O. Moene, and R. Torvik. 2002. "Plunder & Protection Inc." *Journal of Peace Research* 39(4): 447–59.

Midlarsky, M. I. 2000. "Identity and International Conflict." In M. I. Midlarsky, ed., *Handbook of War Studies II.* Ann Arbor, Mich.: University of Michigan Press.

Moore, B., Jr. 1966. *Social Origins of Dictatorship and Democracy: Lord and Peasant in the Making of the Modern World.* Boston: Beacon Press.

Moore, W. H. 1998. "Repression and Dissents: Substitution, Context, and Timing." *American Journal of Political Science* 42(3): 851–73.

Muller, E. N. 1985. "Income Inequality, Regime Repressiveness, and Political Violence." *American Sociological Review* 50(1): 47–61.

_____. 1995. "Economic Determinants of Democracy." *American Sociological Review* 60(6): 966–82.

Muller, E. N., and K.-D. Opp. 1986. "Rational Choice and Rebellious Collective Action." *American Political Science Review* 80(2): 471–87.

Muller, E. N., and M. A. Seligson. 1987. "Inequality and Insurgency." *American Political Science Review* 81(2): 425–51.

Muller, E. N., and E. Weede. 1990. "Cross-National Variation in Political Violence: A Rational Action Approach." *Journal of Conflict Resolution* 34(4): 624–51.

Murdoch, J., and Sandler T. 2002a. "Civil Wars and Economic Growth: A Regional Comparison." *Defense and Peace Economics* 13(6): 451–64.

_____. 2002b. "Economic Growth, Civil Wars, and Spatial Spillovers." *Journal of Conflict Resolution* 46(1): 91–110.

Neumann, S. 1949. "The Structure and Strategy of Revolutions: 1848 and 1948." *Journal of Politics* 11: 532–44.

Newman, S. 1991. "Does Modernization Breed Ethnic Conflict?" *World Politics* 43(3): 451–78.

Odom, W. E. 1992. *On Internal War: American and Soviet Approaches to Third World Clients and Insurgents.* Durham, N.C.: Duke University Press.

Olson, M. 1971. *Logic of Collective Action: Public Goods and the Theory of Groups.* Cambridge, Mass.: Harvard University Press.

_____. 1982. *The Rise and Decline of Nations: Growth, Stagflation, and Social Rigidities.* New Haven, Conn.: Yale University Press.

Olzak, S., and J. Nagel, eds. 1986. *Competitive Ethnic Relations.* New York: Academic Press.

Palmer, R. R. 1954. "The World Revolution in the West." *Political Science Quarterly* 69(1): 1–14.

Paris, R. 1997. "Peacebuilding and the Limits of Liberal Internationalism." *International Security* 22(Fall): 54–89.

Petersen, R. D. 2002. *Understanding Ethnic Violence: Fear, Hatred, and Resentment in 20th-Century Eastern Europe.* Cambridge, U.K.: Cambridge University Press.

Posen, B. 1993. "The Security Dilemma and Ethnic Conflict." In Michael Brown, ed., *Ethnic Conflict and International Security.* Princeton, N.J.: Princeton University Press.

Prendergast, J. 1996. *Frontline Diplomacy: Humanitarian Aid and Conflict in Africa.* Boulder, Colo.: Lynne Rienner.

Przeworski, A., M. E. Alvarez, J. A. Cheibub, and F. Limongi. 2000. *Democracy and Development: Political Institutions and Well-Being in the World, 1950–1990.* Cambridge, U.K.: Cambridge University Press.

Regan, P. M. 2000. *Civil Wars and Foreign Powers.* Ann Arbor, Mich.: Michigan University Press.

_____. 2002. "Third-Party Intervention and the Duration of Intrastate Conflicts." *Journal of Conflict Resolution* 46(1): 55–73.

Reynal-Querol, M. 2002a. "Ethnicity, Political Systems, and Civil War." *Journal of Conflict Resolution* 46(1): 29–54.

_____. 2002b. "Political Systems, Stability, and Civil Wars." *Defence and Peace Economics* 13(6): 465–83.

Riezler, K. 1943. "On the Psychology of Modern Revolutions." *Social Research* 10: 320–36.

Ross, M. L. 2000. "Does Oil Hinder Democracy?" *World Politics* 53(April): 325–61.

_____. 2003. "The Natural Resource Curse: How Wealth Can Make You Poor." In I. Bannon and P. Collier, eds., *Natural Resources and Violent Conflict: Options and Actions*. Washington, D.C.: World Bank.

Sambanis, N. 2000. "Partition as a Solution to Ethnic War." *World Politics* 52(4): 437–83.

Sandler, T. 2000. "Economic Analysis of Conflict." *Journal of Conflict Resolution* 44(6): 723–29.

Schutz, B. M., and R. O. Slater. 1990. *Revolutionary Change in the Third World*. Boulder, Colo.: Lynne Rienner.

Silver, M. 1974. "Political Revolutions and Repression: An Economic Approach." *Public Choice* 14(1): 63–71.

Skaperdas, S. 2001. "An Economic Approach to Analyzing Civil Wars." Paper presented at the World Bank Conference on Civil Wars and Post-War Transitions, May 18–20, University of California at Irvine.

_____. 2002. "Warlord Competition." *Journal of Peace Research* 39(4): 435–46.

Skocpol, T. 1987. *States and Social Revolutions: A Comparative Study of France, Russia, and China*. New York: Cambridge University Press.

Smith, A. D. 1991. *National Identity*. Reno, Nev.: University of Nevada Press.

Snyder, J. 2000. *From Voting to Violence: Democratization and Nationalist Conflict*. New York: Norton.

Sorokin, P. 1925. *The Sociology of Revolution*. New York: Lippincott.

Stedman, S. J., D. Rothschild, and E. N. Cousens, eds. 2002. *Ending Civil Wars: The Implementation of Peace Agreements*. Boulder, Colo.: Lynne Rienner.

Tilly, C. 1978. *From Mobilization to Revolution.* New York: McGraw-Hill.

Tullock, G. 1971. "The Paradox of Revolution." *Public Choice* 11: 89–99.

_____. 1974. *The Social Dilemma: The Economics of War and Peace.* Blacksburg, Va.: Public Choice Center.

_____. 1985. "A New Proposal for Decentralizing Government Activity." In H. Milde and H. G. Monissen, eds., *Rationale Wirtshafts-politik in Komplexen Gesellschaften.* Stuttgart, Germany: Verlag W. Kohlhammer.

_____. 1987. *Autocracy.* Boston: Kluwer Academic Publishers.

Vanhanen, T. 1990. *The Process of Democratization. A Comparative Study of 147 States, 1980–88.* New York: Crane Russak.

_____. 1999. "Domestic Ethnic Conflict and Ethnic Nepotism: A Comparative Analysis." *Journal of Peace Research* 36(1): 55–73.

Varshney, A. 2002. *Ethnic Conflict and Civic Life: Hindus and Muslims in India.* New Haven, Conn.: Yale University Press.

Walter, B. F. 2002. *Committing to Peace.* Princeton, N.J.: Princeton University Press.

Wintrobe, R. 1998. *The Political Economy of Dictatorship.* Cambridge, U.K.: Cambridge University Press.

Wood, E. J. 2000. *Forging Democracy from Below: Insurgent Traditions in South Africa and El Salvador.* Cambridge, U.K.: Cambridge University Press.

Zartman, W. I. 1985. *Ripe for Resolution: Conflict and Intervention in Africa.* Oxford, U.K.: Oxford University Press.

_____, ed. 1995. *Collapsed States: The Disintegration and Restoration of Legitimate Authority.* Boulder, Colo.: Lynne Rienner.

References

The word "processed" describes informally reproduced works that may not be commonly available through libraries.

Acemoglu, D., S. Johnson, and J. A. Robinson. 2001. "The Colonial Origins of Comparative Development: An Empirical Investigation." *American Economic Review* 91(5): 1369–1401.

Andre, C., and J. P. Platteau. 1998. "Land Relations under Unbearable Stress: Rwanda Caught in the Malthusian Trap." *Journal of Economic Behavior and Organization* 34(1): 1–47.

Asia Watch. 1991. *Afghanistan: The Forgotten War.* New York: Human Rights Watch.

Azam, J.-P., and A. Hoeffler. 2002. "Violence against Civilians in Civil Wars: Looting or Terror?" *Journal of Peace Research* 39(4): 461–85.

Balch-Lindsay, D., and A. J. Enterline. 2000. "Killing Time: The World Politics of Civil War Duration, 1820–1992. *International Studies Quarterly* 44(4): 615–42.

Barrett, D. B., ed. 1982. *World Christian Encyclopedia.* Oxford, U.K.: Oxford University Press.

Barro, R. J., ed. 1997. *Determinants of Economic Growth.* Cambridge, Mass. and London: MIT Press.

Bell, Stewart. 2000. "Canadian Financed Terror Bombs, Sri Lankans Say." *National Post.*

Bennett, D. S., and A. Stam. 1996. "The Duration of Interstate Wars, 1816–1985." *American Political Science Review* 90(2): 239–57.

Bigombe, B., P. Collier, and N. Sambanis. 2000. "Policies for Building Post-Conflict Peace." *Journal of African Economies* 9(3): 322–47.

Boyce, J. K. 2002. *Investing in Peace: Aid and Conditionality after Civil Wars.* International Institute for Strategic Studies, Adelphi Paper no. 351. Oxford, U.K.: Oxford University Press.

Brass, P. 1997. *Theft of an Idol.* Princeton, N.J.: Princeton University Press.

Bray, J. 2003. "Attracting Reputable Companies to Risky Environments: Petroleum and Mining Companies." In I. Bannon and P. Collier, eds., *Natural Resources and Violent Conflict: Options and Actions.* Washington, D.C.: World Bank.

Brown, M. E., and R. Rosecrance, eds. 1999. *The Costs of Conflict.* Boulder, Colo.: Rowman & Littlefield.

Brück, T. 2001. "Mozambique: The Economic Effects of the War." In F. Stewart, V. Fitzgerald, and associates, eds., *War and Underdevelopment,* vol. 2. Oxford, U.K.: Oxford University Press.

Buhaug, H., and S. Gates. 2002. "The Geography of Civil War." *Journal of Peace Research* 39(4): 417–33.

Buhaug, H., S. Gates, and P. Lujala. 2002. "Lootable Natural Resources and the Duration of Armed Civil Conflict, 1946–2001." Paper presented at the Annual Meeting of the Peace Science Society (International), November 1–3, Tucson, Ariz.

Cairns, Edmund. 1997. *A Safer Future: Reducing the Human Cost of War.* Oxford, U.K.: Oxfam Publications.

Canning, D. 1998. "A Database of World Stocks of Infrastructure, 1950–95." *World Bank Economic Review* 12(3): 529–47.

Carballo, M., and S. Solby. 2001. "HIV/AIDS, Conflict and Reconstruction in Sub-Saharan Africa." Paper presented at the conference on Preventing and Coping with HIV/AIDS in Post-Conflict Societies: Gender Based Lessons from Sub-Saharan Africa, March 26–28, Durban, South Africa.

Casavant L., and C. Collin. 2001. "Illegal Drug and Crime: A Complex Relationship." Prepared for the U.S. Senate Special Committee on Illegal Drugs.

Centre for Research on the Epidemiology of Disasters. 2001. Data presented to the workshop on Filling Knowledge Gaps: A Research Agenda on the Impact of Armed Conflict on Children, July 2–4, Florence, Italy.

Chadhury, N., and J. S. Hammer. 2002. "Ghost Doctors: Absenteeism in Bangladesh Health Facilities." Development Research Group, World Bank, Washington, D.C. Processed.

Colletta, Nat J., and Michelle L. Cullen. 2000. *Violent Conflict and the Transformation of Social Capital.* Washington, D.C.: World Bank.

Collier, P. 1994. "Demobilization and Insecurity: A Study in the Economics of the Transition from War to Peace." *Journal of International Development* 6.

_____. 1999. "On the Economic Consequences of Civil War." *Oxford Economic Papers* 51: 168–83.

_____. 2001. "Ethnic Diversity: An Economic Analysis." *Economic Policy* 32(2):129–66.

Collier, P., and J. Dehn. 2001. "Aid, Shocks, and Growth." Policy Research Working Paper no. 2688. World Bank, Washington, D.C.

Collier, P., and D. Dollar. 2002. "Aid Allocation and Poverty Reduction." *European Economic Review* 46(8):1475–1500.

Collier, P. and A. Hoeffler. 2002a. "Aid, Policy, and Growth in Post-Conflict Societies." Policy Research Working Paper no. 2902. World Bank, Washington, D.C.

_____. 2002b. "Aid, Policy, and Peace: Reducing the Risks of Civil Conflict." *Defence and Peace Economics* 13(6): 435–50.

_____. 2002c. "Greed and Grievance in Civil Wars." Working Paper Series 2002–01. Centre for the Study of African Economies, Oxford, U.K. Available on: http://www.csae.ox.ac.uk.

_____. 2002d. "Military Expenditure: Threats, Aid, and Arms Races." Policy Research Working Paper no. 2927. World Bank, Washington, D.C.

_____. 2002e. "On the Incidence of Civil War in Africa." *Journal of Conflict Resolution* 46(1): 13–28.

_____. 2003. "The Political Economy of Secession." Centre for the Study of African Economies, Oxford, U.K. Processed. Available on: http://users.ox.ac.uk/~ball0144.

Collier, P., A. Hoeffler, and C. Pattillo. 2002. "Africa's Exodus: Capital Flight and the Brain Drain as Portfolio Decisions." World Bank, Washington, D.C. Processed.

Collier, P., A. Hoeffler, and M. Söderbom. 2003. "On the Duration of Civil War." Centre for the Study of African Economies, Oxford, U.K. Processed. Available on: http://users.ox.ac.uk/~ball0144.

Cortright, D., and G. A. Lopez 2002. *Sanctions and the Search for Security: Challenges to UN Action, a Project of the International Peace Academy.* Boulder, Colo.: Lynne Rienner.

Crossin, C. G. Hayman and S. Taylor. 2003. "Where Did It Come From? Commodity Tracking Systems." In I. Bannon and P. Collier, eds., *Natural Resources and Violent Conflict: Options and Actions.* Washington, D.C.: World Bank.

Davies, V. A. B., and A. Fofana. 2002. "Diamonds, Crime, and Civil War in Sierra Leone." Paper prepared for the World Bank and Yale University case study project The Political Economy of Civil Wars. Processed.

DeRouen, K., Jr. 2003. "A Competing Risks Model of Civil War Duration and Outcome: Implications for Rebel Decision Making." Paper presented to the Gilman/Curiel Conference on New Directions in International Relations, February, Yale University.

Doyle, M. W., and N. Sambanis. 2000. "International Peace Building: A Theoretical and Quantitative Analysis." *American Political Science Review* 94(4): 779–801.

_____. 2003. "Alternative Measures and Estimates of Peace Building Success." Yale University, Department of Political Science, New Haven, Conn. Processed.

Economist, The. 2001. "Hitting the Tigers in their Pockets." March 10.

Elbadawi, I., and N. Sambanis. 2000. "External Interventions and the Duration of Civil Wars." Paper presented at World Bank DECRG conference on The Economics and Politics of Civil Conflicts, March, Princeton University, Princeton, N.J.

_____. 2002. "How Much Civil War Will We See? Explaining the Prevalence of Civil War." *Journal of Conflict Resolution* 46(3): 307–34.

Elbadawi, I., A. A. Ali, and A. Al Battahani. 2002. "On the Causes, Consequences, and Resolution of the Civil War in Sudan." Processed.

Elbe, S. 2002. "HIV/AIDS and the Changing Landscape of War in Africa." *International Security* 27(2): 159–77.

Esman, M. J., and R. J. Herring, eds. 2001. *Carrots, Sticks, and Ethnic Conflict: Rethinking Development Assistance.* Ann Arbor, Mich.: University of Michigan Press.

Esty, D. C., J. A. Goldstone, T. R. Gurr, B. Harff, M. Levy, G. D. Dabelko, P. T. Surko, and A. N. Unger. 1998. *State Failure Task Force Report: Phase II Findings.* McLean, Va.: Science Applications International Corporation.

Farah, Douglas. 2002. "Al Qaeda Cash Tied to Diamond Trade." *Washington Post,* November 1. Available on: http://www.washingtonpost.com/wp-dyn/articles/A27281-2001Nov1.html.

Fearon, J. D. 2002. "Why Do Some Civil Wars Last So Much Longer Than Others?" Stanford University, Palo Alto, Calif. Processed. Available on: http://econ.worldbank.org/files/18171_Fearon Dur3. pdf.

Fearon, J. D., and D. Laitin. 1996. "Explaining Interethnic Cooperation." *American Political Science Review* 90(4): 715–35.

_____. 2003. "Ethnicity, Insurgency, and Civil War." *American Political Science Review* 97(1): 75–90.

Figes, O. 1996. *A People's Tragedy: The Russian Revolution 1891–1924.* London: Pimlico.

Gates, S. 2002. "Recruitment and Allegiance: The Microfoundations of Rebellion." *Journal of Conflict Resolution* 46(1): 111–30.

Gates, S., H. Hegre, M. P. Jones, and H. Strand. 2003. "Institutional Inconsistency and Political Instability: Persistence and Change in Political Systems Revisited, 1800–1998." International Peace Research Institute, Oslo, Norway. Processed.

Ghobarah, H. A., P. Huth, and B. Russett. 2003. "Civil Wars Kill and Maim People—Long after Shooting Stops." *American Political Science Review* 97(2).

Gleditsch, N. P. 1998. "Armed Conflict and the Environment: A Critique of the Literature." *Journal of Peace Research* 35(3): 381–400.

Gleditsch, N. P., O. Bjerkholt, Å. Cappelen, R. P. Smith, and J. P. Dunne. 1996. *The Peace Dividend.* Amsterdam: Elsevier.

Gleditsch, N. P., P. Wallensteen, M. Eriksson, M. Sollenberg, and H. Strand. 2002. "Armed Conflict 1946–2001: A New Dataset." *Journal of Peace Research* 39(5): 615–37.

Global Witness. 2002. *The Logs of War. The Timber Trade and Armed Conflict.* Report no. 379. Fafo Institute for Applied Social Science, Oslo, Norway. Available on: http://www.fafo.no/pub/ rapp/379/379.pdf.

Goldstein, P. 1985. "The Drug/Violence Nexus: A Tripartite Conceptual Framework." *Journal of Drug Issues* 39: 143–74. Available on: http://www.lindesmith.org/library/tlcgolds.html.

Graduate Institute of International Studies. 2001. *Small Arms Survey 2001. Profiling the Problem.* Oxford, U.K.: Oxford University Press. Available on: http://www.smallarmssurvey.org/Yearbook2001.html.

Grossman, H. I. 1991. "A General Equilibrium Model of Insurrections." *American Economic Review* 81(4): 912–21.

_____. 1992. "Foreign Aid and Insurrection." *Defense Economics* 3(4): 275–88.

_____. 1995. "Insurrections." In K. Hartley and T. Sandler, eds., *Handbook of Defense Economics*, vol. 1. New York: Elsevier Science.

_____. 1999. "Kleptocracy and Revolutions." *Oxford Economic Papers* 51(2): 267–83.

Guha-Sapir, D., and Emanuela Forcella. 2001. "The Reproductive Health Needs of Refugees: Evidence from Three Camps in Ethiopia." Centre for Research on the Epidemiology of Disasters, Brussels. Processed.

Guha-Sapir, D., and W. G. Van Panhuis. 2002. "Mortality Risks in Recent Civil Conflicts: A Comparative Analysis." Centre for Research on the Epidemiology of Disasters, Brussels. Processed.

Guillaumont, P. and S. G. Jeanneney. 2003. "Dampening Price Shocks." In I. Bannon and P. Collier, eds., *Natural Resources and Violent Conflict: Options and Actions.* Washington, D.C.: World Bank.

Gurr, T. R. 1974. "Persistence and Change in Political Systems, 1800–1971." *American Political Science Review* 68(4): 1482–1504.

_____. 2000. *Peoples Versus States: Minorities at Risk in the New Century.* Washington, D.C.: United States Institute of Peace.

Gurr, Ted Robert, Monty G. Marshall, and Deepa Khosla. 2001. *Peace and Conflict 2001: A Global Survey of Armed Conflicts, Self-Determination Movements, and Democracy.* College Park, Md.: Center for International Development and Conflict Management.

Hammer, J. S. 1993. "The Economics of Malaria Control." *World Bank Research Observer* 8(1): 1–22.

Hardin, R. 1995. *One for All: The Logic of Group Conflict.* Princeton, N.J.: Princeton University Press.

Harvey, C. 1992. "Botswana: Is the Economic Miracle Over?" *Journal of African Economies* 1(3): 335–68.

Hechter, M. 2001. *Containing Nationalism.* Oxford, U.K.: Oxford University Press.

Hegre, H. 2003. "Disentangling Democracy and Development as Determinants of Armed Conflict." Paper presented at the Annual Meeting of International Studies Association, February 27, Portland, Oreg. Available on: http://econ.worldbank.org/files/ 24637_ddcwwb.PDF.

Hegre, H., T. Ellingsen, S. Gates, and N. P. Gleditsch. 2001. "Toward a Democratic Civil

Peace? Democracy, Political Change, and Civil War, 1816–1992." *American Political Science Review* 95(1): 33–48.

Heston, A., R. Summers, and B. Aten, 2002. *Penn World Table Version 6.1.* Center for International Comparisons at the University of Pennsylvania. Available on: http://pwt.econ.upenn.edu/.

Hiltermann, Joost. 2002. "Incorporating Human Rights in the Study of Civil Wars." Georgetown University, Washington, D.C. Processed.

Hirsch, J. L. 2001. *Sierra Leone: Diamonds and the Struggle for Democracy.* International Peace Academy Occasional Paper Series. Boulder, Colo.: Lynne Rienner:

Hirshleifer, J. 2001. *The Dark Side of the Force. Economic Foundations of Conflict Theory.* Cambridge, U.K.: Cambridge University Press.

Hoeffler, A., and M. Reynal-Querol. 2003. "Measuring the Cost of Conflict." Oxford University, Oxford, U.K. Processed. Available on: http://users.ox.ac.uk/~ball0144.

Holt, K. 2003. "Once They Were Girls. Now They Are Slaves." *The Observer.* February 2, p. 23.

Homer-Dixon, T. F. 1991. "On the Threshold: Environmental Changes as Causes of Acute Conflict." *International Security* 19(1): 5–40.

Horowitz, D. L. 1991. "Self-Determination: Politics, Philosophy, and Law." *NOMOS* 39: 421–63.

_____. 1998. "Structure and Strategy in Ethnic Conflict." Paper presented at the Annual Bank Conference on Development Eco-

nomics, April 20–21, World Bank, Washington, D.C.

ICBL (International Campaign to Ban Landmines). 2002. *Landmine Monitor Report 2002: Toward a Mine Free World.* New York: Human Rights Watch. Available on: http://www.icbl.org.

Keely, C. B., H. E. Reed, and R. J. Waldman. 2000. "Understanding Mortality Patterns in Complex Humanitarian Emergencies." In H. E. Reed and C. B. Keely, eds., *Forced Migration and Mortality.* Washington, D.C.: The National Academies Press. Available on: http://www.nap.edu/openbook/0309073340/html/1.html.

Kingma. K. 2002. "Improving External Support to Reintegration of Ex-Combatants into Civilian Life." Bonn International Center for Conversion, Bonn, Germany. Processed.

Klare, M. 2001. *Natural Resource Wars: The New Landscape of Global Conflict.* New York: Metropolitan Books.

Knight, M., N. Loayza, and D. Villanueva. 1996. "The Peace Dividend: Military Spending Cuts and Economic Growth." *IMF Staff Papers* 43(1): 1–37.

Le Billon, P. 2003. "Getting It Done: Instruments of Enforcement." In I. Bannon and P. Collier, eds., *Natural Resources and Violent Conflict: Options and Actions.* Washington, D.C.: World Bank.

Leith, C. J. 2002. "Why Botswana Prospered." University of Western Ontario, London, Ontario, Canada. Processed.

Licklider, R. 1993. *Stopping the Killing.* New York: New York University Press.

_____. 1995. "The Consequences of Negotiated Settlements in Civil Wars, 1945–1993." *American Political Science Review* 89(3).

Lijphart, A. 1984. *Democracies: Patterns of Majoritarian and Consensus Government in Twenty-One Countries.* New Haven, Conn.: Yale University Press.

Lipset, S. M. 1959. "Some Social Requisites of Democracy: Economic Development and Political Legitimacy." *American Political Science Review* 53(1): 69–106.

Lunde, L., and P. Swanson. 2003. "Who Gets the Money? Reporting Resource Revenues." In I. Bannon and P. Collier, eds., *Natural Resources and Violent Conflict: Options and Actions.* Washington, D.C.: World Bank.

Machel, G. 2002. "Conflict Fuels HIV/AIDS Crisis." Available on: http://www.IPsnews.net/hivaids/section1_2.shtml.

Matovu, J. M,. and F. Stewart. 2001. "Uganda: The Social and Economic Costs of Conflict." In F. Stewart, V. Fitzgerald, and associates. *War and Underdevelopment,* vol. 2. Oxford, U.K.: Oxford University Press.

Mauro, P. 1995. "Corruption and Growth." *Quarterly Journal of Economics* 110(3): 681–712.

McDonald, L. 2002. "The International Operational Response to the Psychological Wounds of War: Understanding and Improving Psychosocial Interventions." Working Paper no. 7. Feinstein International Famine Center, Tufts University.

Mearsheimer, J. J. 1990. "Back to the Future: Instability in Europe after the Cold War." *International Security* 15(1): 5–56.

Mollica, R. F., K. McInnes, N. Sarajlić, J. Lavelle, I. Sarajlić, and M. P. Massagli. 1999. "Disability Associated with Psychiatric Comorbidity and Health Status in Bosnian Refugees Living in Croatia." *Journal of the American Medical Association* 281(5): 433–39.

Montalvo, Jose G., and M. Reynal-Querol. 2002. "Fighting against Malaria: Prevent Wars while Waiting for the Miraculous Vaccine." Working Paper. University of Pompeu Fabra, Barcelona, Spain. Processed.

Mueller, J. 2000. "The Banality of 'Ethnic War.' " *International Security* 25(1): 42–70.

Murdoch, J., and Sandler T. 2002. "Economic Growth, Civil Wars, and Spatial Spillovers." *Journal of Conflict Resolution* 46(1): 91–110.

Ndikumana, L., and K. Emizet. 2002. "The Economics of Civil War: The Case of the Democratic Republic of Congo." World Bank and Yale University case study project The Political Economy of Civil Wars. Processed.

Ngaruko, F., and J. D. Nkurunziza. 2002. "Civil War and Its Duration in Burundi." Paper prepared for the World Bank and Yale University case study project The Political Economy of Civil Wars. Processed.

Ogen, J. K., and N. Loy. 1996. "AIDS and the Military: Implications of Demobilisation."

Paper presented at the International Conference on AIDS, July 7–12.

Olson, M. 1993. "Dictatorship, Democracy, and Development." *American Political Science Review* 87(3): 567–76.

Over, M. 2003. "The Effects of Societal Variables on Urban Rates of HIV Infection in Developing Countries: An Exploratory Analysis. Confronting AIDS." In M. Ainsworth, L. Fransen, and M. Over, eds., *Evidence from the Developing World.* Washington, D.C. and Brussels, Belgium: European Commission and World Bank.

Parker, K., A. Heindel, and A. Branch. 2000. "Armed Conflict in the World Today: A Country by Country Review." Written for the Humanitarian Law Project/International Educational Development and Parliamentary Human Rights Group, U.K. Available on: http://www.hri.ca/doccentre/docs/cpr/armedconflict2000. shtml#_Toc486401419.

Pax Christi Netherlands. 2001. "Peace in Colombia: A Matter of Civil Initiatives." Available on: http://www.paxchristi.net.

Pinker, S. 2002. *The Blank Slate. The Modern Denial of Human Nature.* Viking Press.

Prunier, G. 1995. *The Rwanda Crisis: History of a Genocide.* New York: Columbia University Press.

Przeworski, A. 1991. *Democracy and the Market: Political and Economic Reforms in Eastern Europe and Latin America.* Cambridge, U.K.: Cambridge University Press.

Przeworski, A., M. E. Alvarez, J. A. Cheibub, and F. Limongi. 2000. *Democracy and Development: Political Institutions and Well-Being in the World, 1950–1990.* Cambridge, U.K.: Cambridge University Press.

Rawls, J. 1971. *A Theory of Justice.* Cambridge, Mass.: Harvard University Press.

Regan, P. 2002. "Third-Party Intervention and the Duration of Intrastate Conflicts." *Journal of Conflict Resolution* 46(1): 55–73.

Reinikka, R., and J. Svensson. 2002. "Coping with Poor Public Capital." *Journal of Development Economics* 69(1): 51–69.

Reuter, P. 2001. "The Need for Dynamic Models of Drug Markets." *Bulletin of Narcotics* LIII (1–2).

Reynal-Querol, M. 2002a. "Ethnicity, Political Systems, and Civil War." *Journal of Conflict Resolution* 46(1): 29–54.

_____. 2002b. "Political Systems, Stability, and Civil Wars." *Defence and Peace Economics* 13(6): 465–83.

Ross, M. L. 2000. "Does Oil Hinder Democracy?" *World Politics* 53(April): 325–61.

_____. 2002a. "Booty Futures: Africa's Civil Wars and the Futures Market for Natural Resources." Department of Political Science, University of California, Los Angeles. Processed. Available on: http://www.polisci.ucla.edu/faculty/ross/bootyfutures.pdf.

_____. 2002b. "Resources and Rebellion in Aceh, Indonesia." Paper prepared for the World

Bank and Yale University case study project The Political Economy of Civil Wars. Processed. Available on: http://www.polisci.ucla.edu/faculty/ross.

Ross, M. 2003. "The Natural Resource Curse: How Wealth Can Make You Poor." Ch. 2 in I. Bannon and P. Collier, eds, *Natural Resources and Violent Conflict: Options and Actions.* Washington, DC: The World Bank.

Ruiz, Hiram A. 1998. "The Sudan: Cradle of Displacement." In R. Cohen and M. F. Deng, eds., *The Forsaken People: Case Studies of the Internally Displaced.* Washington, D.C.: The Brookings Institution.

Sambanis, N. 2000. "Partition as a Solution to Ethnic War." *World Politics* 52: 437–83.

_____. 2003. "Using Case Studies to Expand the Theory of Civil War." Paper prepared for the World Bank and Yale University case study project The Political Economy of Civil Wars. Processed.

Scott, Colin. 1998. "Liberia: A Nation Displaced." In R. Cohen and M. F. Deng, eds., *The Forsaken People: Case Studies of the Internally Displaced.* Washington, D.C.: The Brookings Institution.

Sherman, J. 2002. *Policies and Practices for Controlling Resource Flows in Armed Conflict.* New York: International Peace Academy. Available on: http://www.ipacademy.org.

Singer, D. J., and Small, M. 1994. *Correlates of War Project: International and Civil War Data, 1816–1992.* Ann Arbor, Michigan: Inter-University Consortium for Political and Social Research.

Small, M., and Singer, J. D. 1982. *Resort to Arms: International and Civil War, 1816–1980.* Beverly Hills, Calif.: Sage.

Smallman-Raynor, M. R. and A. D. Cliff. 1991. "Civil War and the Spread of AIDS in Central Africa." *Epidemiology and Infection* 107 (1): 69–80.

Stedman, S. J. 2001. "Implementing Peace Agreements in Civil Wars: Lessons and Recommendations for Policymakers." Policy Paper Series on Peace Implementation. New York: International Peace Academy.

Stewart, F., C. Huang, and M. Wang. 2001. *Internal Wars in Developing Countries: An Empirical Overview of Economic and Social Consequences.* In F. Stewart, V. Fitzgerald, and associates, eds., *War and Underdevelopment,* vol. 1. Oxford, U.K.: Oxford University Press.

Summers, R., and A. Heston. 1991. "The Penn World Table (Mark 5): An Expanded Set of International Comparisons, 1950–1988." *Quarterly Journal of Economics* 99(2): 327–68.

Taylor, H. M., and S. Karlin. 1998. *An Introduction to Stochastic Modeling.* 3rd. ed. San Diego, Calif.: Academic Press.

UN (United Nations). 1999. *Consolidated Inter-Agency Appeal for Angola, 2000.* New York and Geneva: Office for the Coordination of Humanitarian Affairs. Available on: http://www.reliefweb.int.

_____. 2000. *Humanitarian Context.*

_____. 2002. *Consolidated Inter-Agency Appeal for Eritrea, 2003.* New York and Geneva: for the Coordination of Humanitarian Affairs. Available on: http://www.reliefweb.int.

UNHCR (United Nations High Commission for Refugees). 2002. "Refugees by Numbers." Available on: http://www.unhrc.ch/.

UNODCCP (United Nations Office for Drug Control and Crime Prevention). 2002. "Global Illicit Drugs Trends 2002." In *ODCCP Studies on Drugs and Crime.* New York.

_____. 2003. *The Opium Economy in Afghanistan: An International Problem.* New York.

U.S. Bureau of Justice and Statistics. 2002. "Drugs and Crime Facts." Available on: http://www.ojp.usdoj.gov/bjs/spectps.htm.

U.S. Department of State. 1999. "Arms and Conflict in Africa." Available on: http://www.state.gov/www/global/arms/reports/arms_conflict.html.

USSR. 1964. *Atlas Narodov Mira.* Moscow: Department of Geodesy and Cartography of the State Geological Committee.

Walter, B. F. 1997. "The Critical Barrier to Civil War Settlement." *International Organization* 51(3): 335–65.

_____. 2002. *Committing to Peace.* Princeton, N.J.: Princeton University Press.

Weingast, B. R. 1997. "The Political Foundations of Democracy and the Rule of Law." *American Political Science Review* 91(2): 245–63.

Weiss, Thomas G. 1998. *Beyond UN Subcontracting: Task-Sharing with Regional Security Arrangements and Service-Providing NGOs.* New York: St. Martin's Press.

WHO (World Health Organization). 1983. *World Health Statistics Annual.* Geneva.

_____. 1999. "Malaria 1982–1997." *Weekly Epidemiological Record* 74(32): 265–70.

_____. 2000. *The World Health Report 2000: Health Systems: Improving Performance.* Geneva.

_____. 2001. *Reproductive Health during Conflict and Displacement.* Available on: http://www.who.int/reproductive_health/publi…/RHR_00_13_RH_conflict_and_displacemnet.

Winer, J. M. and T. J. Roule. 2003. "Follow the Money: The Finance of Illicit Resource Extraction." In I. Bannon and P. Collier, eds., *Natural Resources and Violent Conflict: Options and Actions.* Washington, D.C.: World Bank.

World Bank. 1997. *Confronting Aids: Public Priorities in a Global Epidemic.* Oxford, U.K.: Oxford University Press.

_____. 2002a. *World Development Indicators.* Washington, D.C.

_____. 2002b. *World Bank Work in Low-Income Countries under Stress: A Task Force Report.* Washington, D.C. Available on: http://www1.worldbank.org/operations/licus/documents/licus.pdf.

_____. 2003.

Zartman, William I. 1995. "Putting Things Back Together." In *Collapsed States: The Disintegration and Restoration of Legitimate Authority.* Boulder, Colo.: Lynne Rienner.

Zinn, A. 2002. "Theory Versus Reality: Civil War Onset and Avoidance in Nigeria, 1960–1999." Paper prepared for the World Bank and Yale University case study project The Political Economy of Civil Wars. Processed.

Zürcher, C., J. Koehler, and P. Baev. 2002. "Civil Wars in the Caucasus." Paper prepared for the World Bank and Yale University case study project The Political Economy of Civil Wars. Processed.